JUDAISM AND ZOROASTRIANISM
AT THE DUSK OF LATE ANTIQUITY

SOUTH FLORIDA STUDIES IN THE HISTORY OF JUDAISM

Edited by
Jacob Neusner
William Scott Green, James Strange
Darrell J. Fasching, Sara Mandell

Number 87
JUDAISM AND ZOROASTRIANISM
AT THE DUSK OF LATE ANTIQUITY
How Two Ancient Faiths Wrote
Down their Great Traditions

by
Jacob Neusner

JUDAISM AND ZOROASTRIANISM AT THE DUSK OF LATE ANTIQUITY

How Two Ancient Faiths Wrote
Down their Great Traditions

by
Jacob Neusner

Scholars Press
Atlanta, Georgia

JUDAISM AND ZOROASTRIANISM
AT THE DUSK OF LATE ANTIQUITY

©1993
University of South Florida

Publication of this book was made possible by a grant from the Tisch Family Foundation, New York City. The University of South Florida acknowledges with thanks this important support for its scholarly projects.

Library of Congress Cataloging in Publication Data
Neusner, Jacob, 1932–
    Judaism and Zoroastrianism at the dusk of late antiquity: how two ancient faiths wrote down their great traditions/ by Jacob Neusner.
        p. cm. — (South Florida studies in the history of Judaism; no. 87)
    Includes index.
    ISBN 1-55540-889-3
    1. Judaism—Relations—Zoroastrianism. 2. Zoroastrianism—Relations—Judaism. 3. Pahlavi rivayat of Aturfarnbag. 4. Pahlavi rivayat. 5. Talmud—Comparative studies.   I. Title.   II. Series.
BL1566.J8N48 1993
296.1'2506—dc20   93-5615
                                                    CIP

Printed in the United States of America
on acid-free paper

Table of Contents

Preface ix
1. Judaism and Zoroastrianism at the Dusk of Late Antiquity 1
2. Writing Down the Great Tradition... 17
3. The Bavli: Form and Program. A Sample 33

Part One
THE PAHLAVI RIVAYAT OF ATURFARNBAG AND THE TALMUD

4. The Pahlavi Rivayat of Aturfarnbag and the Bavli: Description and Comparison 53
5. Episodic Comparisons: The Family... 87
    I.   Exercising the Right of Refusal... 89
    II.   When Equal Shares in an Inheritance Have Been Guaranteed.. 94
    III. Disposing of an Inheritance of Thievery........................... 98
6. Episodic Comparisons: The Social Order...................................105
    I.   Relations to the Outside World 106
    II.   Oaths Imposed on Children in Connection with the Father's Estate's Debts..113
    III. Can One Transfer Ownership of What Has Not Yet Come into Existence? 116
    IV. Some Preliminary Generalizations 122

Part Two
THE PAHLAVI RIVAYAT ACCOMPANYING THE DADESTAN I DENIG AND THE TALMUD

7. The Pahlavi Rivayat Accompanying the Dadestan i Denig: Form and Program Compared to the Bavli 127

8. Episodic Comparisons 143
   - I. The Transmission of Uncleanness 143
   - II. Master-Disciple Relationships 145
   - III. Father-Son or Master-Disciple Relationships 149
   - IV. Husband-Wife Relationships: The Wife's Perfect Obedience 152
   - V. Commercial Relationships: True Value 156
   - VI. The Relationship between Zoroaster and God, and between Our Sages of Blessed Memory and God 159

Part Three
PERSPECTIVE ON THE GREAT TRADITIONS

9. Ways of Writing Down Great Traditions in Israel and Iran 165
   - I. [1] The Rule Unadorned, [2] the Rule Attached to a Myth, and [3] the Rule Joined to Its Reason: The Three Types of Re-Presenting Great Tradition in Late Antique Iran and Israel 165
   - II. Myth and Rule in the Rivayats and in the Torah (Exodus, Leviticus, Deuteronomy). The Mishnah 168
   - III. The Rule and Its Amplification in the Yerushalmi 170
   - IV. The Rule and Its Reason in the Bavli 177
   - V. The Bavli's Definition of Tradition 191

Index 193

Preface

In this book I invoke for purposes of preliminary comparison and contrast the testimonies of two sets of writings intended to solve one and the same problem: how to write down a great and ancient tradition. Sometime somewhat before 700 in the case of Judaism, and somewhat after 800 in the case of Zoroastrianism – during a span of approximately a century and a half in all – massive efforts of Judaic sages and Zoroastrian priests accomplished the writing down of centuries of tradition, in the Talmud of Babylonia, ca. 600, on the one side, and the Pahlavi books through which we know Zoroastrianism, on the other. That Talmud, a.k.a. the Bavli, took over the received heritage, reshaping the whole into a new and authoritative, persuasive statement. The Pahlavi books composed by a family of priests formed the canon of Zoroastrianism from that time onward. The Bavli defined Judaism, serving as its summa, from the time of its closure to our own day. And, along these same lines, it is the simple fact that almost all the Zoroastrian Middle Persian writings that we possess are, in their final form at least, products of the ninth and tenth centuries. That is when the scholar-priests of the declining Zoroastrian communities of Iran made a notable effort through a literary exercise to defend the faith and instruct the faithful.[1]

My purpose here is to compare the Talmud of Babylonia, a.k.a. the Bavli, to two counterpart documents of Zoroastrianism, both called Rivayat, "tradition," the Pahlavi Rivayat of Aturfarnbag and the Rivayat that accompanies the Dadestan i Denig. The uniform purpose and task undertaken by the respective religions' authors and editors form the basis for comparison. In both cases the purpose was the same: write down the truth handed on from of old, protect the fundament of the faith

---

[1] E. Yarshater in his introduction to J.P. de Menasce, "Zoroastrian Pahlavi Writings," in Ehsan Yarshater, ed., *The Cambridge History of Iran,* vol. 3 (2), *The Seleucid, Parthian, and Sasanian Periods* (Cambridge, 1983: Cambridge University Press), p. 1166.

for generations to come, say it all in some coherent manner, prepare for an uncertain future. When we see how one set solved its problem of transcribing a vast heritage, we gain perspective on the work of the other. In particular, I aim at gaining perspective on the intellectual and literary character of the Talmud of Babylonia by examining how others in roughly the same time and circumstance solved the same problem, namely, the authoritative (re)statement of all that was known out of an ancient tradition for transmission to an unknown world to come. Only by comparison will I discern what is distinctive in that Talmud.

This is not a work in comparative literature, religion, or law, whole or in part, but only the comparison and contrast of ways in which Judaic sages and Zoroastrian priests formulated and handed on (part of) their respective traditions, hence the subtitle of this book, *How Two Ancient Faiths Wrote Down Their (Respective) Great Traditions.* What it means to accomplish such a comparison, the limited but precise scale on which I carry out the project, and what I hope to achieve, are all spelled out in the shank of the book.

I happily acknowledge the collegiality, support, and long-time friendship of the luminary of Iranian studies, Professor Mary Boyce, London. Her writings provide a synthetic account, up to date and interesting, as we now have, for example, for Zoroastrianism up to Parthian and Sasanian times. Her vast learning is matched by her generosity to all comers, which makes her a legend in her field. Reading her books and articles, models of not only learning, commonplace in this field, but also exemplary writings for their rarer virtues of clarity, wit, and intelligence – that reading, for all its pleasures, scarcely compares to the advantage of conversation with her on her field. There her full mastery, mordant wit, and profound wisdom come into play as well. It goes without saying that I should never have contemplated the adventure at hand without her counsel, though I do not claim to have taken all of her sage advice, and certainly absolve her of responsibility for all but those results offered here that may be found reliable.

A second exemplary colleague is her pupil, Dr. A.V. Williams, University of Manchester, who not only guided me through his scholarship, but even provided a computer disc of his translation, to make it easier for me to use his work. He is a worthy disciple of a great scholar, exhibiting those same virtues of intellect and collegiality that make his master the luminary of an otherwise darkening field. One of the few Iranists with a keen interest in religion and even theology, he has already made an important contribution and shown himself an important scholar.

Preface

I enjoyed access, while writing this book, to the Cambridge University Library and the hospitality, also, of the Institute for Ancient Indian and Iranian Studies, Cambridge, the latter through the good offices of Professor H.W. Bailey, whose warm hospitality to my wife and myself is one of my many good memories of Cambridge. To meet Professor Bailey is to sit in the presence of an immortal, and I value the time he gave me there.

I wrote most of this book while a visiting fellow at Clare Hall, Cambridge. To many good friends at that delightful place I owe thanks for intellectual stimulation and generous friendship.

My study-mate there for the period in which I wrote this book was Professor David Gunby, University of Canterbury, Christchurch, New Zealand, whose sage counsel and engaging wit made the work still more enjoyable than my research ordinarily is for me. He was always ready to tell me about his two massive projects, one in English literature, the other in English military history, and to help me solve problems of thought and expression in connection with mine, too.

Association with him, among a number of intellectually stimulating colleagues, is only the most important among the many advantages conferred on me, among all its Visiting Fellows, by Clare Hall. I value many other memories of that wonderful seat of learning. Let me dwell on the virtues of that remarkable institution, which proves that, in the academic world, we really can set out to accomplish a goal and then actually achieve it. I cannot imagine a more congenial place in which to write a book or conduct intellectual experiments. The humble facilities of that research center conceal the wealth of spirit and intellect that flourish there.

To the president and his remarkable wife, Professor Anthony Low and Mrs. Belle Low, and to the staff of Clare Hall – one and all – and to the many friends and colleagues who accorded a warm welcome to my wife and myself, I express thanks. For thirty years now, a group of highly conscientious academicians, with much goodwill aforethought, conceived of a truly international community of scholars, encompassing humanities, social sciences, natural sciences, law and jurisprudence, and many other areas of learning, in which the resources of an ancient university would be made available to foreigners and home-born alike.

None of the many things that work well at Clare Hall is an accident. Knowing, as I do, the present and the several past presidents, recognizing the warm and constructive collegiality of the Permanent Fellows and the wonderful staff as well, I realize none of this is an accident. It is the result of hard work and deep thought about the nature of an academic community that really is a community. I express my admiration and thanks for all that I have enjoyed on account of the work of these many men and women of goodwill.

I have further to express my thanks to the University of South Florida for affording to me an ongoing research fund, enabling me to do my work summer as well as winter, providing for research costs and expenses. Not only so, but on account of a benign administration and more than a few engaged colleagues, I am perpetually aware of my good fortune to teach and pursue research at that excellent place. It strikes me as providential that, at just the point in my life that I found, at University of South Florida, a community of learning colleagues, including my dean and president and many others in the College of Letters and Science, the College of Education, and elsewhere on our vast and diverse campus, colleagues one and all capable of genuine intellectual exchange and cordiality, too, in Clare Hall I found here in Cambridge a similar community. For the unusually comfortable situation – material, intellectual, and social – in which to pursue my work I am thankful.

JACOB NEUSNER

Visiting Fellow
CLARE HALL
Cambridge University

Distinguished Research Professor of Religious Studies
UNIVERSITY OF SOUTH FLORIDA
Tampa, FL 33620-5550 USA

July 28, 1992
My sixtieth birthday

1

Judaism and Zoroastrianism at the Dusk of Late Antiquity

At the dusk of late antiquity, in the century and a half just before and just after the rise of Islam and the Muslim conquest of the Near and Middle East, two of the region's most ancient religious traditions, Judaism and Zoroastrianism, succeeded in writing down such of their great traditions in books as would endure for all time, to the present. In both cases, circumstances were the same. Each tradition faced a crisis at once political and religious, the Jews prior to the fall of Zoroastrian Iran because of unfavorable political circumstances, the Zoroastrians after the rise of Islamic Iran because of the disestablishment of the faith and massive apostasy. For both groups, the future looked uncertain. At that moment, the Judaic sages and Zoroastrian priests wrote the Talmud of Babylonia and the bulk of the Pahlavi books of Zoroastrianism, respectively. During the final stages of Iranian rule of Babylonia, the Judaic sages met conditions of instability; ancient settlements were disturbed and long-standing arrangements upset.[1] After the Islamic conquest of Iran, the Zoroastrian priests saw huge numbers of the faithful abandon the fire temples in favor of Islam, a common motif of their writings being the practical consequences for families and society alike of apostasy.

Under these comparable conditions and aiming at the same goal, both groups of intellectuals determined to make a statement out of the past for the future: to write down their respective great traditions. Both succeeded, each in its own way. For the coming ages, no one would gain access to the past other than through the writings given form in the darkening, closing years of late antiquity and just beyond. The Talmud

---

[1] I discuss this topic at length in my *History of the Jews in Babylonia. V. Later Sasanian Times* (Leiden, 1970: E.J. Brill), Chapters One and Two.

defined Judaism. Without the work of the ninth-century Zoroastrian priests, such remnants of the "good religion of the worshippers of Mazda" as endured would have perished. Any account of how antiquity's successful religions – the ones that endured to the present day, which are Judaism, Zoroastrianism, Christianity, and, at the end, Islam – prepared themselves for the long passage through medieval and modern, and into even contemporary, times will pay close attention to the writings that for Judaism and Zoroastrianism formed the chosen and the sole medium of tradition.

These writings therefore show us the way chosen by the respective sets of priests and sages to continue the progress through time of the traditions (they held to endure) unbroken and wholly continuous from the time of God's revelation to the prophet (whether Moses, whether Zoroaster) into the very world in which they lived. What makes these writings interesting is, first of all, the very fact that it was through writing down the tradition, rather than choosing some other form for preservation and transmission, that the priests and sages did their work. What makes them important is that the documents did succeed in realizing their writers' goals: Zoroastrians to our own century have valued and consulted writings of the ninth century, such as we examine here, and the Talmud of Babylonia remains the point at which the classical writings come together and from which all normative accounts of doctrine and law begin.

These writings of closure and continuation attained success beyond what their authors could have imagined: to guide people in worlds the writers could not have conceived, under circumstances they could not have understood – but in a way entirely consistent with what was represented as God's revealed will. A tradition demands our attention when it exhibits the marks of success in the very group that was supposed to value and conform thereto. Zoroastrian and contemporary Judaic norms, reaching into the documents treated here, justify an inquiry into the comparison of the character of these writings, the choices their authors made in preserving precisely the traditions they wished to preserve for that very posterity that even today appreciates them: why this, not that? And in the end, in the comparison and contrast we shall discern the choices people made and so gain perspective on the ways taken by each group.

So what? An account of the way such writings were so shaped as to form links in the chain of receiving and handing on the great tradition opens the question of how a grand civilization secures its own future through the frail medium of writing. Why preserve the received truth in one form, rather than in some other, through one medium, in one institutionalized form, and for one purpose, rather than through, in, and

Judaism and Zoroastrianism at the Dusk of Late Antiquity

for some other? We have no reason to take for granted the choice these writers made for either Judaism or Zoroastrianism. They could have carved their words in stone, or made mosaics, or written prayers for the faithful to recite; in the case of Judaism, we have others' formulations of the tradition in all three media, but, from the Judaic sages, only the medium of writing. There were Jews – sages, by definition – who made inscriptions and mosaics, composed prayers and poems, and in other ways supposed they made their lasting statement and handed it on. And, so far as we now know, those Jews who painted on walls or made mosaics are not the ones who wrote the books we have in hand, and the opposite is also the case; we cannot, therefore, take for granted writing was the only way people considered, or that it was the best way that, in their minds, they could have chosen. Other people made other decisions. The writers succeeded, we know, because we have their work; we have these books because for long centuries afterward people valued the writing, copied it over and over again, and handed it on as the record of not history but divine truth: what we are to believe and practice. So these works proved persuasive and therefore endured, and we want to know why. So far as the traits of the documents testify (over and above the accidents of time and taste), we shall find out.

Further, when two sets of people set out to do the same thing under comparable conditions and within a determinate period of time, the choices they made about how to do the work surely demands not only description – how each group did the work, with attention to the rhetorical, logical, and topical rules of composition – but also comparison and contrast. That is to say, trying to make sense of what was done to accomplish a single goal, in the nature of things, requires not only description and analysis of a piece of writing in its own terms and its own documentary context, but also comparison in the setting of other writings that accomplished the same end. What justifies the work is not only that the writers of each community shared a goal of the same sort, but that the two religions in fact bear a range of affinities. These range from the rather general to the very specific. Take, for example, the following:

Offering stolen firewood unto the fire

Question: If one offers unto the fire libation and fuel that are stolen and robbed and obtained through deceit and wickedness, then does any meritorious deed accrue therefrom or not?

Answer: No, surely it is a sin. The fire of Ohrmazd scorches him just as when he holds heat. And he who would offer me the libations procured through theft, robbery, ravishing, raid, and brought from a liar. He who offers libation unto my fire originating from theft, robbery, ravishing, deceiving, depriving men [they deprive mankind in price] and carrying through fraudulence, Burns me thus with so much burning, just as thereby...and defilement of the Evil Spirit comes upon men. My fire scorches that man with so much scorching, just as mankind whom the Destructive Spirit defiles.[2]

And, along these same lines:

A. A stolen or dried-up willow branch is invalid.
B. And one deriving from an asherah or an apostate town is invalid.

M. Sukkah 3:3A-B

Now the sentiment is the same: one cannot serve God through things gained unlawfully. That commonplace need not capture our attention; what makes it interesting is that the same idea is expressed through the same medium: a case that, changing the details, proves interchangeable from writing to writing. The setting is of course particular, each to its own system. The Zoroastrian formulation has God instruct Zoroaster, the Judaic one just states a rule in a laconic, factual way – a mighty difference indeed. It follows that, at particular points – a great many, as a matter of fact, as we shall see even in the severely curtailed survey given here – Judaism and Zoroastrianism intersect and commonly concur on the same principle, each making the same point through its own idiom. But that is not the main consideration here.

The meeting is not solely an invention of our own making; these two traditions lived for a long time together, in the same country – Iranian Babylonia – and under an enduring political arrangement: the Zoroastrians running the state, the Jews their own affairs, the one seldom interfering with the other, the other seldom troubling the one. The two traditions by the end of late antiquity and the rise of Islam had coexisted for at least a thousand years, with Jews in Babylonia in Achaemenid, Parthian, and Sasanian times subject to Iranian, therefore Zoroastrian, rulers. The confluence that concerns me – a shared project of composing for posterity an account of the received tradition – is only the latest (though, it turns out, the last) of the points of intersection of the two ancient faiths.

They had met before, at the beginning and the end of their formation in the ancient world, at the sixth century B.C., with the intersection of parts of the Pentateuch of ancient Israel with Zoroastrian conceptions of the same period; they cohabited for the long centuries of Parthian and Sasanian rule of Babylonia, then the westernmost satrapy of the Iranian

---

[2]Kaikhusroo M. Jamaspa and Helmut Humbach, *Pursishniha. A Zoroastrian Catechism* (Wiesbaden, 1971: Otto Harrassowitz), *Part I. Text, Translation, Notes*, pp. 36-37.

empire, from the second century B.C., when the Parthians took over Babylonia, through the seventh century A.D., when the Sasanians lost the region, along with their throne, and the Zoroastrians lost control of Iran. And now they met again, sharing as they did the same circumstance, at the seventh (for Judaism) through the ninth (for Zoroastrianism) centuries, that is, the time just before and after the rise of Islam. It as then – the seventh century for Judaism, the ninth century for Zoroastrianism – that priests and sages of both religions undertook in writing to make for posterity systematic statements of the faith. Just as the pentateuchal writings sustain comparison with the Gathas and Avesta, particularly the priestly code and other priestly writings contained in the pentateuchal books of Leviticus and Numbers at the beginning. And so, too, the Talmud of Babylonia bears comparison and contrast with Pahlavi legal and theological books at the end of the millennial coexistence of these particular religions.

And, it goes without saying, this rather restricted comparison stands only at the threshold of a much more sustained and systematic comparison, since no two religions have more in common than the Zoroastrianism of the Avesta and the Pahlavi books and the Judaism of the Pentateuch ("Written Torah") and the Talmud. To begin with comparable in substance, at the end in form and purpose, the writings of the two religions afford more than adventitious occasion for that kind of analysis. For, alike in their interests in purity, at the outset, and in their professed intention of writing down the great traditions of the two religions, respectively, at the end, the writings of the two contiguous religious systems furthermore share common topics, on the one side, and accomplish common purposes, on the other side of late antiquity.

While alike, the two traditions also are unlike in the vast middle: the systemic statement and program that each brings to full, written expression. The differences become consequential because of the similarities; the similarities take on nuance because of the differences, and the process illuminates throughout. The two religions' considerable, shared interest in the theme of purity comes to expression in details that intersect only casually and not systemically. Their shared devotion to principles of justice, their conviction that God intervenes in human affairs, so as to repay acts of decency but also acts of unfairness and evil – that point in common (also with Islam and Christianity) conceals massive differences at the theological foundations of the conviction viewed in its own systemic setting. So it is the fact that each set of sages speaks to its own group about its own concerns. The likenesses and differences afford the opportunity for comparison, therefore also contrast. That is to say, alike but not alike, these writings allow for the comparison and contrast of influential world religions at critical turnings in their parallel histories of beginning, growth, and renewal. These two facts – alike in some ways, different in others – make possible the kind of work presented, if only in an initial probe, in this book.

Let me spell out the kind of comparison I do not propose to undertake, so that readers will not expect what I do not promise. This is not an essay in the comparison of Zoroastrianism and Judaism. Comparison of intellectual and consequent literary formal programs, involving theological and legal texts, such as I do define for myself, is not the same as an essay in comparative theology, which, in its own terms, is incomprehensible. For knowing what two distinct writings say about a common set of theological questions, for example, the nature of God, the will of God for the social order, the program of God for the individual life and conscience, by itself yields chaos: no basis for intelligible conclusions, but only the facts that religion A thinks this, and religion B thinks that. Only systemic comparison of theologies in broad context of religious systems and structures permits making sense of the results of comparison, whether similarities or differences.

And the same is so for comparative law. While, for my own purposes, I do compare law to law, it is with an interest in the way the same law is formulated by the respective writers. That is not the same thing as comparative law. Knowing a detail of one system is like, or not like, a detail of another presents us with inert facts, not active and formative insight into why this, not that. When I ask, therefore, for points at which the two sets of sages talk about the same problem and reach conclusions that intersect (whether like or unlike), I do not propose to draw conclusions for comparison of laws or of law, still less of legal systems. This second question is important to me not because I conduct a sustained and systematic account of comparative law, Zoroastrian and Talmudic (though I see such a comparison as illuminating). A labor of comparison of theology or of law cannot define its agenda in a single, partial representation of the theology or the law to be compared, but only whole theological structures or whole law systems against whole other systems.

Comparison must be systemic or accept dismissal as disproportionate and uncomprehending. Comparison out of whole, systemic context promises ordering insight but in the end delivers chaos: information, no interpretation; and that is not my purpose here. I compare the treatments of the same problem and solution only because I want to see how the several documents discuss the same topic and formulate their statements upon it. As I said, my primary interest directs attention to the modes of thought and expression that serve two distinct groups of sages in making their statements. That is because the Bavli's modes of thought and expression, already shown by me to define the power of the document, will be illuminated by comparison and contrast to those of the two rivayats where they intersect with the Bavli – not comparison of law at all, only of laws in situ and for a distinctive purpose.

So the kind of comparison I undertake is not systemic but only documentary. For systemic comparison must take up the whole of that statement and program, and the evidence considered here, and presently available for consideration at all, does not encompass the whole of the Zoroastrian system, even for the ninth century alone. While, for the Bavli, our document tells us everything there is to know, for the two Zoroastrian writings considered here, we have only a small part of a vast library of writings that contain the great tradition. But we can compare completed writings that accomplish the same purpose, if not the entire systems of which they form important parts. So, to state my purpose as clearly as I can: it is solely the comparison of two ways of writing traditions, the classification of the types and possibilities of those ways, yielding the possibility of the analysis of similarity and difference aimed at drawing conclusions about how each religion made its concluding statement.

Why do the work at all? My particular interest requires explanation, since the mere comparison of how two distinct religions that bear affinities undertake a common literary task, by itself, would not have drawn me to this work. For that purpose, it would have sufficed to list the titles of the Pahlavi books of the ninth century and say, the Talmud of Babylonia is different. The detailed documentary comparison, by the neutral and ubiquitously applicable criteria spelled out in Chapter Four, aims at providing a hitherto unseen perspective on the Bavli. That is, as is now clear, the perspective afforded by comparison with another book that aimed at the same goal, with equivalent success, as some of the Pahlavi books of the ninth century did. The rivayats or tradition writings afford perspective upon that document through comparison and contrast because, in the context in which they were created, they were meant to accomplish the same goal. It was systematically and comprehensively to set out how things are supposed to be: this way, not that way. More to the point, both sets of writings did so in the acute detail of concrete situations and everyday problems. Both sets of writers wish to summarize and restate theology and law in the here and now of what the faithful are to do this morning. The concreteness of the two writings, their focus upon specific problems and disinterest in vast abstractions – these, too, show us different people trying to solve the same sort of problem, each group in its own context.

My primary interest narrows down to the comparison and contrast of the modes of thought and expression of the respective writings. What captures my attention are three traits of these writings (or any other): their rhetoric, their logic of coherent discourse, and their topical or proposition program, its traits, its plan of organization and exposition, its general foci. The data afforded by analysis of the writings' manner of formulating the task, choice of means for stating and solving concrete problems, way of saying much the same thing in response to much the same specific problem yields the possibility of classifying the ways of re-presenting great traditions. That classification then shows us how to frame our question: why this, not that; and then, speaking to the Bavli, I am able to ask, so what if it is this, not that? That forms the entire program of this book.

So I take the natural next step in my systematic description of the Bavli. I have already proceeded from the sustained analysis of the document's own evidence to the comparison of that writing with the other one of its class, the Talmud of the Land of Israel or Yerushalmi, and now move forward to the comparison of writings with which the Bavli forms yet another class, the writings that (claim to) set down ancient and great traditions, as I said. The description and analysis of the Talmud of Babylonia has involved describing and analyzing that vast writing out of its own resources: its topical program, its principles of logical coherence and discourse, and its rhetorical characteristics; its philosophical program and generative problematic. As my first act of comparison, I also have compared that Talmud with the other, earlier one, the Talmud of the Land of Israel. So I have a clear picture of what the Bavli is, described in its own terms, and also of how the Bavli is to be analyzed, through comparison to another species of its genus. Now, as I move to the work of interpretation, I require a broader sense for the possibilities of making a systemic statement, as the Bavli does, and for other ways of doing the same thing. And that third stage in presenting a document, besides description and analysis, involves interpretation, meaning, comparison and contrast beyond the limits of the genus.

In this setting the program of the book is a simple, natural one. I take up for purposes of comparison two systematic exercises of comparison, addressing two Zoroastrian writings out of the enormous corpus produced in the ninth century, after the challenge of Islam required of the Zoroastrian sages a complete restatement of the ancient tradition. In Chapter Three I describe the Bavli as I now see it, so framing the question that draws attention to comparison and contrast with other systemic statements of law and theology, and then in Parts One, Chapters Four through Six, and Two, Chapters Seven through Eight, I address an identical and simple program to two rivayats (which will be identified in due course): [1] how do the forms and the topical program of this document compare and contrast to the Bavli; [2] are there specific points

Judaism and Zoroastrianism at the Dusk of Late Antiquity 9

of legal intersection, and how do the laws compare in formulation and logic? That accounts for the simple program of Parts One and Two: formal comparison, two points of substantive comparison, with an eye to how the same problem is expressed in diverse ways in the two documents under study. Chapter Nine then identifies the results of comparison and places the Bavli into its correct context: compared with the two rivayats, on the one side, and with the Yerushalmi, on the other; the upshot is a taxonomic system that, I maintain, ought to make sense of a broad variety of writings of the classification at hand.

Which of the many Pahlavi books have I chosen for comparison and contrast? I have chosen two, both of them as a matter of fact simply called "Tradition," Rivayat, [1] the Pahlavi Rivayat of Aturfarnbag, and [2] the Pahlavi Rivayat Accompanying the Dadestan i Denig. Among the Pahlavi books available to us in suitable translations into European languages,[3] these two contain a sufficiency of legal and theological writings to form rough counterparts to the Bavli, in ways in which writings of a more sustainedly theological character do not.[4]

Why among the many legal documents did I choose these two rivayats in particular? My choice of documents was dictated by three considerations, all of them (alas) extrinsic to the work: [1] I looked for texts in accessible form, meaning, in a Western language, completely and competently presented as presently known; [2] I sought texts that center on law with concern for theology as well, as does the Bavli, and that, further, are alleged, as is the Bavli, to stand upon a rich received tradition of law and propose to continue that tradition; [3] I required texts that cover, among their laws, topics that are important, also, to the Bavli. These requirements are met by the two rivayats, or traditions, I have selected, the one of Aturfarnbag, the other associated with the Datastan i Denig. I systematically examined a third, Pursishniha, "a Zoroastrian catechism," but it did not differ in materially important ways from the

---

[3]My knowledge of Pahlavi, such as it is, derives from three years of study, in 1960-1961 with Ilya Gershevitch at Columbia University, and 1962-1964 with Richard N. Frye at Harvard University. I do not present myself as a scholar in Middle Iranian studies.

[4]I could not find grounds for comparing wholly theological texts with the Bavli, which is both legal and theological, since I do not know how to compare the theologies of different religions. I cannot identify a viable model for myself, one that I should like to follow. Laws, by contrast, do sustain comparison when they identify the same case and define the issues in the same way. But, as I stressed in Chapter One, the purpose of comparing laws in the present study is solely to gain perspective on the kind of writing the Bavli is, and also is not.

first-named, and the results of comparison did not tell me more than I already knew, so I repeat only a few of them.[5]

These stringently limiting criteria admittedly excluded many important documents, some of them considerably more representative of the state of Zoroastrian writing in the ninth century than the ones before us. In fact not many Zoroastrian texts meet these conditions, for I found I did not have to sift among many candidates. The principal ones, the great law code, Matakdan i hazar datastan, the book of a thousand decisions,[6] and the huge encyclopaedia, the Denkart,[7] did not qualify for my purpose. The Denkart is not suited by the character of its contents to comparison with the Bavli (though other sorts of comparison – episodic, not systematic, and certainly not systemic – prove feasible). The great law code is not yet fully translated into a Western language. The descriptions and the accounts we now have show that it would sustain literary but not systemic comparison, for which a much larger sample of the Pahlavi books will be needed. In any event, to my good fortune, the two documents I chose do meet my requirements. Both mix law and theology. Both set forth norms of action and belief. Both make possible documentary comparison, because we can describe their contents and literary character and can also identify, in them, occasions for episodic comparison of how shared viewpoints or details are dealt with by the respective writers. Both rivayats, but particularly the second treated here, are available in accessible versions; the one that accompanies the Dadestan i Denig is exemplary.

---

[5]Cited above, n. 2.
[6]Maria Macuch, *Das sasanidische Rechtsbuch, "Matakdan i hazar Datatistan." Teil II. Abhandlungen für die Kunde des Morgenlandes XLV.1. Deutsche Morgenländische Gesellschaft* (Wiesbaden, 1981: Kommissionsverlag Franz Steiner); and Sohrab J. Bulsara, *The Laws of the Ancient Persians as Found in the Matikan e hazar Datastan, or the Digest of a Thousand Points of Law.* Translated with introduction, glossary, and index (Bombay, 1937: Hoshag T. Anklesaria). I do not read Russian and therefore could not use A. Perikhanian's edition and translation of this document. Macuch makes ample reference to it. I admired Macuch's translation and explanation of part of the Matigan, but I wanted to see a complete document, and that was not possible in this case.
[7] See Jean Pierre de Menasce, *Le troisième livre du Denkart* (Paris, 1973: Travaux de l'Institut d'Études Iranniennes de l'Université de Paris), and his *Une encycopédie mazdéenne: le Denkart; quatre conférences* (Paris, 1958: Bibliotheque de l'École des Hautes Études, Section des Sciences Religieuses, 69). Note also Saul Shaked, *The Wisdom of the Sasanian Sages: Denkart VI. By Aturpat-i Emetan* (Boulder, 1979: Westview Press). Neither book of the Denkart makes possible productive comparison with the Bavli, though the latter bears some comparison with tractate Abot, ca. 250 C.E. These documents focus on questions of metaphysics and theology, not law and norms of proper conduct.

Both rivayats treat law, including specific legal problems the Bavli's compositions' authors would have found entirely familiar, along with much theology. Both moreover serve as restatements of a received tradition and say so. That is why I chose them. The comparison with the Bavli then rests on these points of legitimation: [1] the writings undertake a common problem, re-presentation of the great tradition; [2] they present their materials in a common spirit, one of authoritative restatement in a form meant to persuade, not merely inform (of which more in due course); [3] they deal at some points with common concrete cases or principles. Thus [1] in purpose, [2] in formulary program, and [3] episodically at least, also in subject matter, they sustain comparison.

The first, the Rivayat of Aturfarnbag, comes to us in the edition and translation of Behramgore Tahmuras Anklesaria.[8] While that edition and translation do not conform in all respects to the norms of Western Iranology, they do serve for our purpose.[9] The text covers 147 questions and answers assigned to Aturfarnbag and one of the oldest Pahlavi expositions extant today of the legal, religious and social customs, usages, and practices of devout Zoroastrians about two centuries after the downfall of the Sasanian Empire.[10] We survey only the 147 questions of Aturfarnbag, dealing with those that cover topics important to Mishnaic and Talmudic law.

The second, the Pahlavi Rivayat Accompanying the Dadestan i Denig, in the opinion of the authority on the document, A.V. Williams, dates from the late part of the ninth or first quarter of the tenth century.[11] Williams's edition and translation provide by far the best edition of a Pahlavi text that we have in the English language, far superior for any

---

[8]Kaikhusroo M. Jamasp Asam, who published this work, explains that Behramgore Tahmuras Anklesaria, who died in 1944, left for posthumous publication a variety of works, most of which were burned in a fire at the Fort Printing Press, Bombay, in 1945. He submitted this text for a prize in 1938.

[9]Would that we could say the same of Bulsara's edition of the Matigan i Hazar Datastan, cited in the introduction, n. 1, but Macuch's simple statement to the contrary sufficed to warn me off. Her translation covers only a part of the document, and though I greatly admire her work, I could not claim to describe a document, as to its program, only part of which was accessible to me in a reliable form.

[10]The work also contains 34 other questions put to Farnbag-Srosh i Vahram by herpat Spenddat Farroxuborzin. These date from 1000; I pass by that part of Anklesaria's edition.

[11]A.V. Williams, *The Pahlavi Rivayat Accompanying the Dadestan i Denig* (Copenhagen, 1990: The Royal Danish Academy of Sciences and Letters). I. *Transliteration, Transcription, and Glossary.* II. *Translation, Commentary, and Pahlavi Text.*

substantive purpose[12] to any other systematic presentation of an entire document out of the Zoroastrian tradition in that language, and the standard by which, from now on, all others will be measured. That we have here a writing down of the great tradition is clear, in Williams's words: "Much of the material appears to come directly from a knowledge of the Pahlavi versions of the Avesta with the Zand, either oral or written."

A further, important point of the pertinence of this document to the Bavli is that both the Judaic and Zoroastrian compilations are organized in relationship to a prior writing, hence as "commentaries" of one sort of another, again Williams: "...in structure PRDd. [Pahlavi Rivayat accompanying the Dadestan i Denig] resembles the Dadestan i Denig, insofar as most of the chapters are in some way answers either to a question, explicit or implied, or to a predicament." Williams finds the voice of the document that of a priest.[13] The work is "neither speculative, philosophical, nor in any narrow sense theological; it is pedagogical, for here, above all, the doctrines of purity, righteousness, and just meritorious action are extolled to the reader by every available means." The authority of the document "musters old scriptural authority to urge reader and listener to practical religion and recounts well-known mythological narratives to provide the traditional context of faith."[14] Williams explains, "The purpose of the text is not only to impart information, whether practical, ritual, or theological, to the community; rather it tends to preach solidarity and faithfulness in the community." An authority behind the Bavli could not have said things better.

The Bavli and these two Rivayats therefore undertake the common task of stating the tradition, inclusive of its laws, for coming generations. But they bear significant parallels in other ways. A further point of intersection with the Bavli derives from the fact that both Rivayats that we shall consider take the form of questions and answers, a form of formulating ideas that plays an important role in the Bavli, but is rare in the Yerushalmi.[15]

---

[12]As distinct from a merely philological purpose, for which a number of other European language editions serve as well, I suppose. But for the humanistic learning that asks other than questions of philology, I know of no better presentation of a Pahlavi text than Williams, but a great many that are at best pedestrian.
[13]Vol. I, p. 9.
[14]Ibid.
[15]Whether the question-answer form for the presentation of laws and legal principles was borrowed by the Bavli's sages from their Iranian counterparts, whether both derived the form from a prior, third source, or whether each party made it up for itself as part of its repertoire of media for the formulation of ideas

Each of them turns out to exhibit the traits of a systemic statement, since both formulate in numerous concrete details a few main points. In a variety of works I have shown that fact for the Bavli.[16] Williams establishes that fact for his Rivayat:

> The traditions of PRDd. presented the community with the means to revitalize the principles and practice of the...Good Religion....: this is done by treating of a large number of problems, both perennial and particular to the time. All are characterized in Zoroastrian thought as stemming from the duality of worldly existence...in the material state of the world – i.e., the state of opposition and strife of the hostile and heterogeneous forces of Ahriman against the creations of Ohrmazd. This duality is perceived in all aspects of life, personal, public, and spiritual, and PRDd. deals with a range of oppositions. Each chapter of PRDd. has one or more of these dualities as its explicit theme. In most cases the text attempts to resolve the duality either explicitly in doctrinal or ritual prescriptions from the orthodox tradition, or more allusively in legendary narrative, cosmological symbolism, or religious mythology.[17]

The importance of this observation for gaining perspective on the Bavli is obvious: that document, too, finds a great many ways of saying some very few things, and it makes its statement, in the aggregate, in terms of the everyday world.

Clearly, the document before us exhibits the same basic program: large conceptions writ small. Williams finds the contrasts, for example,

---

is inconsequential in the present context. The near absence of the same form from the Yerushalmi does not strike me as evidence for a Babylonian venue, simply because the well-known yelammedenu form ("May our master teach us" + question + answer) is well established in the writings of the Judaic sages of both the Land of Israel and Babylonia. No successful form history has been accomplished with rabbinic texts, or with the literature as a whole.

[16] Among the score of monographs, see in particular *The Bavli's One Voice: Types and Forms of Analytical Discourse and Their Fixed Order of Appearance* (Atlanta, 1991: Scholars Press for South Florida Studies in the History of Judaism); *The Bavli's One Statement. The Metapropositional Program of Babylonian Talmud Tractate Zebahim Chapters One and Five* (Atlanta, 1991: Scholars Press for South Florida Studies in the History of Judaism); *The Law behind the Laws. The Bavli's Essential Discourse* (Atlanta, 1992: Scholars Press for South Florida Studies in the History of Judaism); *The Bavli's Intellectual Character. The Generative Problematic in Bavli Baba Qamma Chapter One and Bavli Shabbat Chapter One* (Atlanta, 1992: Scholars Press for South Florida Studies in the History of Judaism); *The Principal Parts of the Bavli's Discourse: A Final Taxonomy. Mishnah Commentary, Sources, Traditions, and Agglutinative Miscellanies* (Atlanta, 1992: Scholars Press for South Florida Studies in the History of Judaism); *The Torah in the Talmud. A Taxonomy of the Uses of Scripture in the Talmuds. Tractate Qiddushin in the Talmud of Babylonia and the Talmud of the Land of Israel.* I-II; and *The Bavli's Unique Voice. A Systematic Comparison of the Talmud of Babylonia and the Talmud of the Land of Israel* (Atlanta, 1993: Scholars Press for South Florida Studies in the History of Judaism), I-VII.

[17] Vol. I, pp. 10-11.

between trade and greed, sexual relations in marriage as against sexual relations when a woman is menstruating; the Bavli's sages likewise make their abstract points in their modes of analyzing quite concrete problems of trade and family relationships (among other things). Among the "five main religious resolutions" listed by Williams in descending order of emphasis, righteousness, practical observance, retribution and reward, wisdom, eschatological hope, the Bavli would have chosen the first two as the focus for its exhibition of applied reason and practical logic in the analysis of the principles of being: the social order, the life of the family, and the like. So much for the theory of the comparison undertaken here.

A third candidate, as noted, is Pursishniha, a compilation of nearly five dozen questions and answers much like Aturfarnbag's rivayat.[18] Let us glance at that text, since we shall not return to it. Its forms and program fall well within the framework of the two rivayats I have chosen, the form appearing similar to Aturfarnbag's rivayat, the theological program, the other rivayat, as the following survey shows:

> Duties of the Raspiks
> Punishment in hell till resurrection
> Regarding and disregarding a lord and Dastur
> Evil conduct through conspiracy with Devs
> Paradise for those who worship Ohrmazd...
> Penalty for vilification
> Gomez of animals...
> Excellent meritorious deed according to the Good Religion
> Worst sin against the Good Religion
> Meritorious deed performed without a Dastur
> On meritorious deeds...
> On the disciple and the teacher
> Sin of placing on fire a pot full of water
> Offering stolen firewood unto the fire [cited above]
> Sin of touching fire with soiled hands
> Performing meritorious deeds to eradicate sins
> Best existence for performing meritorious deeds...
> Composition of thought, conscience, and wisdom

---

[18]Kaikhusroo M. Jamaspa and Helmut Humbach, *Pursishniha. A Zoroastrian Catechism* (Wiesbaden, 1971: Otto Harrassowitz), *Part I. Text, Translation, Notes.*

Improper drinking of Parahom
Non-recital of the Ashem Vohus by the Raspik....
Reward after death and related matters
On the Yazat who comforts and leads the soul
Praiseful charity and its dispensation
Degree of sin and judgment for haughtiness...
Demerit for not diffusing the Religion
Discernment of a righteous man
Consequences of helping the wicked enemies of Religion
Righteousness – the best possession for both worlds

The list extends over a variety of other matters, a potpourri of laws and doctrines required for the faithful. Comparing this document to the Bavli would not have given us a richer repertoire of like and unlike traits than the two subject to detailed study in the shank of this book. Still, the way in which the Zoroastrian priest and the Judaic sage make the same point, that one cannot act as a judge in his own case, signals what is at stake throughout:

> Question: A judge, if it is his own affair, is it proper for him to act as witness or not?
>
> Answer: No. Even if the inquest has fallen to him on account of appointment. Even if he is that one who as judge by appointment should inquire into it. He shall not act as inquirer nor shall he take an oath. It is not he who should inquire into that, and it does not pertain to him.[19]

The same position is taken by the Mishnah in the following language:

A. All marks of skin uncleanness [such as are described at Lev. 13-14] does a man examine, except for his own.
B. R. Meir says, "Also not those of his relatives."
C. All vows does a man release, except for his own vows.
D. R. Judah says, "Also not the vows of his wife so far as they apply to matters between her and third parties."
E. All firstlings does a man examine, except for his own.

Mishnah-tractate Negaim 2:5A-E

The point is the same, the context different. A judge may not bear witness in his own case. The list of those who, in the Judaic court, may not testify does not include the judge of the case, since a judge could not participate in the judgment of such a case. The counterpart is a different

---

[19]Kaikhusroo M. Jamaspa and Helmut Humbach, *Pursishniha*, p. 77.

one: one may not reach a decision in a case involving his own, or his family's, uncleanness, vows, or firstlings (in this case, so as to declare them permanently blemished and so suitable for secular use). The basic principle is the same, which is hardly surprising, the sense of what is fair and unfair being broadly diffused. But the details are different, and no important conclusions may be drawn from the commonplace that both systems aim at both fairness and the appearance of fairness. But where do we identify points of significant comparison and contrast? That is the program of our reading of the two rivayats. Now to the work itself.

So, as I said, the bulk of Parts Two and Three is then devoted to the detailed treatment of the second, then the third points of comparison: the documents' topical and organizational principles, and the documents' respective ways of saying the same thing. Now let us turn to the dusk of late antiquity, the dawn of another world altogether, when four massive formations of antiquity, Christianity, Judaism, Zoroastrianism, joined by Islam, made the move – alone of all the religions from recorded time onward – to the medieval world, and thence in unbroken line to our own day.

2

Writing Down the Great Tradition

When, just before and after the advent of Islam, between the seventh and the ninth centuries, authorities of two of the Near and Middle East's four ancient, enduring religious traditions, Judaism and Zoroastrianism, undertook to save what was known and hand over to a new generation in a systematic and comprehensive way the law and theology of the faith, they continued a long story of those religions' parallel, if separate, development. In the case of Iran's Judaic sages, living in Sasanian Babylonia in the final century of Iranian rule of what became Iraq, and the Zoroastrian ones, living in other parts of the empire after Islam had conquered Iran itself, the task was the same. It was to recast a vast and complex heritage of learning, law, and lore, in so cogent and systematic a form that new ages might gain access to the great tradition. The circumstances in which the work was done varied; the work was the same. The basis for comparison is, first, the work was done in comparable circumstances, at the end of a very long period of stable development (Sasanian Iran, in both cases); and second, the work was done to attain, in each case, a comparable purpose: to lay the foundations for the holy community's long future in good thoughts (right attitude "in the heart" in the idiom of the Talmud), good words (right doctrinal viewpoint), good deeds (right action).

For the disciples of Moses, our rabbi, our date for their writing proves less certain. The purpose, moreover, is not so readily identified. The earliest date conventionally assigned to the Talmud of Babylonia, a.k.a. the Bavli, the sole, but sufficient, counterpart to the ninth century Pahlavi books, is 500; with as much, or as little, reason I have used the date of 600, the beginning of the seventh century, meaning, just prior to the Muslim conquest. The first external evidence to the existence of the Bavli, that is, a reference to the document outside of its own pages or datable manuscript evidence of its existence, is ca. 800. Since the document remains cogently within its own framework, referring to documents outside of itself only if they derive from the remote past – Scripture, the Mishnah, Tosefta, Sifra, the two Sifrés, for instance, but not referring in so many words or otherwise to the prior talmud, the Talmud of the Land of Israel of ca. A.D. 400 – the absence of response to the critical moment of Islam's advent by itself yields no conclusion.[1] The Pahlavi books treated here belong to the ninth century, the Talmud, possibly to the sixth, probably to the late seventh or early eighth; we cannot then dismiss a difference of from a hundred to three hundred years as trivial. Our information for the Zoroastrian enterprise rests on firm ground, that for the Judaic, somewhat less so.

More to the point than temporal coincidence is a compelling parallel in circumstances: impending crisis. While the Bavli never hints at the circumstances in which it was composed or the reason for its writing, we know exactly why the Zoroastrian priests did the work. They not only tell us in so many words, but the frequent references to a pervasive social problem, widespread apostasy (to Islam) and the intervention of non-Iranians into Iranian family life, provide ample substantive evidence of the same fact. In the disaster represented by the Muslim conquest of Iran and the mass defections, to Islam, of former Zoroastrians, a handful of sages – of a single family as a matter of fact – determined to preserve in writing what had been received, whether in the medium of memory or in writing, from time immemorial, so to hand on to an indeterminate future the fundament of truth they cherished. If the Bavli were demonstrated to constitute a work composed after the rise of Islam, we should surely imagine that the same world-shaking event led the Judaic sages to hasten to write things down. But, as a matter of fact, while the document itself

---

[1] In any event, absence of reference to Islam by itself proves nothing, for the reason specified by A.V. Williams, *The Pahlavi Rivayat Accompanying the Dadestan i Denig* (Copenhagen, 1990: The Royal Danish Academy of Sciences and Letters). I. *Transliteration, Transcription, and Glossary*. II. *Translation, Commentary, and Pahlavi Text*. I, p. 15: "Nowhere in the text is anything Islamic mentioned directly – for this would have been to invite persecution – yet the text emphasizes the stark polarity of *weh denih* [the good religion] and ag-denih throughout. The term *ag-denih* clearly refers to Islam." But Williams notes that "abhorrence of contact with Muslims is a theme which pervades much of the text," while in the Bavli, the counterpart is loathing of "Rome," meaning Byzantine and Christian Rome; there are less consistent evaluations of Iran, some of them complaining of problems and even persecution, some of them praising various kings of kings. "Arabs" are always Tai-Arabs, and there is not a single reference in the Bavli, or in any other document of this particular Judaism in late antiquity, to Arabs in any other role but despised and lowly outsider; "Ishmael" is not equated with "Rome" as Israel's persecutor. In a moment I shall explain why this entire issue – the Talmud as pre- or post-Islamic – has no bearing on my comparisons here.

preserves silence on the matter, the received accounts of the writing down of the Talmud, as we shall see, intimate that it was after the great tradition found itself threatened by the fragility of its own systemic medium. The story of the Talmud is told in terms of the death of the last named authorities – and then they wrote it all down.

That story certainly does correspond to the little that we know as fact about late Sasanian policy toward the Jews (among others), which no longer accorded to them conditions of secure and stable life and self-government, such as they had enjoyed over centuries of Parthian and then Sasanian rule.[2] The advent of Islam came as a relief to Jewry in both the Land of Israel under Roman (Byzantine) rule and Babylonia under Iranian (Sasanian) government, and if "our sages of blessed memory" responded to the crisis of continuity by writing down what they knew, then the circumstance corresponded to that brought about by the advent of Islam and mass apostasy in Zoroastrian Iran, even though the time was not the same.

Beyond the correspondence of circumstances what further justifies the comparison is that through writing down traditions in books both the Zoroastrian priests and the Judaic sages accomplished the same goal, that of organizing and putting down in fixed and official writing a full and authoritative statement of the received tradition and faith. Not only so, but these books – rather than agreed upon creeds set forth by councils of authorities, for example, as in the Christian case – were meant to provide reliable information, settling questions left open so that the faithful should know what they were to believe and do (in the Zoroastrian case) or how they were to think and what they should do (in the Judaic one). And they in particular bore the task – rather than the preachments of great preachers, or the exemplary lives of saints, as in the Christian case – of persuading the faithful to think good thoughts and do right deeds.

Note the contrast with Christianity (which wrote books, too). Neither religion chose to rely upon synods of ecclesiastical authorities. Neither one, so far as available evidence suggests, laid heavy emphasis on the exemplary behavior of holy men and women, though, of course, both knew such figures; the writings of neither religion in this phase lay heavy emphasis on the great deeds, including miracles, of saints, though, in the case of the Talmud, stories about rabbis did serve the purpose of setting good examples. And, most important, neither religion made its points through the actions of political figures, heads of states and governors, such as Islam and Christian could and did do, for the enforcement of uniform right belief and practice. Neither created great

---

[2] I survey these matters in the opening chapter of each of the volumes of my *History of the Jews in Babylonia* (Leiden, 1965-1970: E.J. Brill) I-V.

centers of pilgrimage. Neither built counterparts to cathedrals or other holy places. Neither constructed ecclesial structures. That is not to say they would not have done any of these things if they could have. They could not do some of them, they did not do others of them.

That is not to suggest, of course, that, had they the power, the two religions would have refrained from preserving the tradition through politics; to the contrary, the Talmud's sages recognized the legitimacy of violence when they could utilize violent means, or the threat thereof, to gain their purpose of conformity; the Zoroastrian writers looked back on the glory days of the Sasanians and blessed the memory of kings of kings whom Israel or Christendom remembered in an altogether different spirit. But in the circumstances in which the Bavli and the Pahlavi books came to be written down, the respective writers had to persuade, because they could not coerce in any other way than through right reason and compelling argument. So both writings, the Judaic and the Zoroastrian, pay close attention to considerations of persuasion, power, whether political and legitimate, or otherwise, not being available.

For our inquiry, the upshot is the same. Writing is the instrument of choice of those who cannot resort to coercion; the mode of constructing monuments for those who have no place in which to build. For good and sufficient reasons we are justified to undertake the comparison of the writings of two groups of sages whose sole means of accomplishing their goal, the reform of the holy community, lay in plausible appeal to the authority of revelation, the prestige of great learning, the precision of clear decisions, and the compelling force of persuasive presentation, questions with self-evidently valid answers, on the Zoroastrian side, propositional formulations joined to penetrating and fair and compelling argument, on the Judaic. In both instances, the stakes were defined in terms of not what I may rightly do to you, but what you must think in response to my arguments: the formation of attitudes, leading to actions. So what validates comparison is the choice of the one medium to which the two sets of sages gained recourse: the shaping of attitudes through learning and the moral authority of sound knowledge, the coercion deriving from uncompelled assent to persuasive argument: the things that, in general, intellectuals use to shape the world the way they want it to be. But the writing of books to accomplish much the same goal by two distinct groups forms no guarantee that the books will look alike, only that they will be used in like ways.

The two sets of writings differ in interesting ways; part of our task is to explain, and draw perspective from, the difference. Let me now point to some substantive and telling contrasts, besides the certainty of a date for the one writing, the uncertainty of a provenance for the other, to bear in mind as we compare writings that in some basic ways sustained comparison, but in other, also important ways, are different from one another.

The first contrast is simple: we do not know who wrote the Bavli, or when the work was done. By contrast, the bulk of the Pahlavi books come to us in the names of specific persons, who lived at identifiable times. Aturfarnbag,[3] responsible for the Pahlavi Rivayat that we shall consider in Part One, flourished in the first half of the ninth century. His descendant, Manushchihr, high priest of Pars and Kirman, responsible for Dadestan i Denig, followed in the second. The voice of the Bavli is anonymous, that of Aturfarnbag and Manushchihr, clearly identified; the Judaic sages speak as a collegium, the Zoroastrian ones as individuals. That contrast demands attention.

A second point of contrast, closely related to the foregoing, is that the Bavli apparently comes to us from a collectivity of writers, which I call "an authorship," while in the case of the Pahlavi books a single family is mainly responsible. These were two brothers, who were high priests, Manushchihr, high priest of Shiraz and Kirman, and Zatspram, high priest of Sirkan.[4] Manushchihr produced an authoritative statement of the faith, Datastan i Denik, "the Religious Norm."[5] Dated in the ninth century are the following: Namakiha, Datastan i denik, Vicitakiha, Bundahishn, and Denkart.[6]

Before proceeding, let us briefly take note of just two of their more important writings. Among the ninth-century books, the most important is the Denkart, described by Zaehner as "a corpus of religious knowledge that runs into nearly a thousand printed pages." The Denkart, made up of nine volumes, of which seven survive, "is an encyclopaedia of Mazdean knowledge."[7] Book Three is "an original contribution to Mazdean theology and its defense against Islam." Book Four takes up theological problems of Sasanian times, Book Five, of Islamic ones. Book Six compiles moral precepts; Book Seven, the legend of Zoroaster; Book Eight, "a detailed table of contents of the Nasks of the Avesta, with their divisions and sub-divisions." Book Nine details with "the contents of the three Nasks which appear as commentaries linked with the Gathas."

---

[3]Since this book of mine is not concerned with problems of philology, with which I am not competent to deal, I give a simple phonetic rendering of the various Pahlavi and Aramaic words and titles that are cited throughout. For people likely to find this book useful, that suffices. Consultation with the editions that I reproduce will give further phonetic information if needed.
[4]Zaehner, p. 194.
[5]Ibid.
[6]H.W. Bailey, p. li.
[7]De Menasce, in *Cambridge History of Iran*, vol. 3 (2), p. 1170. All further quotations from de Menasce are from this article.

None of this could have yielded productive comparison and contrast with the Bavli. Nor would the Andarz literature, even though its wisdom traditions derive from an international genre in Middle Eastern writing; for the Bavli is not a compilation of wisdom sayings, though it includes many of them. Documentary comparison requires that the genres intersect in some important ways. "Testaments" presented, in de Menasce's words, "as spiritual declarations made before death by a person, historical or otherwise," do not correspond in form or in intent with the writing down of the great tradition that the Bavli's authors accomplished.

An ideal candidate for comparison, alas not accessible as yet, is the law code, Matakdan i hazar datastan, the book of a thousand decisions.[8] This is described by de Menasce as follows:

> This is not a codex but a collection of laws and decrees, often accompanied by jurists' precepts, grouped into subjects but without any definition or explanation of the legal principles involved. Here it does not differ from the 'codices' of ancient Mesopotamian civilizations, neither does it cover the whole of Sasanian law; penal and agrarian law is almost entirely omitted. But on the subject of civil and family law and the law of contractual obligations, it is the only book that gives us a true idea of social relations in Sasanian society as seen from within.

The subjects that are covered are these:

> Evidence, advocates, plaintiffs, slaves, societies, divorce, the representative, deterioration and other hazards to which legal documents may be subject, interdiction, ordeal and oath, payments to be made on family wealth, the transfer of property, the daughter "evakenm," the potestas, preliminary payment without security, food and maintenance, the establishment of fires and sacrifices, marriage with a *patixshayiha* woman, the *guharen* (exchange, compensation), pawning, partnership of two men for the construction of a qanat, the *sturih*, sharing and participation, the performance of an obligation contracted with associates, the half-portion and declared value, security binding on several, declaration of possession, possession of property, association, words designating a contractual agreement, adoption, fines and contracts specifying them in case of non-performance, earnest money, profits and their division, disobedience of women and children in

---

[8]Maria Macuch, *Das sasanidische Rechtsbuch, "Matakdan i hazar Datatistan." Teil II. Abhandlungen für die Kunde des Morgenlandes XLV.1. Deutsche Morgenländische Gesellschaft* (Wiesbaden, 1981: Kommissionsverlag Franz Steiner); and Sohrab J. Bulsara, *The Laws of the Ancient Persians as Found in the Matikan e hazar Datastan, or the Digest of a Thousand Points of Law*. Translated with introduction, glossary, and index (Bombay, 1937: Hoshag T. Anklesaria). The Russian translation by A.G. Perikanian was published in Yerevan in 1973; an English translation by N. Garsoian is announced as "in press" in *The Cambridge History of Iran*, vol. 3 (2), p. 1389, but so far as I know, it has not yet come out of press.

respect of their sardar, formulas describing effective possession, specific legal formulas, the competence of officials, written and sealed documents, judgments in accord, judgments known through old documents, written and sealed, judgments giving the opinion of dasturs.[9]

From this list, it is clear that the document is not organized around a topical program in the way that the Mishnah is, for example, by divisions and subdivisions (seder/masekhet); the sequence of topics, neither random nor cogently arranged, corresponds to the way in which the two rivayats we shall examine are laid out: materials grouped, but no overriding principle of organization to be discerned.

The body of books produced at this time hardly finds adequate description in these few brief allusions, but the point is clear, that while the Judaic sages put forth a single document, the Zoroastrian priests created an entire library. And, again, while the Bavli contains within itself ample citations of the Written Torah (Scripture) not to mention massive parts of the Mishnah, its framers (so far as we know) put forth as their statement that one document alone. By contrast, the Pahlavi books preserve passages in translation from Avestan books, both lost and surviving; commentaries on received writings; and a vast body of law and doctrine. The contrast between a single enormous document and numerous, equally ambitious writings has also to be explained.

Reverting to our list of fundamental contrasts, we come to the third, which is equally simple. For Judaism in the Bavli we have one authoritative writing, a summa. There are no other extant documents produced by this authorship or in this period. By contrast, for Zoroastrianism, we have numerous writings. That difference matches the first and the second: a collegium of Judaic sages produces one authoritative document, while various Zoroastrian priestly writers write various books. The difference in volume is noteworthy.

Fourth, and closely correlated with the third, while both traditions claim for their final statements a long antecedent heritage of tradition, most of it oral, the Bavli rests upon a single piece of writing, the Pahlavi books refer to a variety of writings but do not organize themselves as commentaries on only one of them. Specifically, the Bavli draws upon the Mishnah as its organizing and definitive document. The Zoroastrian tradition is repeatedly described as oral prior to being written down, alongside writings that were accessible in scrolls. But that tradition comprises far more than a single prior writing. And this difference coheres with the first and the second. These points of contrast underscore the basic difference between the two versions of great

---

[9]De Menasce, pp. 1189-1190.

traditions, the Judaic and the Zoroastrian. A collegium [1] anonymously, therefore unanimously states [2] a consensus, identifying [3] a single received authority for the organizing of [4] its utterly uniform and unique lessons. By contrast, [1] individual writers quote [2] what or whom they wish, [3] to make the point each has in mind. May we account for the differences?

A fifth point of contrast derives from the disparity of size and diversity of the statements in conclusion that the two religious traditions were given. The Judaic summa came forth in a single, free-standing, authoritative statement; the Zoroastrian one emerged in a vast and various set of writings. The Bavli – as we shall see in Chapter Two – forms a single, sustained, and utterly coherent work. We have not got a trace of evidence of any other writing of its kind out of late antiquity, save the prior talmud, the Talmud of the Land of Israel or Yerushalmi. That Talmud lies in the distant past of the Bavli, at least two hundred years earlier, and exercised no influence whatsoever upon this one. It follows that so far as the framers of the Bavli were concerned, their summa would come forth in a single, unique writing, and while a variety of prior Judaic writings is quoted in the Bavli, and certainly a whole library of prior writings survived along with the Bavli, the Bavli was meant to stand on its own and from its own time for all time actually did occupy a unique place in the canon of Judaism.

It is clear, by contrast, that no one imagined any Pahlavi document would form the entirety of the final statement. And, again, the Bavli is huge, but singular, while the Pahlavi books include writings approximately as voluminous, but many more of them. That is to say, in volume, the Bavli, covering 37 tractates, some of them huge, competes with any one of the more massive Pahlavi books, but taken altogether, the sheer volume of writings of the family of Zoroastrian priests responsible for what we have vastly exceeds the Judaic counterpart.[10]

One may well wonder whether the reason behind these interesting points of difference derives from the generative point of difference: on the Judaic side, a concern with schism and heresy that can provoke rigid uniformity of discourse, as against, on the Zoroastrian side, a different sort of problem altogether. Specifically, the Pahlavi books are written against a background of mass apostasy, as Islam rapidly captured the vast majority of the formerly Zoroastrian Iranian peoples. In that context, avoiding schism and suppressing heresy form costly luxuries;

---

[10]For brief surveys, see Otakar Klíma, "Das mittelpersische Schrifttum," in J. Rypka, ed., *Iranische Literaturgeschichte* (Leipzig, 1959: Otto Harrassowitz), p. 34; R.C. Zaehner, *The Dawn and Twilight of Zoroastrianism* (London, 1961: Weidenfeld and Nicolson), p. 193.

defense of the faith itself defines what is necessary to do. And whoever successfully defends the faith – a variety of named, prestigious authorities – gains his hearing among the faithful, without too much concern for the niceties of consistency and doctrinal coherence, beyond the obvious requirements of the normally defined orthodoxy. The contrast is between Talmudic sages, heirs of a vast inheritance that they seek to organize, harmonize, and restate in a coherent and authoritative form, and Zoroastrian sages, heirs to an equally vast inheritance, now demanding defense. These contrasts strongly suggest that the one group wrote down the great tradition for its reasons and in response to its interior considerations, and the other group for its reasons, provoked by exterior provocations.[11]

And this brings us to the point in common to which I made allusion a moment ago. In both instances, when people justified making a permanent, written copy of what (so they maintained at any rate) had been preserved solely as an oral tradition, they pointed to impending loss of the tradition altogether. In neither case does the issue make its appearance in connection with the period at hand – Judaism just prior to, Zoroastrianism just after, the advent of Islam; in both they speak of generalized threats to the tradition, whether deriving from internal forgetfulness or external enemies. Why write things down? We know the reason they gave.

Let us dwell for a moment on the Zoroastrian theory of how documents came to be written down, as set forth in a writing of this period, the Denkart. In his study of the word tradition, the great Iranist and Indologist H.W. Bailey identifies with the word *patvand* the problem of the transmission of the religious tradition: "This tradition, the *patvand*, is the means by which the formation of an authoritative canon of writings is attained, whereon philosophical conclusions can be based, and the ritual and the customary religious law and the accepted ethics can be founded."[12] Bailey sets forth how "the Zoroastrian writers of the ninth century A.D. viewed the transmission of their religious traditions as contained in their authoritative works."[13] The parallel between the task undertaken by the authors of the Bavli and that addressed by the Pahlavi books' writers runs closer than the general one of formulating the great tradition, since the Middle Persian word *patvand* has its Sanskrit

---

[11]Why, at the advent of Islam, Zoroastrianism and Christianity crumbled wherever Muslim armies prevailed, while (so far as we know) Judaism stood firm, remains to be considered.
[12]H.W. Bailey, *Zoroastrian Problems in the Ninth-Century Books*. Ratanbai Katrak Lectures (Oxford, 1971: Clarendon), p. 149.
[13]Ibid., p. 149.

counterpart in a word, amnaya, that stands for "tradition preserved by memory." In both traditions, therefore, the task of writing down was linked to the origin of what was to be written down, which was, a tradition hitherto preserved in another medium altogether.

Much the same explanation for the writing down of the great tradition seems to me is implied by the ninth-century Pahlavi texts and by the ninth-century Judaic authority Sherira, c. 906-1006, in his famous letter,[14] for the writing down of the oral tradition of the Torah. He notes, "In the year 871 [= 470] all the synagogues of Babylonia were closed, and the children of Jews were seized by the magi...and in the year 787 [476] R. Sama b. Raba died. After him ruled R. Yosé; in his days came the end of instruction, and the Talmud was completed."[15] *Seder Tannaim veAmoraim*, along the same lines, "In the year 782 [471] was gathered in R. Hama b. Raba, an Huna b. Mar Zutra was killed....In the year 811 [= 500] Rabina was gathered in, which marked the end of instruction, and the Talmud was completed."[16] To be sure, whether the intention is to say, post hoc, ergo propter hoc, is not clear; only the context is. But the conception that what is preserved in memory may easily be lost is a commonplace in the Talmudic writings.[17]

Bailey cites a number of accounts of how the writing down of the great tradition was to be explained: the tradition came under severe threat, so, to prevent its being lost, it had to be written down; not only so, but schism called into question the unity of the truth; it became necessary to write things down to establish a single valid statement of the whole. That explanation referred to times in the distant past, but certainly could have served for the more immediate labor of the ninth century. Here are Bailey's translations of pertinent allegations to that effect:

> Thus they relate: once the righteous Zoroaster received the faith and made it current in the world and to the end of 300 years the faith was uncontaminated and men were free from doubt. Afterwards the accursed Destructive spirit, holder of lies, to cause doubt of this faith among men deluded the accursed Alexander the Roman, who dwelt in

---

[14]A. Hyman, *Iggeret deRabenu Sherira Gaon* (London, 1911).
[15]See my *History of the Jews in Babylonia* (Leiden, 1970: E.J. Brill), 5:137.
[16]Ibid.
[17]Stories about how evil Israelite monarchs tried to wipe out all the sages, corresponding to stories about how their earlier counterparts tried to wipe out all the prophets, are routine. "And as to the Torah, what will become of it" – if the schools are neglected, the sages killed, and the like forms a recurrent refrain. Justification for writing down what was given by God to Moses in solely memorized form, for oral formulation and oral transmission, appeals to the possibility of forgetting the Torah. We need not make more of that fact, or invoke it to explain why the authorship of the Talmud wrote the document, to sustain the simple point at hand.

Egypt, who came with grievous mischief and strife and trouble to Eran shahr. He slew the ruler of Eran and destroyed the court and sovereignty and laid it waste. The faith of which the whole Avesta and Zand had been prepared on ox hides and written with liquid gold and had been placed in Istakhr of Papak in the house of Archives, Alexander the Roman, the ill-fortuned adversary, heretic, and holder of lies, doer of evil, who dwelt in Egypt, carried off and burnt. Many of the teachers, lawyers, herbads and mobads, the supporters of the faith, the rich and the wise of Eran shahr, he slew. The great ones and governors of Eran shahr fell into feud and strife with one another openly....Since they had no sovereign lord, chief, or teacher who knew the faith, and were doubtful in things relating to the yazds, many sorts of doctrine and belief, wrong custom, doubt, and false decisions appeared in the world, till there was born Aturpat i Mahraspandan, of noble fravat and of immortal soul, who in the ordeal which he endured for the faith poured molten copper on his breast. He did much work of law and judging in strife with those of false doctrine and false belief.[18]

Alexander is credited with the loss of the old texts elsewhere as well:

> It [the knowledge of the faith and teaching of Zoroaster] was known in Eran shahr 1,000 years. After the coming of the destruction wrought by the ill-fortuned Alexander, created of wrath, thereof such was not to be found that it could have been preserved through the teachers.[19]

The loss of the oral tradition is a matter of concern in the following:

> You know that of our book of the faith Alexander burnt up 12,000 ox hides in Istakhr. One third of those chapters remained in their heart, but all that was legends and traditions; they did not know the laws and decisions; until those tales and traditions also passed from folk's memory through the decadence of the men of that time, the loss of the kingdom, and the craving for novelty and falsifications and prideful desire; so far it went that not a tittle of righteousness remained.

Now, that the texts were preserved orally, in memory, is well known and fully documented: "The ideal to be attained was a complete memorizing of the whole Apastak and Zand." The remedy for Alexander's destruction is explicit:

> When the accursed Alexander the Roman came to Eran shahr, he took and slew those who walked on the path of the magians. Some men and boys came to Sagastan. The one nask existed. With the women was a young child who had memorized the nask....In this way the faith returned to Sagastan. He arranged and ordered it afresh, but except in Sagastan, there was no memory of it elsewhere.

What is important is that by the ninth century a clear tradition maintained much was preserved orally, in memory. Not only so, but the

---

[18]Pp. 151-153.
[19]Bailey, pp. 154-155.

memorized text was held in the highest regard.[20] A more immediate consideration, to be sure, may have come into play, whatever happened in the distant past. By the ninth century, Christians, Manichaeans, and Jews referred to writings of divine authority.[21] The Muslims of course claimed the same. They treated Judaism and Christianity with respect, as religions of the book. The Zoroastrians then faced the task of establishing their bona fides in such a context. One obvious solution is to write up one's own traditions. But on what basis are people going to explain for themselves why they are writing down what countless prior generations memorized? The precedent of how people had dealt with the wicked Alexander ("the Great") certainly placed matters in proper perspective.

It follows that both the Bavli and the variety of Pahlavi books are represented in somewhat the same light at much the same time: in response to the threat to the ancient tradition, handed on from the founders – Moses, Zoroaster, respectively – through oral formulation and oral transmission, that is, in the medium of memory, learned sages at the last wrote down in final form what had endured so long in the minds of the great sages of the ages. So much for the contrasts. Then what validates the comparison, rendering the two sets of writings sufficiently like so that observations on how they are unlike prove illuminating?

It is the simple fact that both sets of documents – the Bavli's thirty-seven tractates, the large, more numerous and more various Pahlavi books – accomplished the same purpose, and were meant to. And if, as is the fact, two sets of writers undertake to do the same thing, then comparing and contrasting the diverse ways in which they proposed to do that one thing is entirely in order. And the one thing the Judaic sages and Zoroastrian priests proposed to accomplish was to set forth the tradition, both law and theology, in a form that later generations would find readily accessible. Both sets of writings, viewed overall and in context, aimed at that one goal: to formulate the entire received heritage to be handed to the indeterminate future. Whether provoked by a threat to the continuity of tradition, as the Pahlavi tradition tells of itself in an earlier phase, and as the Talmudic sages' seem to me to imply, or whether drawn by the intellectual challenge of putting everything together, the upshot was the same. In both Judaism and Zoroastrianism, some few documents made all the difference.

We see that fact in the contrast between the situation prevailing before and after the advent of the two sets of writings. Before the Bavli,

---

[20]Bailey, p. 166. Nonetheless, Bailey maintains, the first complete writing down of the Avesta may be "about the middle of the sixth century A.D."
[21]Ibid., p. 151.

the Judaic writings formed a various and discrete set of writings – in the canon summarized by the Bavli, encompassing the Mishnah, the Tosefta, the Yerushalmi (which we shall meet presently), Sifra, the two Sifrés, and another dozen or so Midrash compilations formulated at various times over centuries. All of these writings enjoyed the status of forming part of "the Torah," meaning, the canon of God's revelation to Moses at Sinai. But, altogether, they did not coalesce to make a single, coherent statement. There was nothing to which sages could point as "the one whole Torah of Moses, our rabbi," as their myth required them to do. But after the Bavli people could and did identify such a single, cogent and authoritative statement. Consequently, the Bavli formed the prism.

In more concrete terms, from the advent of the Bavli, for all time, when people wanted to know law or theology, they turned first to the Bavli, then its commentaries, its codes, response to questions referred initially to it. So the Bavli accomplished its writers' goal: to present the diverse writings from the Mishnah forward in a uniform and harmonious statement. So far as Judaism endured through the ages as a coherent and entirely cogent religious tradition, wherever, and under whatever circumstances, Jews made their lives, it was because of the Bavli, which defined the norms, and did so in such a way that, everywhere and at any time, people could and did conform to them. Then for us the issue is, how was this accomplished, and in the concluding chapter, in comparison with other writings, both within and without the Judaic tradition itself, we shall see the answer.

And along these same lines, before the work of the family graced with figures such as Aturfarnbag and Manushchihr, there was no well-crafted library of the received books and traditions; afterward, there was. It suffices to state very simply that every account of the history of Zoroastrianism makes that point. So far as Zoroastrianism survived the crisis precipitated by Islam's success in Iran, it was because in books the faith found a refuge, and in reading those books, the survivors recovered the faith. The many books the priests wrote did survive, and, in them, the faith endured, as they hoped it would; the great tradition was not lost. So, as I have stressed, the Pahlavi books and the Bavli undertook parallel tasks and performed them with parallel, and successful, results.

There is a further, obvious point that demands a brief glance. Writing down the great tradition for both Judaic and Zoroastrian sages transformed what had been a locative into a utopian system. Books move, their contents in secure, permanent form. If sages do not move, what they know stays put as well. From the centuries just before and just after the advent of Islam, the now written great traditions would make their movement from Iran. That was, respectively, from Iranian Babylonia, the locus of Israel, to all parts of the Muslim and Christian worlds, and from the Iran-proper locus of Zoroastrianism to India. The Zoroastrian priests' books left Iran with the Zoroastrians, finding their home in India. Whether or not before the ninth century Zoroastrians had taken refuge abroad, after that time they had in hand a full statement of the faith and how to keep it. The books made the faith portable in a way in which preservation in the frail persons of sages did not – if the knowledgeable sage did not leave, the tradition would be lost to those who did – and that fact proved adventitious. As it turned out, Zoroastrianism endured principally in a land beyond Iran.

For the Judaic sages of Babylonia, by the seventh century, there could have been no doubt that, short of the advent of the Messiah, Israel would live outside of the Land of Israel. By the advent of Islam, Israelites in the Land of Israel were few and diminishing. People fled the brutal wars of Byzantine, Christian Rome, and Zoroastrian Iran, fought for, among other things, control of the Land of Israel and Jerusalem; Jews could scarcely recover from the massacres that accompanied victory, whether Roman, whether Iranian. In the debilitating, last wars that set the stage for Islam's rapid conquest of the Near and Middle East, Jewish settlement in the Land of Israel rapidly declined. More to the point, few came from overseas to live in the Holy Land. For the Israelite sages of Iranian Babylonia, therefore, it was equally clear, much of the Torah, though not all of its rules, could be kept, and was kept, overseas and in alien land. Their restatement of the great tradition took a shape in response to the requirement that the Torah accompany Israel in not only the exile of Babylonia, now home for more than a millennium, but also those other exiles to which, from the Babylonian exile, they would make their way in the future. Wherever Jews would settle, it would not, for a very long time, be in the Land of Israel.

The writing down of the great tradition of Israel in its way accomplished that task of making the Torah portable by recasting the Mishnah, a highly locative document of the Land of Israel, into a statement relevant to utopian Israel. Those parts of the Oral and Written Torah that depended upon dwelling in the Holy Land they neglected in their (re)statement; those parts that spoke of how things are supposed to be anywhere, without regard to the particular location, they vastly extended and in detail restated. So they attended to laws governing holy time, the family and personal status, and the civil order. True, they read with equal, detailed interest the laws on the conduct of the everyday rites of the Temple, so allowing for preparation for the restoration of the holy city, Jerusalem, and the rebuilding of the holy place, the Temple or house of the sanctuary (as they called it), and the reconstitution of the holy rites of animal sacrifice. But the Messianic hope was never locative, animating only Jews in the Land of Israel, not at all. The upshot is that both great traditions in written form made possible that very kind of life – the utopian kind, not limited to location – that the faithful then lived and would continue to live, in the case of Judaism, and realized they would have to live, in the case of Zoroastrianism.

3

The Bavli:
Form and Program

A rivayat, as we shall see, with suitable abstracts, in Chapters Four and Seven, is a set of episodic questions and answers, a compilation of little essays on topics of law or theology, alluding to a tradition but not formed as a commentary on a received document. Utterly different in literary genre from a rivayat, a talmud is a sustained, analytical reading and interpretation of a received law code, the Mishnah. We have two Talmuds, species of the common genus, talmud. The genus, in particular, is formed of a compilations of comments upon paragraphs of chapters of a chosen Mishnah tractate (neither Talmud takes responsibility for the whole of the Mishnah). In a talmud a systematic and critical program aims at explaining the meaning and concrete application of the Mishnah rule, on the one side, and harmonizing one Mishnah rule with others with which it intersects, on the other. So "a talmud" accomplishes the work of Mishnah commentary and explanation by forming a moving ("dialectical") argument, from point to point, in which all possibilities are systematically taken up and examined.

The two Talmuds speciate the genus, then, the one the Talmud of Babylonia, the other, of the Land of Israel. What besides the common form defines the genus, that is, what is Talmudic about the two Talmuds is that shared mode of thought, which is a critical, systematic application of applied reason and practical logic, moving from a point starting with a proposition and (ordinarily) ending with a firm and articulated conclusion. The Talmud of the Land of Israel (a.k.a. the Yerushalmi, or the Jerusalem Talmud, or the Palestinian Talmud), ca. 400 C.E., and the Talmud of Babylonia (a.k.a. the Bavli), ca. 600, share many formal traits, though, in character and most of their contents they differ radically.

Like the Talmud of the Land of Israel, ca. 400, the Talmud of Babylonia, ca. 600, is formed as a commentary to parts of the Mishnah, ca. 200. The Mishnah is not presented as a coherent document but is broken up into bits and pieces; not only so, but some tractates are analyzed, others are ignored altogether. The Talmud of Babylonia serves the Mishnah's second through fifth divisions; the Talmud of the Land of Israel, the first through the fourth; both ignore the sixth division, purities, except for the tractate Niddah, on a woman's status when menstruating (sexual relations being prohibited at that time). Consequently, even at its simplest element, the very contents, the Mishnah is recast in the two Talmuds, reshaped into something other than what it is when read on its own. Nonetheless, the Talmud – severely intratextual, and, unlike all other rabbinic writings, never intertextual – always identifies the Mishnah paragraph under discussion in intrinsic ways of both language and form. The Mishnah is in Hebrew, the two Talmuds in Aramaic, citing large sections in Hebrew as well; the Mishnah is descriptive and sets forth simple declarative statements; the Talmuds are analytical, full of questions and answers, and make their points in an unfolding argument. The Mishnah means to provide information, well organized and coherent; the Talmuds give not information but interpretation of information.

Validating the formation of the two Talmuds into a single genus, talmud, is validated by another fact drawn from the context of the Mishnah and both Talmuds: the two Talmuds are not only like one another in form but they are different from every other document in their shared context, that of the canon of the Judaism of the Dual Torah that reached closure in ancient times, down to the seventh century. There are four other documents that respond to the Mishnah in explicit terms, the Tosefta (supplements to the Mishnah organized around the Mishnah), Sifra (organized around Leviticus), Sifré to Numbers (organized around the book of Numbers), and Sifré to Deuteronomy. None of these documents compares in any way to the Yerushalmi or the Bavli, both of which, as a matter of fact, cite verbatim from all four compilations. None pretends to provide the Mishnah with a sustained, line-by-line or paragraph-by-paragraph commentary; none conducts a sustained analytical-exegetical essay (though Sifra and the two Sifrés are rich in sustained arguments). By contrast, no composite passage of the two Talmuds is exhaustively comprehensible without knowledge of the passage of the Mishnah around which the two Talmuds' discourse centers. So the two Talmuds are like one another and unlike all other writings of their class.

Yet in describing and defining the two Talmuds, we should grossly err if we were to say they are only, or mainly, a step-by-step commentary

The Bavli: Form and Program

on the Mishnah, defined solely by the Mishnah's interests. Speaking of both documents for the present purpose as "the Talmud,"[1] we may say very simply: The Talmud is in full command of its own program of thought and inquiry. Its framers, responsible for the units of discourse, chose what in the Mishnah will be analyzed and what ignored. True, there could be no Talmud without the Mishnah and Tosefta, heavily cited as they are in the Talmuds. But knowing only those two works, we could never have predicted in a systematic way the character of the Talmuds' discourse at any point.

The Talmuds invariably do to the Mishnah one of these four things: (l) text criticism, (2) exegesis of the meaning of the Mishnah, including glosses and amplifications, (3) addition of scriptural prooftexts of the Mishnah's central propositions, and (4) harmonization of one Mishnah passage with another such passage or with a statement of Tosefta. The first two of these four procedures remain wholly within the narrow frame of the Mishnah passage subject to discussion. The second pair take an essentially independent stance vis-à-vis the Mishnah pericope at hand. The Mishnah is read by the Talmuds as a composite of discrete and essentially autonomous rules, a set of atoms, not an integrated molecule, so to speak. In so doing, the most striking formal traits of the Mishnah are obliterated. It follows that the Talmuds are a composite of three kinds of materials: [1] exegeses of the Mishnah, [2] exegeses of Scripture, and [3] accounts of the men who provide both. Perhaps one might wish to see the Talmud as a reworking of its two antecedent documents: the Mishnah, lacking much reference to Scripture, and the Scripture itself. The Talmuds bring the two together into a synthesis of their own making, both in reading Scripture into Mishnah, and in reading Scripture alongside of, and separate from, Mishnah.

What legitimates comparing a talmud to a rivayat – to backtrack briefly – is that both constitute (re)statements of practical law, gained through applied logic. Not only so, but a concern critical to each kind of writing involves the question, what is justice in the context of practical life. To facilitate the literary comparisons that follow in the shank of the book, I give a sizable sample of Talmudic discourse, to match the samples that are coming of rivayat discourse. The sample will further serve in the exposition at Chapter Nine.

---

[1] In the last chapter, when I ask, what does the comparative perspective teach me about the Bavli, I shall turn back and compare the Bavli to the Yerushalmi, turning to the Yerushalmi's reading of the same Mishnah paragraphs treated here, and thus completing the comparative exercise of the present study by turning from external writings to a close affine of the Bavli.

I give the citations from the Mishnah and Tosefta in boldface type. Since the Talmud is in Aramaic, but the formulated rules, for example, Tosefta, Mishnah, and other rules of the same status, ordinarily are given in Mishnaic Hebrew, I give the Aramaic in italics, the Hebrew in plain type. Aramaic bears the analytical discussion, the Hebrew, the rules. My sample derives from the Babylonian Talmud, the fourth division, Neziqin or damages, which deals with civil law and justice, tractate Baba Mesia, chapter one, Mishnah paragraphs one and two. The figure in square brackets, [2A] and so on, refers to the printed page, second page, obverse side; [2B] then is the reverse side, and so on throughout. All editions of the Talmud of Babylonia follow the same pagination.

Babylonian Talmud to Mishnah-tractate Baba Mesia 1:1-2

1:1

- A. **[2A] Two lay hold of a cloak –**
- B. **this one says, "I found it!" –**
- C. **and that one says, "I found it!" –**
- D. **this one says, "It's all mine!" –**
- E. **and that one says, "It's all mine!" –**
- F. **this one takes an oath that he possesses no less a share of it than half,**
- G. **and that one takes an oath that he possesses no less a share of it than half,**
- H. **and they divide it up.**
- I. **This one says, "It's all mine!" –**
- J. **and that one says, "Half of it is mine!" –**
- K. **the one who says, "It's all mine!" takes an oath that he possesses no less of a share of it than three parts,**
- L. **and the one who says, "Half of it is mine!" takes an oath that he possesses no less a share of it than a fourth part.**
- M. **This one then takes three shares, and that one takes the fourth.**

1:2

- A. **Two were riding on a beast,**
- B. **or one was riding and one was leading it –**
- C. **this one says, "It's all mine!" –**
- D. **and that one says, "It's all mine!" –**
- E. **this one takes an oath that he possesses no less a share of it than half,**
- F. **and that one takes an oath that he possesses no less a share of it than half.**
- G. **And they divide it.**
- H. **But when they concede [that they found it together] or have witnesses to prove it, they divide [the beast's value] without taking an oath.**

I.1
- A. *What need do I have to repeat in the Mishnah,*
- B. **this one says, "I found it!" –**
- C. **and that one says, "I found it!" –**

The Bavli: Form and Program

	D.	**this one says, "It's all mine!"** –
	E.	**and that one says, "It's all mine!"?**
	F.	*Let the Tanna repeat only a single* [plea] [surely one plea would have been sufficient].
	G.	*It is only a single [formulation] that the Tanna has repeated* [Daiches: It is only one plea], *namely,*
	H.	*"This one says, 'I found it and it's all mine...,' and that one says, 'I found it and it's all mine....'"*
I.2	A.	*Then let the Tanna repeat [the plea],* "I found it," *and I shall [naturally] know the fact [that the litigant has claimed],* "It's all mine"!
	B.	*Had the Tanna [repeated the formulation solely as,]* "I have found it," *I might have reached the conclusion, "What is the sense of* 'I have found it'? *'I saw it, even though it did not actually come into my hands. Through merely seeing the object, I have effected acquisition of it.'"*
	C.	*The Tanna [has formulated the rule in the language of]* **"It's all mine!"** *to indicate that merely by seeing the object, the man has not made acquisition of it.*
I.3	A.	*But can you really maintain that the sense of* "I have found it" *must be* "I saw it"?
	B.	*Now lo,* Rabbanai has said, "'And you find' (Deut. 22:3: 'And so shall you do with any lost thing of your brother's, which he loses and you find') – [that is to say,] *that it has come into his possession."*
	C.	*Indeed so, when Scripture says,* "And you find," *the sense is, that it has come into his possession."*
	D.	*Nonetheless, [in the passage at hand,] the Tanna has employed the [commonplace and] prevailing usage.*
	E.	*[And, in accord with that usage, once] one has seen [an object], he takes the view, "I have found it," so that even though the object has not actually come into the man's possession, [he supposes that merely because] he has seen the object, he has effected possession of it.*
	F.	*The Tanna [has formulated the rule in the language of]* **"It's all mine!"** *to indicate that merely by seeing the object, the man has not made acquisition of it.*
I.4	A.	*Then let the Tanna repeat [the plea],* "It's all mine," *and he then need not repeat in the passage the wording,* "It's all mine"!
	B.	*Had the Tanna [repeated the formulation solely as,]* "It's all mine," *I might have reached the conclusion that in general, when the Tanna uses the language,* "I have found it," *the sense is that merely by sighting an object in general, one has acquired possession of it.*
	C.	*He has formulated matters in the language of* **"I have found it,"** *and then gone and formulated the passage further,* **"It's all mine,"** *so that, from this repetition we should draw the conclusion that merely by the act of sighting an object, one has not acquired possession of it.*
I.5	A.	*But can you really maintain that it is only a single [formulation] that the Tanna has repeated,* namely, ["This one says, 'I found it and it's all mine...,' and that one says, 'I found it and it's all mine....'"]? [Up to this point in its analysis of the Mishnah, the Talmud has sought to establish that the first two clauses, "I found it," and "All of it is mine," are two necessary features of a single, integral unit, dealing with one particular case. The Talmud now proceeds to attack this basic assumption and asks, Can you say that the Mishnah in its two

opening statements is teaching one particular case with one particular claim? Surely the wording indicates that the Mishnah is referring not to one but to two separate and distinct cases.]

B. Lo, the Tanna has repeated matters in the language, "This one says...and that one says...": [Steinsaltz: The implication of this language is that there are two separate and distinct claims, and not the same claim repeated in different terms!]

C. [thus:] **This one says, "I found it!"** –
D. **and that one says, "I found it!"** –
E. **this one says, "It's all mine!"** –
F. **and that one says, "It's all mine!"**?
G. *Said R. Pappa, and some attribute the statement to R. Shimi b. R. Ashi, or assign it to Kadi, "The initial case involves an object that has been found, the succeeding one, a case of purchase and sale."*
H. *And both of these cases had to be addressed individually.*
I. *[2B] For if the Tanna had repeated the rule only concerning the case of a conflict over an object that has been found, I might have reached the conclusion that it is specifically in the case of an object that has been found that rabbis have imposed the requirement of taking an oath, since each party might allow himself to lay claim, saying, "My fellow loses nothing if I go and take possession of the object and split the object with him, [since the other never owned the garment to begin with and paid nothing for it]. But in the case of a dispute over who has purchased a given object, where there can be no such calculation, I might say that [sages have] not imposed [the requirement of an oath.]*
J. *And if the Tanna had repeated the rule only concerning the case of conflict over an object that has been purchased [in which both parties claim to have purchased the same thing], the reason that rabbis have imposed the requirement of taking an oath in such a case in particular is this: The litigant may permit himself to lay claim, saying, "My fellow has paid for the object, and I can go and pay for the object. Now that I need it, I'll grab it, and let the fellow go and take the trouble to buy another object." But in the case of a dispute over an object that has been found, in which case such reasoning will not apply, I might say that that is not the rule. Accordingly, it was necessary [to impose the same rule in the case of a conflict over an object that has been purchased].*

I.6 A. *But in a case of an object that has been purchased, then [why should there be such a conflict between two equally valid claims, without evidence available to settle matters]?*
B. *Just see from whom [the seller] has accepted the money [and when he indicates who paid for the cloak, we know the resolution of the conflict].*
C. *Not at all, the [oath is] required in a case in which the seller has taken money from them both, one of them willingly, one of them under constraint, and we do now know from whom it was taken willingly, and from whom under constraint.*

Let me now explain what we have read. The analysis of the Mishnah paragraph on the part of the Bavli begins with the analysis of the way in which it is formulated. The premise of the Bavli is that the Mishnah's framers do not repeat themselves, so that if there is what appears to be repetition, it is to make a point, for example, deal with a case that for

The Bavli: Form and Program

some reason differs from the initial one. We begin with the question, 1.F, why has the matter been repeated, in that each party is assigned two pleas, first, I found the object, second, I wholly possess it. The first answer is as given at G-H. This is challenged at 2.B and the reason for the specific wording is then adduced. It is to exclude misinterpretation of the law. Had the language been other than what it is, we should have misinformation on the rule. This position is again challenged and reinforced at No. 3 and No. 4, which goes over familiar materials.

The second fresh initiative commences at No. 5, which revises the grounds of analysis. Up to this point, we have assumed that we deal with a single case, one in which two people contest the possession of a single object, both of them claiming to have found it. But the language "It's all mine" can be read to speak of a quite distinct situation from one involving lost-and-found. Now we have two people who contest ownership of an object both claim to have purchased. This second initiative, fully worked out, is then challenged on the obvious ground that someone out there should have the facts, so why bother with an oath? Then, 6.C, we create a situation in which the seller cannot supply the required testimony, so we still are in a case of equally valid claims and so invoke the oath. This concludes the analysis of the Mishnah's paragraph pretty much in its own terms.

But the Mishnah's rule and case(s) bear a variety of implications, some of them right on the surface, and one of them demands analysis in its turn. It is that an oath is imposed in a case such as this – which is the absolute given of our Mishnah paragraph and the purpose for which that paragraph of three cases has been composed. But are we not then engaged in a kind of entrapment, since we are imposing an oath on two parties in the certain knowledge that one of the two parties is going to swear falsely? That question now demands attention in its own terms.

II.1   A.   [2B] *May one claim that the Mishnah passage before us* [in requiring the taking of an oath to settle the matter] *does not accord with the principle of Ben Nannus?*
       B.   For **Ben Nannus has said, "How is it possible that this party and that that party should be brought into the state of taking a false oath?" (M. Shebu. 7:5)** [The reference is to M. Shebu. 7:1A, C: These are the ones who take an oath and collect what is owing to him:...a shopkeeper concerning what is written in his account book. M. Shebu. 7:5: A shopkeeper concerning what is written in his account book – how so? It is not that he may say to him, "It is written in my account book that you owe me two hundred zuz." But if the householder said to him, "Give my son two seahs of wheat," "Give my worker change for a sela," and he says, "I already gave it to him," and they say, "We never got it" – the storekeeper takes an oath and collects what is owing to him, and

the workers take an oath and collect what they claim from the householder. Said Ben Nannus, "How so? But these or those then are taking a vain oath! Rather, the storekeeper collects what is owing to him without taking an oath at all, and the workers collect what they claim not to have received without taking an oath."]

C. [The case before us may accord] *even with the principle of Ben Nannus* [who will not impose an oath in a case in which it is clear one or another party will be taking the oath falsely].

D. *In the case to which Ben Nannus refers* [in stating his principle], *there is most assuredly going to be a false oath.*

E. *But in the present case, there is the possibility of claiming that there is no false oath.*

F. *One may say that the two of them at the same instant raised up the object* [and thereby effected possession of it, so both can be telling the truth].

II.2 A. *May one claim that the Mishnah passage* [in requiring the taking of an oath to settle the matter] *before us does not accord with the principle of Sumkhos (Symmachus)?*

B. *For if it were to accord with Sumkhos, has he not said,* "As to money that is subject to doubt [and therefore contested ownership], that money is divided without the taking of an oath"?

C. *But then what* [alternative do you propose? Is it that the Mishnah passage before us accords with the principle of] *sages* [vis-à-vis Symmachus]?

D. *Lo, they have maintained,* He who proposes to take away [the property of another] bears the burden of bringing proof of the validity of his claim. [So they, too, will not concur that an oath will serve to settle the issue here.]

E. *Now if, as a matter of fact, you introduce the position of sages* [vis-à-vis Symmachus], *in that case, in which both parties have not seized hold of the property that is disputed, rabbis indeed rule,* He who proposes to take away [the property of another] bears the burden of bringing proof of the validity of his claim.

F. *But in this case, in which both parties have seized hold of the property that is disputed, they indeed will divide the object upon the taking of an oath.*

G. *But if, on the other hand, you maintain that [the Mishnah passage at hand] accords with the principle of Sumkhos,* [we may formulate matters in this way and so demonstrate the contradiction between his principle and the ruling before us]:

H. *If in such a situation, in which both parties have not in fact seized hold of the disputed object, they are to divide the object without the taking of an oath, here, in which both parties have seized hold of the disputed property, is it not an argument a fortiori* [that they should divide the object without taking an oath! Accordingly, the present ruling cannot accord with the position of Sumkhos].

I. *You may even take the view that the Mishnah passage before us accords with the principle of Sumkhos.*

J. *When Sumkhos took the view that he did, it is in the situation in which each party is uncertain* [as to the facts of the matter, so neither of them can be made to take an oath], *but in a case, such as this one, in*

The Bavli: Form and Program

which both parties express certainty about their rights of ownership, he would take a different view.

K. And in the view of Rabbah bar R. Huna, who stated, "Sumkhos said, 'Even in a case in which both parties express certainty about their rights of ownership [an oath is taken to settle the conflicting claims], what is there to be said?

L. You may even maintain that in such a case, it is still in accord with the view of Sumkhos.

M. When Sumkhos took the view he did, it was in a case in which there would be a loss of money.

N. But does that view not yield an argument a fortiori [which will prove that Sumkhos does not accord with our Mishnah paragraph]?

O. If in the case to which reference is made, a loss of money to one party is involved, and a loss of money to the other party is equally involved, [3A]

P. and, further, one may maintain that the whole of the disputed item may belong to one party, and one may maintain that the whole of the disputed item may belong to the other party, and, in such a case, Sumkhos has adopted the principle, "As to money that is subject to doubt [and therefore contested ownership], that money is divided without the taking of an oath," here [in the case of the Mishnah's rule],

Q. in which case there is no question of a loss of money to either party, for one may rule that the disputed property belongs to both parties [and so may be divided without an oath taken by either one], is it not an argument a fortiori [and hence the Mishnah cannot accord with Sumkhos, who will have the property equally divided without the taking of an oath]!

R. You may, indeed, still hold [that the Mishnah passage accords with the principle of] Sumkhos.

S. This oath [of which the Mishnah speaks] is imposed only by the authority of the rabbis [and not on the authority of the Torah. There are then two kinds of oath, and when Sumkhos avoids imposing an oath, as in the cases just now discussed, it is an oath on the authority of the Torah. The distinction between the two kinds of oaths permits us to allow that, in the present case, Sumkhos would concur that an oath is invoked, while in the cases of which he speaks elsewhere, it is not invoked. The difference then vitiates the argument a fortiori].

T. And that accords with the view of R. Yohanan, for said R. Yohanan, "This oath [to which our Mishnah passage refers] happens to be an ordinance imposed only by rabbis,

U. "so that people should not go around grabbing the cloaks of other people and saying, 'It's mine!'" [But, as a matter of fact, the oath that is imposed in our Mishnah passage is not legitimate by the law of the Torah. It is an act taken by sages to maintain the social order.]

III.3 A. May one claim that the Mishnah passage [in requiring the taking of an oath to settle the matter] before us does not accord with the principle of R. Yosé?

B. For if it were to accord with R. Yosé, has he not said, **[Two who deposited something with one person, this one leaving a maneh [one hundred zuz], and that one leaving two hundred zuz – this** one says, "Mine is the deposit of two hundred zuz," and that one says, "Mine is the deposit of two hundred zuz" — he pays off a maneh to this one and a maneh to that one, and the rest is left until Elijah comes. Said R. Yosé,] "If that is the case [that one may take an oath and (merely in that way) acquire possession of property subject to dispute], then what does a liar lose? But let everything be left until Elijah comes [and settles matters]"? [M. B.M. 3:4F-G].

C. But with whom then may we say the passage accords? Is it with the possession of rabbis vis-à-vis R. Yosé?

D. But since rabbis [vis-à-vis R. Yosé] have said, "**Let the remainder [of the property under dispute in the cited passage] remain until Elijah comes [and settles matters],**" lo, [the cloak in the Mishnah paragraph before us is in the status of] the remainder [in the case under discussion, for it is subject to doubt.

E. How now! [Daiches: What a comparison!] If you have invoked the position of rabbis in that other case, in which the money at issue assuredly belongs to one of the two parties, so that, in that case, sages have ruled, "**Let the remainder [of the property under dispute in the cited passage] remain until Elijah comes [and settles matters],**" in the present case, in which there is the possibility of claiming that it belongs to both of the claimants, rabbis would [reasonably] take the position that it should indeed be divided upon the taking of an oath.

F. But if you take the position that the passage before us accords with R. Yosé, [that is quite a difficult view, for] if in the case [of M. B.M. 3:4], where it is certain that each claimant beyond doubt is entitled to a maneh, R. Yosé has said, "**Let the remainder [of the property under dispute in the cited passage] remain until Elijah comes [and settles matters],**" in the present case, in which one may claim that the cloak belongs to only one of the two parties, is it not an argument a fortiori [that the property should be left in the custody of the court and not divided by means of an oath]?

G. [To the contrary,] you may even maintain that the Mishnah paragraph represents the view of R. Yosé. In that other case, there most assuredly is a liar. But here, who will say with certainty that there is a liar? I should claim that the two of them at one and the same moment raised up the cloak.

H. Or in that other case, R. Yosé imposed an extrajudicial fine upon the liar so that he would be impelled to confess his deceit, while here, what loss is incurred that would impel the deceiver to confess? [He will incur no loss if he forfeits the garment.]

I. That argument suffices for the case of an object that has been found [to which the two lay claim], but what is there to be said about the case of an object that has been purchased [and subject to dispute as to who has paid for it]?

J. But the initial answer [Daiches: that in the other case one claimant is certainly fraudulent, while in our case both may be honest] is the better one.

III.4 A. [With reference to M. Shebu. 7:5, cited above, **A shopkeeper concerning what is written in his account book – how so?** It is not that he may say to him, "It is written in my account book that you owe me two hundred zuz." But if the householder said to him,

The Bavli: Form and Program 43

"Give my son two seahs of wheat," "Give my worker change for a sela," and he says, "I already gave it to him," and they say, "We never got it" – the storekeeper takes an oath and collects what is owing to him, and the workers take an oath and collect what they claim from the householder. Said Ben Nannus, "How so? But these or those then are taking a vain oath! Rather, the storekeeper collects what is owing to him without taking an oath at all, and the workers collect what they claim not to have received without taking an oath,"] *whether with regard to the position of rabbis or to that of R. Yosé* [who concur that the liar should not profit from his lying], *in the case involving the storekeeper, at which it is repeated,* **the storekeeper takes an oath and collects what is owing to him, and the workers take an oath and collect what they claim from the householder,** *how is that case to be differentiated from this one, in that there we do not rule, let the money be taken from the householder [who certainly owes it to either the storekeeper or the workers, who were to be paid in kind through their purchases at the company store], and* **Let the remainder [of the property under dispute in the cited passage] remain until Elijah comes [and settles matters]**?

B. *For lo, in that case,* [one or another of the parties to the dispute] *most certainly is a liar!*

C. *In that case, here is the reason [for the ruling as it is given]: The storekeeper may say to the householder, "I was your agent in this matter and have carried out your mission. What business have I to do with the worker* [who claims not to have been paid]? *Even though he may take an oath to me, even when he takes an oath, he is not credible to me. You were the one who laid your trust in him, for you did not say to me, 'Only in the presence of witnesses are you to pay him off.'"* ["You were the one who trusted the worker, now you are the one who has to be penalized if he takes the oath."]

D. *And along these same lines the worker may say to the householder, "I did my work for you. What business do I have with the storekeeper? Even though he takes an oath to me, he is not credible to me."*

E. *Therefore both claimants are to take oaths and collect what is owing from the householder.* [In that way we differentiate the case cited in connection with Ben Nannus from the case at hand involving Yosé. The two cases have nothing to do with each other, by reason of differing circumstances.]

To take up the task of exposition once more: The sustained exposition of II.1-4 shows how a single hand – one editor or a hundred, it hardly matters – has put together a systematic study of the problem of settling a dispute by taking an oath. Framing matters in terms of named authorities, the author before us has raised principles that must be brought into relationship, and if possible harmonized, with the rule before us. The Talmud therefore engages in a vast labor of detailed comparison and contrast of cases and rules, aiming at a single cogent statement of the whole. No. 1 raises the question of allowing an oath to settle a dispute, since liars take oaths as much as do God-fearing folk. At

No. 1 we point out how our passage accords with – does not contradict – the view of Ben Nannus. Where there is the certainty that one party to a dispute must be lying, we do not invoke the oath; but here there is no such certainty.

But, quite to the contrary, No. 2 asks, why require an oath at all? If both parties can be telling the truth, then let them divide the disputed property without the fearsome procedure. The solution to this problem is to differentiate the cases. No. 3 proceeds to a third authority, Yosé, who raises the same question as Ben Nannus: Why permit a liar to benefit? The solution once again is to differentiate the cases. And, No. 4 shows, we may also harmonize the views of Ben Nannus and Yosé and our passage. I cannot think of a more perfect execution of the task, which is to introduce all pertinent cases and principles and show how they either accord with one another or do not contradict one another. Nothing is omitted; everything is satisfactorily ordered.

IV.1   A.   [5B] **This one takes an oath that he possesses no less a share of it than half, [and that one takes an oath that he possesses no less a share of it than half, and they divide it up]:**
       B.   *Is it concerning the portion that he claims he possesses that he takes the oath, or concerning the portion that he does not claim to possess?*
       C.   *Said R. Huna, "It is that he says, 'By an oath! I possess in it a portion, and I possess in it a portion that is no less than half a share of it.'"* [The claimant swears that his share is at least half (Daiches).]
       D.   *Then let him say, "By an oath! The whole of it is mine!"*
       E.   *But are we going to give him the whole of it?* [Obviously not, there is another claimant, also taking an oath.]
       F.   *Then let him say, "By an oath! Half of it is mine!"*
       G.   *That would damage his own claim* [which was that he owned the whole of the cloak, not only half of it].
       H.   *But here, too, is it not the fact that, in the oath that he is taking, he impairs his own claim?* [After all, he here makes explicit the fact that he owns at least half of it. What happened to the other half?]
       I.   *[Not at all.] For he has said, "The whole of it is mine!"* [And, he further proceeds,] *"And as to your contrary view, By an oath, I do have a share in it, and that share is no less than half!"*

IV.2   A.   Now, since this one is possessed of the cloak and standing right there, and that one is possessed of the cloak and is standing right there, why in the world do I require this oath?
       B.   Said R. Yohanan, "This oath [to which our Mishnah passage refers] happens to be an ordinance imposed only by rabbis,
       C.   "so that people should not go around grabbing the cloaks of other people and saying, 'It's mine!'" [But, as a matter of fact, the oath that is imposed in our Mishnah passage is not legitimate by the law of the Torah. It is an act taken by sages to maintain the social order.]

The Bavli: Form and Program 45

D. *But why then not advance the following argument: Since such a one is suspect as to fraud in a property claim, he also should be suspect as to fraud in oath-taking?*

E. *In point of fact, we do not advance the following argument: Since such a one is suspect as to fraud in a property claim, he also should be suspect as to fraud in oath-taking, for if you do not concede that fact, then how is it possible that the All-Merciful has ruled, "One who has conceded part of a claim against himself must take an oath as to the remainder of what is subject to claim"?*

F. *Why not simply maintain, since such a one is suspect as to fraud in a property claim, he also should be suspect as to fraud in oath-taking?*

G. *In that other case, [the reason for the denial of part of the claim and the admission of part is not the intent to commit fraud, but rather,] the defendant is just trying to put off the claim for a spell.*

H. *This concurs with the position of Rabbah. [For Rabbah has said, "On what account has the Torah imposed the requirement of an oath on one who confesses to only part of a claim against him? It is by reason of the presumption that a person will not insolently deny the truth about the whole of a loan in the very presence of the creditor and so entirely deny the debt. He will admit to part of the debt and deny part of it. Hence we invoke an oath in a case in which one does so, to coax out the truth of the matter."]*

I. *For you may know, [in support of the foregoing,] that R. Idi bar Abin said R. Hisda [said]: "He who [falsely] denies owing money on a loan nonetheless is suitable to give testimony, but he who denies that he holds a bailment for another party cannot give testimony."*

J. *But what about that which R. Ammi bar Hama repeated on Tannaite authority: "[If they are to be subjected to an oath,] four sorts of bailees have to have denied part of the bailment and conceded part of the bailment, namely, the unpaid bailee, the borrower, the paid bailee, and the one who rents."*

K. *Why not simply maintain, since such a one is suspect as to fraud in a property claim, he also should be suspect as to fraud in oath-taking?*

L. *In that case as well, [the reason for the denial of part of the claim and the admission of part is not the intent to commit fraud, but rather,] the defendant is just trying to put off the claim for a spell.*

M. *He reasons as follows: "I'm going to find the thief and arrest him." Or: "I'll find [the beast] in the field and return it to the owner."*

N. *If that is the case, then why should one who denies holding a bailment ever be unsuitable to give testimony? How come we don't just maintain that the defendant is just trying to put off the claim for a spell. He reasons as follows: "I'm going to look for the thing and find it."*

O. *When in point of fact we do rule, He who denies holding a bailment is unfit to give testimony, it is in a case in which witnesses come and give testimony against him that at that very moment, the bailment is located in the bailee's domain, and he fully is informed of that fact, or, alternatively, he has the object in his possession at that very moment.*

IV.3 A. *But as to that which R. Huna has said [when we have a bailee who offers to pay compensation for a lost bailment rather than swear it has been lost, since he wishes to appropriate the article by paying*

		for it, (Daiches)], "They impose upon him the oath that the bailment is not in his possession at all,"
	B.	*why not in that case invoke the principle, since such a one is suspect as to fraud in a property claim, he also should be suspect as to fraud in oath-taking?*
	C.	*In that case also, he may rule in his own behalf, "I'll give him the money."*
IV.4	A.	*Said R. Aha of Difti to Rabina, "But then the man clearly transgresses the negative commandment: 'You shall not covet.'"*
	B.	*"You shall not covet" is generally understood by people to pertain to something for which one is not ready to pay.*
IV.5	A.	[6A] *But as to that which R. Nahman said,* "They impose upon him [who denies the whole of a claim] an oath of inducement," *why not in that case invoke the principle, since such a one is suspect as to fraud in a property claim, he also should be suspect as to fraud in oath-taking?*
	B.	*And furthermore, there is that which R. Hiyya taught on Tannaite authority:* "Both parties [employee, supposed to have been paid out of an account set up by the employer at a local store, and storekeeper] take an oath and collect what each claims from the employer," *why not in that case invoke the principle, since such a one is suspect as to fraud in a property claim, he also should be suspect as to fraud in oath-taking?*
	C.	*And furthermore, there is that which R. Sheshet said,* "We impose upon an unpaid bailee [who claims that the animal has been lost] three distinct oaths: first, an oath that I have not deliberately caused the loss, that I did not put a hand on it, and that it is not in my domain at all," *why not in that case invoke the principle, since such a one is suspect as to fraud in a property claim, he also should be suspect as to fraud in oath-taking?*
	D.	*It must follow that we do not invoke the principle at all, since such a one is suspect as to fraud in a property claim, he also should be suspect as to fraud in oath-taking.*
IV.6	A.	[Reverting to the issue of 2A, explaining why the oath is required, we have an explanation alternative to that of Yohanan in what] Abbayye said, [namely,] "*We take account of the possibility that the plaintiff may intend to lay claim for repayment of a defunct loan.*" [Daiches: A litigant may deem himself entitled to an article found by his opponent, on the ground that the latter had borrowed money from him a long time ago and had forgotten about it. Such a litigant would not hesitate to plead that he had found the garment, or that it was all his, in the hope that at least half the value of the garment would be awarded to him. Hence the need for an oath.]
	B.	*If that is the case, then let him keep the cloak without taking an oath at all?*
	C.	*Rather, the reason is,* "*We take account of the possibility that the plaintiff may intend to lay a doubtful claim for repayment of a defunct loan.*"
	D.	*But do we not maintain that one who maintains possession of property on account of a matter of doubt also is subject to doubt as to an oath that he may take?*
	E.	*Said R. Sheshet son of R. Idi,* "People keep far from taking an oath by reason of doubtful claims, while they do not keep far from holding on to property even though their right to it is subject to doubt. What's the

> *difference? You can give back the money, but you can't give back the false oath!"*

To conclude this presentation of a sample of the Talmud: The exposition is cogent and to the point. A single question predominates, which is, why impose this oath? The first issue, predictably, is one of clarification, and No. 1 answers the question. The oath pertains to what the man claims he owns, not to the part he does not own. No. 2 then asks why this oath is imposed, but with a separate issue in mind: Does the oath tell me something I otherwise would not have known? Clearly, not. Yohanan's answer then proposes the reason for the oath; we see that the answer goes over familiar grounds, but it is challenged by a fresh consideration. If someone is suspect as to fraud, so that an oath is required, then why believe his oath at all? No. 2 works out that consideration. No. 3 goes over the same issue, and No. 4 repeats the issue but in a new context. No. 5 proceeds along these same lines. Then No. 6 continues the same discussion, again with a new argument. So the whole is remarkably cogent, beginning to end. So much for our sample.

To conclude the presentation in more general terms: The purpose of the Talmud is to clarify and amplify selected passages of the Mishnah. We may say very simply that the Mishnah is about life, and the Talmud is about the Mishnah. While the Mishnah records rules governing the conduct of the holy life of Israel, the holy people, the Talmud concerns itself with the details of the Mishnah. The one is descriptive and free-standing, the other analytical and contingent. Were there no Mishnah, there would be no Talmud. But the Talmud of Babylonia in fact vastly transcends the Mishnah and forms an eloquent statement of its own.

Our sample leaves a single strong impression: The Talmud of Babylonia speaks in one voice. Quite how a vast and dense writing turns out to say some few things, and to say them with such power as to impose its judgment upon an entire prior writing and on the intellect of an entire religious world to come, requires attention. For it is the fact that, in the Judaism of the Dual Torah, the faithful meet God in the Torah, and the Talmud of Babylonia forms the centerpiece of the Torah. The Bavli's compilers and the writers of its compositions found the way to form the mind and define the intellect of the faithful. And this they did not through statements of doctrine or law, but through the public display of right reasoning, the exposition of argument; to state what I conceive to have been their conviction: If you can show people how to think, then, in the context of a revealed Torah, you can also guide them to what to think: right thoughts, right deeds, right attitudes.

The Bavli is a uniform document, beginning to end. Different from, much more than, a haphazard compilation of traditions, this Talmud shows itself upon examination to be a cogent and purposive writing, in which through a single determinate set of rhetoric devices, a single program of inquiry is brought to bear on many and diverse passages of two inherited documents, the Mishnah and Scripture. The voice is one and single because it is a voice that everywhere expresses the same limited set of sounds. It is singular because these notes are arranged in one and the same way throughout. The Bavli's one voice, sounding through all tractates, is the voice of exegetes of the Mishnah. The document is organized around the Mishnah, and that order is not merely formal, but substantive. At *every* point, if the framers have chosen a passage of Mishnah exegesis, that passage will stand at the head of all further discussion. *Every* turning point in every sustained composition and even in a large composite of compositions brings the editors back to the Mishnah, *always* read in its own order and *invariably* arranged in its own sequence.

So the Bavli's speaks in a single way about some few things. It follows that well-crafted and orderly rules governed the character of the sustained discourse that the writing in the Bavli sets forth. All framers of composites and editors of sequences of composites found guidance in the same limited repertoire of rules of analytical rhetoric: some few questions or procedures, directed always toward one and the same prior writing. Not only so, but a fixed order of discourse dictated that a composition of one sort, A, always come prior to a composite of another type, B. A simple logic instructed framers of composites, who sometimes also were authors of compositions, and who sometimes drew upon available compositions in the making of their cogent composites. So we have now to see the Bavli as entirely of a piece, cogent and coherent, made up of well-composed large-scale constructions. Three generalizations suffice.

First, we are able to classify *all* composites (among the more than three thousand that I examined for the purpose of this description of the document) in three principal categories: [1] exegesis and amplification of the law of the Mishnah; [2] exegesis and exposition of verses of, or topics in, Scripture; [3] free-standing composites devoted to topics other than those defined by the Mishnah or Scripture. These classifications were not forced or subtle; the grounds for making them were consistent; appeal throughout was to gross and merely formal characteristics, not to subjective judgments of what unstipulated consideration might underlie, or define, the intention of the framer of a passage.

Second, with that classification in place, it is a matter of simple fact that much more than four-fifths of all composites of the Bavli address the Mishnah and systematically expound that document. These composites are subject to subclassification in two ways: Mishnah exegesis and speculation and abstract theorizing about the implications of the

Mishnah's statements. The former type of composite, further, is to be classified in a few and simple taxa, for example, composites organized around [1] clarification of the statements of the Mishnah, [2] identification of the authority behind an anonymous statement in the Mishnah, [3] scriptural foundation for the Mishnah's rules, [4] citation and not seldom systematic exposition of the Tosefta's amplification of the Mishnah. That means that most of the Bavli is a systematic exposition of the Mishnah.

Third, the other fifth (or still less) of a given tractate will comprise composites that take shape around [1] Scripture or [2] themes or topics of a generally theological or moral character. Distinguishing the latter from the former, of course, is merely formal; very often a scriptural topic will be set forth in a theological or moral framework, and very seldom does a composite on a topic omit all reference to the amplification of a verse or topic of Scripture. The proportion of a given tractate devoted to other-than-Mishnah exegesis and amplification is generally not more than 10 percent.

The upshot is simple and demands heavy emphasis: *The Bavli speaks about the Mishnah in essentially a single voice, about fundamentally few things.* Its mode of speech as much as of thought is uniform throughout. Diverse topics produce slight differentiation in modes of analysis. The same sorts of questions phrased in the same rhetoric – a moving, or dialectical, argument, composed of questions and answers – turn out to pertain equally well to every subject and problem. The Talmud's discourse forms a closed system, in which people say the same thing about everything. The fact that the Talmud speaks in a single voice supplies striking evidence (1) that the Talmud does speak in particular for the age in which its units of discourse took shape, and (2) that that work was done toward the end of that long period of Mishnah reception that began at the end of the second century and came to an end at the conclusion of the sixth century, at the dusk of late antiquity, the eve of the Muslim conquest of Iran, including Babylonia. Now to the work at hand: the comparison of the two Rivayats with the Bavli.

Part One

THE PAHLAVI RIVAYAT OF
ATURFARNBAG AND THE TALMUD

4

The Pahlavi Rivayat of Aturfarnbag and the Bavli: Description and Comparison

Let us start with a sample of the first of our two rivayats. I reproduce a sizable selection of the complete text in *The Pahlavi Rivayat of Aturfarnbag and Farnbag Srosh,* translated by Behramgore Bahmuras Anklesaria (Bombay, 1969: Kaikhusroo M. Jamasp Asa). Aturfarnbag answers 147 questions, and his questions and answers were collected in book form; but the unit of thought is the question and the answer. Following Anklesaria's summary, we note that Nos. 2-5 deal with the problem of a wife whose husband apostatized, that is, abandoned the religion; what is the status of his wife, who now is without a guardian, her guardianship having been vested in the husband: "As she could not remarry without being given away by her guardian, who could not be an independent wife without being handed over in marriage by her guardian, so she is in the status of one who has married without her guardian's consent." Nos. 6-17, 19-20 deal with guardianship in other aspects. Nos. 18, 21-28 deal with a man who has no son to inherit his wealth and who accepts a person as his adoptive child, male or female. Nos. 29-30 deal with the wickedness of a wife or child. Nos. 31-33, 34-36, 37-50, 54-55, 63-65 deal with purity rules, corpse uncleanness, and the like. Nos. 51, 56-59 deal with personal injuries, 52-53 with those who commit the sin of removing the sacred thread girdle. Nos. 66-69, 72 deal with civil suits, involving lending and borrowing, mortgage of property, and the like; also jailing debtors. Further issues of purity rules follow, to the end.[1]

---

[1] Anklesaria, pp. 36-44.

My sample covers topics addressed, also, by the Bavli to some of which we shall return, for example, questions that have to do with personal status, especially of women, and the social order, for example, property transactions, issues of ethics, and the like.

Several Questions Asked of Aerpat Atar-frenabag Son of Farokhuzat leader of the Faithful

I

Question

1. There is a man who has a daughter; two men desire her in marriage, and the father gives her to one of the men; the daughter does not agree to that man; her liking is towards the other man; does the prerogative rest with the father or with the daughter? And if the father does not fulfill the wish of the daughter, is the daughter entitled to fix her guardian, and to have a husband? And if she does not fix a guardian, can the daughter be an independent wife or not?

Reply

2. As I understand: the father is entitled to assign the guardianship; as long as he is living, he is entitled to withdraw the guardianship, whenever it is necessary, but with the consent of the woman and even that of the guardian; it cannot be otherwise; she cannot have a husband otherwise, but with the consent of the father as long as the father is living, and with the consent of the guardian, after the father's passing away.

II

Question

1. When a man gives away a daughter to a man, that man becomes renegade; with whom rests the guardianship of that woman? And if she marries, can she be an independent wife or not?

Reply

2. There are different views thereon; there is one who said, "Whoever marries her, she is an independent wife"; there is one who said: "She is of ausrain status."

III

Question
1. When all members of a family save a woman become renegade, can that girl have the status of an independent woman or ausrain?

Reply
2. If there be none of the ancestors of this faithful whose lineage can be traced, they shall appoint a guardian in the presence of the "rats" or "magupats" or "dasturs," or they shall prepare a deed thereon, and they shall give her to a husband; if no "rat" or "dastur" be at hand, he who is far-advanced in the discussion of rules, and has most by heart the Avesta and the commentary, shall secure a guardian, and the guardian shall give her to a husband, and he is entitled so to give.

IV

Question
1. A man departs from the earthly existence; he has a wife and a daughter, and, thereafter the wife turns renegade or departs from the earthly existence; what shall be the arrangement for that daughter?

Reply
2. As I understand: if the wife expires, she has that one daughter without issue, the daughter is alive and is not married, the daughter whilst living is of the father; and if the wife be of independent status, and the daughter be alive and marries under the guardianship of the wife, her status as an independent wife is appropriate.

V

Question
1. If there is a man who has a sister or a daughter, that man becomes a renegade, unto whom will their guardianship rest? If they marry, can they be women of independent status or not?

Reply
2. As I understand: if they have relatives of the good religion, that one of the paternal line closely related will be their guardian; if they have no relative, the guardianship will be the mother's guardianship or of him who is well versed in religion.

VI

Question
1. If a man entrusts a daughter in daughterhood to another man, with whom will her guardianship rest?

Reply
2. With him to whom he entrusts her.

VII

Question
1. If a man entrusts a daughter in daughterhood to a woman who will be the guardian?

Reply
2. The husband has the guardianship of the spouse, and one hands over the woman to the woman's husband, and if the spouse be her own guardian, the guardianship rests with the spouse.

VIII

Question
1. There is a woman who hands over a daughter in daughterhood to a woman, who will be the guardian?

Reply
2. As I understand: the spouse cannot give the daughter to another in daughterhood.

IX

Question
1. There is a woman whose guardianship rests with a man; can that man give the woman in guardianship to another? Or when he departs from the earthly existence, he says: "I have made thee guardian of thine own person, and independent." Can she be a woman of independent status or not?

Reply
2. As I understand: an appointed guardian cannot give the guardianship to another; and if he be a guardian made or become, he can entrust his guardianship to a woman; and if that woman to whom he assigns the guardianship dies, it will revert to the original person, and if he makes her guardian of her own self and independent, and she marries, her independent womanhood will be appropriate.

X

Question
1. There is a man who gives a daughter of mature age to a man in wifehood or in guardianship, the daughter does not agree, shall the guardianship have been given to him, or with whom will her guardianship rest?

Reply
2. As I understand: wifehood can never be but with the consent of the daughter; guardianship can be otherwise without the consent of the daughter; so long as the father is living he can withdraw the guardianship whenever it is necessary, and none can withdraw it after the father.

XI

Question
1. There is a woman whose guardianship rests with a man, and that man dies; he does not give her in guardianship to anyone, nor does he make that woman guardian of her own self and independent, and the woman, thereafter, marries: are that man and that woman rightful or not?

Reply
2. As I understand: if the guardian dies, the guardianship of that woman reverts to the world's worthfulness; he who is very worthy will be the guardian of that woman; if she marries under guardianship, her status of an independent woman will be appropriate.

XII

Question
1. When a man gives a three-year-old daughter to a man in wifehood; and that daughter attains to majority, and says: "I do not consent to marry this man," with whom will the guardianship rest? If that man says: "Unless thou wilt be my wife, I will not give thee to anyone under guardianship," can that daughter secure a guardian? If she marries, will her status be of an independent woman or not?

Reply
2. As I understand: the wifehood cannot take place; the guardianship shall have been given; and if her father will not withdraw the guardianship during the length of his life, the guardianship will rest with him to whom he will give after the father; and if he says, "If thou will not be my wife, I will

not give thee to thy husband," he is rightful; if the husband is agreeable to cause the menstruation month to pass in marriage and the spouse be not agreeable, the sin of the menstruation month originates with the spouse.

XIII

Question
1. There is a minor girl who gives herself in wifehood to a man; when she attains to majority, can she turn away from him and have a husband? And can she be that man's wife of independent status or not? And up to what age can she turn away from a man when she has given her person in wifehood to him?

Reply
2. As I understand: when she attains to majority, she can turn away from him, if she did not at all abide by it; if she marries, she will be a wife of independent status; if she be nine years of age, and has attained to puberty, and gives herself in marriage under lawful guardianship, she cannot, thereafter, turn away from marriage.

XIV

Question
1. If a daughter of nine years gives herself in marriage to a man, can she turn away from the contract, when she becomes fifteen years of age, and become the wife of another man? If she turns away from the contract, what is the sin committed by her towards that man? Will she be the wife of independent status of that other man or not?

Reply
2. As I understand: if a girl of nine years has attained to puberty, she cannot give herself in marriage to a man without the consent of a lawful guardian, and turn away from the wifehood of that man; if she turns away, she is a sinner deserving death, after a full year expires thereafter.

XV

Question
1. If a woman of mature age gives herself in marriage to a boy of immature age, who is only ten years of age, and that boy accepts that woman as wife, can he turn away from the contract when he will become of mature age, or not?

Reply
2. As I understand: if the spouse gave herself in marriage under lawful guardianship, the spouse cannot turn away from the contract; and when the boy attains to majority, he cannot turn away from the contract, if he had at all acted according to the contract; and the boy can turn away from the contract when he attains to majority, if he had not at all acted accordingly.

XVI

Question
1. A woman of mature age who gives herself in marriage to a man of mature age, turns away from that man, then what is her sin and punishment of sin committed towards that man? Or if the woman says: "I give myself in marriage unto thee," is it lawful if she does not become his wife?

Reply
2. As I understand: if she gave herself in marriage under lawful guardianship, she cannot turn away from that man; and if she turns away, and will not perform the duties of wife towards that man, and turns away without the consent of her husband, she becomes a tanapohr sinner on the spot, and a sinner deserving death after a full year.

3. And if she says: "I will be thy wife," and is under lawful guardianship, she ought to be asked four times; when asked four times, the spouse cannot but be his wife; if she will not be his wife, she will become a sinner deserving death after a full year.

XVII

Question
1. There is a woman who without the knowledge of her father makes an engagement with a man, saying, "I gave my person to thee as wife"; then, when the father comes to know and says, "Do you turn away from this man?" can she turn away at the command of the father, and become the wife of another man? Is that woman the rightful wife of that other man or not?

Reply
2. As I understand: as her guardianship rests with the father, unless she plights her troth with the consent of the father, she can turn away from the engagement; for if she does not

give her word with the consent of the father, the engagement as wife does not come into being.

XVIII

Question
1. A woman, when her husband dies, has neither issue nor property through that husband, and that woman has her property; thereafter, that woman dies, and has no issue; is that property that of her brother, or ought they to nominate an adopted son out of the property for her husband?

Reply
2. As I understand: it is so manifest in the Scripture that he who as guardian gave the woman to the husband forthwith gave to him a property of hers; the woman's property thereafter is that of her husband; when the man passes away, the woman, so long as living, is necessitated to make a provision of hers out of that property; when the woman dies, the property comes, by adoption, to the nearest relative of the husband; nothing whatsoever comes to the woman's brother, neither by relationship nor by adoption.

XIX

Question
1. There is a man who tells his daughter, "Thou art made by me independent guardian of thine own self," the daughter may be of mature age or a minor – with whom rests her guardianship?

Reply
2. As I understand: if the daughter is of mature age, and the man says: "Thou art made by me independent guardian of thine own self," the guardianship will come over to this daughter; if the daughter be a minor, the statement should not be considered as of any avail.

XX

Question
1. There is a man whom it behooves that he should give his daughter or his sister in marriage; they do not agree; can that man hand them over in marriage with force? If he does, will the meritorious work of the holy communion come into being or not?

Reply
2. As I understand: it is proper to hand over a sister or a daughter as wife; in that way, with force; if one does it, the marriage is appropriate, and the meritorious work of the holy communion does come into being; it is not proper to do it if the husband does not agree, and it is a sin.

XXIX

Question
1. There is a man, who has a wicked, disobedient wife; the man goes out to a place; she offers her person to non-Iranians, and she lies even with non-Iranians several times, and she commits atrocious sins; can that man retain or divorce that wife? And if that wife commits sins, are the sins those of that man or not?

Reply
2. As I understand: if she submitted herself to non-Iranians for sexual intercourse, if the wife agrees, he can divorce her; and if he does not divorce her, he may retain her for the great good, with this intent, that she may commit less sin; if he even retains her as wife, he can, but he cannot cause the menstrual monthly period to be appeased; if he divorces her, as it is said that if there is even the least fear to material life or fear to the soul, he can divorce her.
3. Note this, too, is stated to us, that if she submitted herself once to alien men, one must certainly have fear both of body and soul.
4. And if the wife commits sin after that, it will not have originated with the husband, save at the time if he does not check her when he can check her.
5. If the wife becomes absolved of sin, he can appease the monthly menstrual period.

XXX

Question
1. There is a man who has a boy of ten years, and that man goes out to a place and hands over that boy in guardianship to a man of the good religion; and that boy does not carry out the commandments of that man and becomes non-Iranian; is it the father's sin or not?

Reply
    2.   As I understand: there is no sin.

LI

Question
    1.   When a man wounds his wife and casts off her young, what is that man's sin?

Reply
    2.   It is a sin deserving of death.

LX

Question
    1.   Ought a man, who sees that a person commits sorcery or sins deserving death or other atrocious sins, mention the fact to another? And if he does not mention it, shall a sin accrue or not? And if he has no witness when he speaks, acceptance of the statement of that man is not proper, ought they to consider this man doubtful or not? And what is your view of that man with this man'?

Reply
    2.   If one commits a sin deserving death, or commits such sin wherefrom the sin deserving death arises, or if a man sees a thief or a brigand on the road, or he knows that they are on the road, so long as he does not mention this it is not proper; if he does not speak out all other sins, on account of not knowing which there will be harm, if he does not disclose a sin deserving death when he can disclose it, if he does not make it public, the same will be the case; if one frees from confinement the thief who has not made an assault, all the sins originate with him, which accrue if he had not made a grievous assault, which it was not possible for him to make; in the case when he had made an assault, then, too, he had been able to make an assault, all the sins do not originate with him; if he frees him from confinement, whichever sin he commits by theft accrue to him.

LXI

Question
    1.   What is the sin of a man who tells a falsehood about a man?

Reply
    2.   Whenever the judges so announce that they are taking his evidence, till when he who gives evidence speaks only that

which is a fact wherefrom there is no harm, it is a statement of wicked speech; if harm issues therefrom, it is a sin.

LXII

Question
1. There is a man who makes an agreement with his wife and says: "The children who are born of thee are made co-partners and joint owners"; and thereafter, to the children who are born of that wife; can that man give a greater share of his property to some one of the children, and less to some one? The father hands over to the husband the daughter who is born of that wife; is a share of the property hers after the father or not?

Reply
2. An equal share belongs to sons and daughters, and one cannot do otherwise; if the daughter takes a husband when her father is alive, even then the share goes to her by way of justice and lawfulness.

LXVI

Question
1. There is a man who gives a loan to a man; that man departs from this world; he has wife and children in this family; the widow does not return the loan taken from the man; when she departs from this world, and there are sons and daughters in the family, and the man asks the return of the loan from a son; and the son is perverse and says, "I do not know it"; the man who is this creditor says, "Swear that thy father did not take this loan from me, and I and other heirs of my father have neither to return nor give this property to thee; their returning or giving is not lawful"; the man who took the loan says, "Let us you and I so undergo the ordeal"; "I and other heirs of my father have no knowledge of this event" – what is the advice?

Reply
2. As I understand: then he shall certainly undertake the ordeal, saying, "My father and mother did not take this loan from thee, O Man! And we who are the heirs of our father and mother have not to return this loan to thee."

LXVII

Question
1. There is a man who wants to recover two hundred 'derams' from a man, and that man says: "I have not, I cannot give"; and the man, the creditor, says: "He has, and give the order so that we may search his house, and this capability which he has, is worth so much in lieu of that debt" – can they seize the man's belongings or not?

Reply
2. The man who wants to recover the debt from a man, cannot seize from the property of the man, the debtor, for his own belonging without the order and adjudication of the Dasturs; if he takes away, he becomes a thief or a robber; the judges shall so adjudicate that of the materials in the house of the indebted man, unless he leaves as much for the indebted man that he has no fear of death nor privation from the continual outcome of his property; otherwise, they cannot decide upon seizing and taking away.

LXVIII

Question
1. There is a man who mortgages a property to a man and takes a loan; and he agrees, and mortgages to the man as much property as can redeem the loan for the property, to the satisfaction of the creditor; and the loan becomes one out of two; then the property can redeem the principal, but it cannot redeem the interest; can the man who is the creditor claim additional property, or will it be enough if he, the mortgagor, delivers that mortgaged property? Shall he make any other amends or not?

Reply
2. As the man, who is the creditor, approved the property which he received as mortgage, by the reckoning of the value of the principal and interest as holding good on that day, and he took it; when the property depreciates, the man who received the loan, and mortgaged his property, so long as the principal is equal to that property, the man is unable to return the loan immediately, and the mortgagee has the right to the property which he received as mortgage, until the mortgagor is able to return the principal and the interest, the opinion for return of the land, too, is such, as if he had taken the loan, but then had not made the mortgage; even then, he

shall return the loan and the interest, in accordance with his means and ability.

LXXI

Question
1. There was a man who had a son of mature age; he had estates, and passed away; the father had a son of inferior status, who was held to be an accepted adopted son; and he expires a little while after that; the case is this: does the estate of the father go to the family of that son who expired before the father or not? And if it does go, how much shall go?

Reply
2. A half of the father's estate has to be added on to the gift of the son's family, and one half is to be given to that accepted son.

LXXIV

Question
1. Whoever makes a solemn vow with this sort of colloquy: "I have dedicated to such and such person all acts and good deeds which I may perform from this day onward," what is your opinion of this case: this as to whether they will have been dedicated by him or not?

Reply
2. If he declares as "dedicated" that property which has not come to his possession, it will not have been dedicated; and if he speaks of that good deed which has not become his, he shall not have dedicated in the same manner; if he speaks of that property which has not come to his possession, or of that good deed and property which have not together come to his possession, if a fear, or a difficulty, or a trouble, or depressing thought, or a defect has not come, such as that which is said in detail in the ordeal section of the Husparam, if he speaks of one who is worthy; then when that property came to his possession, or that good deed came to achievement, then he shall have been dedicated, in the same manner, to him to whom they are dedicated, if even now that worthiness has not elapsed; it can be dedicated for that one fear of fears, when one dedicates anything to worthy persons for fear of the wicked existence; if he says, "I will dedicate a good deed, not for any earthly gain, but for the friendship of the soul of a person who is worthy," it will be

his to whom he said, "I will dedicate," when he has performed it; and it will not be the less, of him who performed it; it will come to him in the same manner as if he had performed it for the sake of his own soul; since he declared that colloquy, "I will dedicate," for the love of righteousness, he advances this in the path of a soul, even this munificence which he advances with a good deed will be such as his who performs a worship, without earthly reward and gain, for the souls of persons; then, the recitation by him of what is in the oath ordeal has gone by, which brings out the least preparation of this kind, then he shall recite the words of Rasnu, those which the Avesta has demonstrated, those which he can verily consider, such as one says: (Av.) "Here is such utility," so is this regulation for defense, (Av.) or, "Here is its information unto me," so I have information of it by proof, (Av.) or, "I do not know of it," or I have not that by knowledge, if by non-recitation of it, I am a sinner who misuses a trust; then, I do not know of any formula to explain that he has to take effectively in reckoning those words which it is not according to the law for him to speak, and to decide the matter.

3. It is instituted that if there has been such a man, a man who, on account of fear, speaks in the presence of judges: "This man had smitten me," the judge understands that he spoke on account of fear, he shall release him on the highway.

4. They shall leave the decision of this, as to for what reason that man spoke in dedicating that good deed, to the Yazats who ordain; they can decide; otherwise, since the judges of this world cannot effectively return to the real holder the property which is invisible, which is known to have been in the keeping of one who carried it away with force, therefore, as an invisible good deed becomes requisite by declaration, he has to atone for the false oath; the punishment of the atonement is evident as determined; they shall not mitigate the penalty of that which is indubitable and that which is doubtful, and they shall adjudicate the material person and property; they shall leave the judgment of the soul and the good deed to Him who knows; it is even due to His power that the righteous is inculpated by that over which he has no power.

CXII

Question
1. A man felt, "I will give a thing to a person, poor or rich" – can he alter that thing or not?

Reply
2. He cannot do otherwise than whatever he felt in his mind, except when a contract is made.

CXXIV

Question
1. A man is passing along a road; enemies approach him: can he fight or not?

Reply
2. Unless he indubitably knows it to be rightful, he cannot.

CXXV

Question
1. Can we purchase wine and other eatables from the Christians or not?

Reply
2. We cannot purchase but during helplessness, for they do not abstain from the menstrual impurity which they hold as lawful.

CXXXIX

Question
1. What is your view of a man who is in the company of a woman in her menses, and the woman does not tell him? What is your view if the woman is non-Iranian, and even if he was of the good religion, and she tells him afterwards?

Reply
2. If the woman was such to whom it was lawful to go, and the man was not aware of her condition, and the woman was aware and does not tell him, the woman is sinful, and the man unsinning; and if the woman was not lawful, the man, too, is sinful.

CXLI

Question
1. Can the man who obtains from his father wealth which is accumulated with unrighteousness, enjoy that wealth, and

make a provision for duty and good deeds or not? And if he performs out of it ceremonies for his own soul and even that of his father, will they reach their souls or not?

Reply
2. For all the wealth which the father had accumulated before the coming forth of the child, I cannot understand his child to be a sharer in his sins or good deeds; and then when it comes into the possession and authority of the child, he shall return, whatever he knows as having been obtained from the thief or the robber; a half or one third, just as the Dasturs may direct, and he shall restore the rest, that which is worthy of him; and he shall make provision according to religious usage, just as may be very helpful, for the expiation of the sins of his father; as to that of which he does not know anything, as he himself is authorized to keep the wealth in his possession, it is good that he shall, in all respects perform ceremonies, votive-offerings, and other works of merit for the soul of his father, for making the atonement of the sins of his father and by way of good deeds even for the sake of the soul of his father, so that he may expiate the sins and impurities, and the indebtedness of his father; for the expiation of sin is the most compulsory work of merit, whereby glory and radiance are increased.

On the strength of this sizable sample of the document, we proceed to our analytical, then comparative study.

The Zoroastrian sages before us (others made other choices) selected for the persuasive presentation of information and argument the form of question and answer, and the question derives from the narrative of a case. The answer requires the form, "as I understand," and when two or more opinions occur, the formula is, "there are different views thereon; there is one who said..., there is one who said...." The formulation of questions in the Talmudic corpus follows diverse patterns. A question may elicit information, or it may represent a step in an argument, for instance. Not only so, but even when a question is not asked, one is implied, as in the statement of a case with an implied question mark, what is the rule? Such a formulation may readily serve as the counterpart to the presentation of a case followed by an articulated question, such as this rivayat commonly supplies. The closest counterpart bears examination. First a single example of the routine form in this rivayat:[2]

I

Question
1. There is a man who has a daughter; two men desire her in marriage, and the father gives her to one of the men; the daughter does not agree to that man; her liking is towards the other man; does the prerogative rest with the father or with the daughter? And if the father does not fulfill the wish of the daughter, is the daughter entitled to fix her guardian, and to have a husband? And if she does not fix a guardian, can the daughter be an independent wife or not?

Reply
2. As I understand: the father is entitled to assign the guardianship; as long as he is living, he is entitled to withdraw the guardianship, whenever it is necessary, but with the consent of the woman and even that of the guardian; it cannot be otherwise; she cannot have a husband otherwise, but with the consent of the father as long as the father is living, and with the consent of the guardian, after the father's passing away.

The requirement of the form[3] is simply stated: description of a case, in abstract terms, omitting reference to any particular person, location, or circumstance. "There is a..." or "if there be none...," or "if there is a man who has...," and the other, familiar apodictic case law. The answer is equally laconic and simple: "As I understand...," followed by a set of simple, unpatterned declarative sentences. The convention at hand then is: question, answer; if..., then..., forming the question, a statement of facts, without decoration, comprising the answer. What we have is a powerful mode of conveying information – but still, just another mode. A perfectly simple counterpart is to restate matters as facts, if there is..., the father is.... So we should not be deceived by the compelling quality of the rhetoric – questions, answers – into supposing that what we have is more than an alternative way of setting forth propositions as to matters of fact, just like the Mishnah, as we shall see time and again.

---

[2] The other has its own form, like this one in the question-and-answer model, but unlike it in its insistence upon an attributive component.

[3] By "form" I mean conventional layout of words or components with a single function, e.g., exposition of a case, within a defined syntax, utilizing recurrent patterns to signal stages in a representation of an unfolding thought.

The abstraction effected by omission of concrete details of a particular case does not extend to the formulation of a purely theoretical question, for example, "does the daughter have the right to reject a suitor approved by the father?" Nor is the premise expressed: the daughter must choose among candidates presented by the father; that fact is expressed by the detail of the two men who desire the daughter, a roundabout way of saying the same thing. The consequences are then laid out in dialectical sequence, if this, then what about that, if that, then what about the other thing. The answer always commences, "As I understand." The formulation yields circumlocution. What Aturfarnbag wants to say is, "The daughter's consent is required." What he says is, the father has every right – but with the consent of the woman. All is formulated to underline the father's power – except the conclusion, which is the opposite: the daughter is not a free agent, but neither is the father. The form of the answer is simple declarative sentences. Now that may appear a commonplace, until we ask, what do we not find?

First, we do not find named authorities. Second, we do not find reference to any prior authoritative texts. Third, we do not find any process of reasoning or argument, any give or take, if not between debaters, then between arguments. Fourth, we do not find any analytical process to speak of. The prolixity of the reply masks its plainness: a simple point is expressed in a complicated way. The upshot is, we have a simple exchange of information: the question, the answer.

Among the question-answer formulas of the Bavli, the following strikes me as bearing comparison because it approaches, in its basic problematic, that is, the independent standing of the daughter, Aturfarnbag's question. Furthermore, the example typifies the situation before us: the formulation of a theoretical question, bearing upon numerous cases. The following derives from Bavli Qiddushin 44A-B. Because of the importance of the amplificatory element, with its contention, dialectical movement, thrust and parry, and the like, I give a sizable abstract. We then set the two "questions" side by side, which permits us to see in a clear way the important structural difference.

5. A. *Raba asked this question of R. Nahman:* **[44B]** *"Can a prepubescent girl appoint an agent to accept a writ of divorce from her husband? Is she comparable to her father's hand or her father's courtyard?*
   B. *"Is she comparable to her father's hand: Just as her father may appoint an agent, so she, too, has the power to appoint an agent.*
   C. *"Or perhaps she is comparable to her father's courtyard: Until the writ of divorce actually reaches her hand, she is not divorced."*
   D. *But can Raba really be in doubt on this matter? Lo, hasn't Raba himself stated, "If he wrote a writ of divorce for her and gave it into the hand of her slave while the slave was asleep and she was watching the slave, it is a valid writ of divorce; if he was awake, it is not a*

The Pahlavi Rivayat of Aturfarnbag and the Bavli: Description and Comparison   71

valid writ of divorce"? *Why isn't it a valid writ of divorce if he is awake? Isn't it because what you have is a* courtyard *that, without her knowledge and consent, is guarded? And if you should suppose that she is treated as comparable to her father's courtyard, then, even when the writ of divorce reaches her hand, she still should not be divorced, since she would then be classified as* her father's courtyard *that is guarded not with her father's full knowledge and consent.*

E. *Rather, in point of fact it was obvious to [Raba] that she is comparable to her father's hand, and, therefore, this is the question that he found troubling: Does she have the same power as does her father's hand, so that she, too, can appoint an agent, or is that not the case?*

F. He [Nahman] said to him, "She may not appoint an agent."

G. He raised this objection: "**A minor girl who said, 'Receive my writ of divorce for me'** – **it is not a valid writ of divorce until it reaches her hand [M. Git. 6:3A-B]** – then if it were a prepubescent girl, lo, this would in fact be a valid writ of divorce." [Freedman: Such a girl can appoint an agent, since she is not under paternal authority; but Raba's question refers to such a girl who has a father.]

H. *"Here with what situation do we deal? It is a case in which she has no father."*

I. *"But lo, since the later clause states as the Tannaite rule,* **But if the girl's father said to him, 'Go and receive my daughter's writ of divorce in her behalf,' if he [the husband] wanted to retract, he may not retract** *[M. Git. 6:3E-F], it follows that we deal in the opening clause likewise with a case in which she also has a father."*

J. *"Not at all, the formulation is flawed, and this is the sense of the matter:* **A minor girl who said, 'Receive my writ of divorce for me'** – **it is not a valid writ of divorce until it reaches her hand [M. Git. 6:3A-B]** – then if it were a prepubescent girl, lo, this would in fact be a valid writ of divorce. Under what circumstances? If she has no father. But if she had a father, and **if the girl's father said to him, 'Go and receive my daughter's writ of divorce in her behalf,' if he [the husband] wanted to retract, he may not retract** [M. Git. 6:3E-F]."

The question is, what is the status as to a girl married off by her father before she has come to maturity and so acquired independent standing? The question's sense is spelled out at B, C. If we compare the question part of the exchange with the formulation of Aturfarnbag's, we need only drop *Raba asked this question of R. Nahman* to replicate the Pahlavi form. Translating "can a...," into "there is a..., is she..." seems a minor move. Now, before proceeding, let us see how the components of the two forms compare when set side by side:

| 1. | There is a man who has a daughter; two men desire her in marriage, and the father gives her to one of the men; the daughter does not agree | 5. | A. | *Raba asked this question of R. Nahman:* **[44B]** "Can a prepubescent girl appoint an agent to accept a writ of divorce from her husband? *Is she* |

to that man; her liking is towards the other man; does the prerogative rest with the father or with the daughter? And if the father does not fulfill the wish of the daughter, is the daughter entitled to fix her guardian, and to have a husband? And if she does not fix a guardian, can the daughter be an independent wife or not?

B. comparable to her father's hand or her father's courtyard?

"Is she comparable to her father's hand: Just as her father may appoint an agent, so she, too, has the power to appoint an agent.

C. "Or perhaps she is comparable to her father's courtyard: Until the writ of divorce actually reaches her hand, she is not divorced."

D. But can Raba really be in doubt on this matter? Lo, hasn't Raba himself stated, "If he wrote a writ of divorce for her and gave it into the hand of her slave while the slave was asleep and she was watching the slave, it is a valid writ of divorce; if he was awake, it is not a valid writ of divorce"? Why isn't it a valid writ of divorce if he is awake? Isn't it because what you have is a courtyard that, without her knowledge and consent, is guarded? And if you should suppose that she is treated as comparable to her father's courtyard, then, even when the writ of divorce reaches her hand, she still should not be divorced, since she would then be classified as her father's courtyard that is guarded not with her father's full knowledge and consent.

E. Rather, in point of fact it was obvious to [Raba] that she is comparable to her father's hand, and, therefore, this is the question that he found troubling: Does she have the same power as does her father's

The Pahlavi Rivayat of Aturfarnbag and the Bavli: Description and Comparison 73

	hand, so that she, too, can appoint an agent, or is that not the case?
	F. He [Nahman] said to him, "She may not appoint an agent."

Reply 2. As I understand: the father is entitled to assign the guardianship; as long as he is living, he is entitled to withdraw the guardianship, whenever it is necessary, but with the consent of the woman and even that of the guardian; it cannot be otherwise; she cannot have a husband otherwise, but with the consent of the father as long as the father is living, and with the consent of the guardian, after the father's passing away.

G. *He raised this objection:* "**A minor girl who said, 'Receive my writ of divorce for me'** – **it is not a valid writ of divorce until it reaches her hand [M. Git. 6:3A-B]** – then if it were a prepubescent girl, lo, this would in fact be a valid writ of divorce." [Freedman: Such a girl can appoint an agent, since she is not under paternal authority; but Raba's question refers to such a girl who has a father.]

H. "*Here with what situation do we deal? It is a case in which she has no father.*"

I. "*But lo, since the later clause states as the Tannaite rule,* **But if the girl's father said to him, 'Go and receive my daughter's writ of**

> divorce in her behalf,' if he [the husband] wanted to retract, he may not retract [M. Git. 6:3E-F], *it follows that we deal in the opening clause likewise with a case in which she also has a father."*
>
> J. "Not at all, the formulation is flawed, and this is the sense of the matter: **A minor girl who said, 'Receive my writ of divorce for me' – it is not a valid writ of divorce until it reaches her hand [M. Git. 6:3A-B]** – then if it were a prepubescent girl, lo, this would in fact be a valid writ of divorce. Under what circumstances? If she has no father. But if she had a father, and if the girl's father said to him, 'Go and receive my daughter's writ of divorce in her behalf,' if he [the husband] wanted to retract, he may not retract [M. Git. 6:3E-F]."

Viewed in this way, I see no material difference between A-C and the following:

> There is a woman whose guardianship rests with a man; can that man give the woman in guardianship to another? Or when he departs from the earthly existence, he says: "I have made thee guardian of thine own person, and independent." Can she be a woman of independent status or not?

But the inclusion of who asked him is a very substantial difference, changing the entire character of the exchange. Now we have transformed a request for information into an initiative for a theoretical exchange: *what is your opinion, and the reasoning behind your opinion?* forms a different question from, *what is the prevailing rule?*

That the entire colloquy shifts in character from an exchange of information (whether in fact, whether in theory) is shown by the character of the framing of D: can anyone ask such a dumb question? or: can Raba contradict himself as apparently he does? Then the formulation of the question, rather than the presentation of the answer, takes over, at D-E, and what we have is not a transaction in information at all, but an inquiry into analytical reason. The upshot, E, is a reformulation of the question, now in more abstract form than before. Then comes an absolutely typical trait of the Talmudic exchange of question and answer: the objection! The questioner, in fact, is given an objection based on a cited, established rule, G, then allowed to spell out the consequence of his citation. And the counterargument proceeds, as, by now, one should expect.

In fact, the two forms of question-and-answer scarcely intersect, because the purpose of the one finds no counterpart in that of the other. The one intends to supply information; the questioner is passive, not a participant in the process. There is, indeed, no process of proposition, argument, evidence, and reasoning; the authority for the colloquy rests with the voice of the speaker, who answers the question: Aturfarnbag himself. The other, by contrast, raises the question as an occasion to analyze a problem; the provision of an answer forms a subordinated consideration. The analytical process rests upon an established set of facts, the received sources (for example, the Mishnah, the Tosefta, Scripture), and the task of the sage is to use those facts, following established processes of reason and analysis, to solve a problem. The voice we hear is the one who says, "He said to him...he said to him...," not the implicit "you say" followed by "there is a...," and then the explicit, I, as in "as I understand." So the voice of the Talmud is the voice of a book, anonymous, commanding, in full charge of the exposition before us; the voice of the rivayat is the voice of the one who wrote the book. This is the point of the Talmud's citing named statements, the rivayat's citing no authority at all. The rivayat stands for its author, who is known and named; the Talmud stands for the consensus of the sages, the anonymous collegium, and so names the authorities who participate in its analytical process, on the one side, or the documents that contribute facts, on the other.

Now if we ask ourselves what is critical to the Talmud but of negligible interest to Aturfarnbag, it is contained in these contrasts. The most important is the contrast between presentation of information and exposition of applied reason and practical logic. Aturfarnbag promises to give you the answer to your question, and he does; you then rely upon him, and that is what is to be said; the transaction is one of reliable authority and faithful inquirer. The Talmud (Aturfarnbag's counterpart) promises to show you how to formulate a question coherent with all that is known. Once asked, the question dictates its own course: the recasting of the problem contains its own solution. Shall we then concur that the Talmud concerns process, not proposition? That is the opposite of the case. The Talmud wants us to know how a proposition is attained, not only the proposition that forms the climax of its presentation (to be sure, not always formulated in so many words, but invariably contained in the inexorable course of argument toward one conclusion, rather than some other). The documentary comparison imposes narrow limits on how much of the Bavli we can take into account, because this rivayat contains only one kind of writing, the Talmud, a great many. But there is a second kind of documentary comparison, which draws our attention to the character of not a formalized piece of writing but the document as a whole. And here we may compare the Bavli to this rivayat: one whole writing to another. It may be simply stated: How do the two documents' authors organize their materials?

At issue is the problem every writer (whether named or anonymous) must solve, which is, how to write not just a sequence of episodic sentences but a sustained writing, a paragraph, a chapter, a book? The problem of the logic of coherent discourse requires attention at all three levels of formulation, sentences into a paragraph, paragraphs into a chapter, chapters into a book. A more adequate formulation of "sentences" is, completed whole units of thought, standing on their own, which cannot be reduced to any smaller component and still make sense; a paragraph is, a completed exposition made up of irreducible minima of thought, such that, all units of thought cohere, beginning to end; but (in a protracted writing) no unit of thought (in particular: the theoretical opening unit, the theoretical closing one) coheres, or coheres so well, with what comes before (in the case of the theoretical opening unit) or with what comes afterward (in the theoretical closing unit's instance) as it does with what follows (as qualified) or what precedes (as qualified). That is, in a well-crafted piece of writing, compositions do cohere internally and also distinguish themselves from whatever stands fore or aft. The same sort of (somewhat ungainly, but theoretically more useful) definition of the chapters made up of paragraphs can be made up by the reader; and of course, a book is a book: the Talmud, or the Rivayat of Aturfarnbag, respectively.

As to the first of the three dimensions of coherent discourse in writing, we already know how both writers make up paragraphs. Aturfarnbag achieves perfect coherence: question, then answer. The answer always addresses the question, the sentences of the question hold together because, as in all propositional or syllogistic discourse, one sentence generates the next and is closely tied to its predecessor. We begin with the general, "there is...," which sets the stage for the case and its problem, then "who will be...," or "can she...," and the like. The answer joins the question in a fully articulated way: "As I understand...," followed by the components of the question. For the Talmud, the composition exhibits equally pleasing traits of cogency. But they are different traits.

Raba's statement, A-C, fully spells out the question, with its alternative positions and the reasoning behind it: our problem is selecting the governing analogy. Now, if Aturfarnfag had written the Talmud, A-C would be followed by "as I understand" plus a selection between the choices and an account of the consequences of the choice of governing analogy. But that is never what the Talmud does. Rather, it undertakes what is called, in general, a dialectical argument, meaning (at least, for this purpose) a sustained exchange of thrust and parry, proposal and counterproposal, reason and refutation, an argument that moves from point to point, always exploring unknown territory. The key, in our case, comes at D: a turning back upon the question itself. In our rivayat there is not a single point at which the premise of the question is challenged, let along the question itself. In the Talmud our example is a commonplace. Does D hold tightly to A-C? Of course it does, question, then counterquestion. And how does E join D? It is through a resolution to the tension created by the challenge by D of A-C! Only at that point do we permit the answer to be given, F. I see no material difference between the success at joining sentences into a paragraph achieved by Aturfarnbag and by the Talmud, but the media contrast, even though, in form, they are the same: question, answer. It goes without saying that the remainder of the Talmud's composition ("paragraph") sustains a single, cogent discourse, each sentence in its proper place. The criterion for success that applies to both writings is simple: If we were to take out one sentence from its present position and put it elsewhere, would the passage still make as much, or as little, sense? And the answer for both writings is, absolutely not. So both documents' writers may claim considerable success in the formulation of intelligible thought in paragraphs.

Now we have to ask ourselves, do our writers aspire to compose larger units than paragraphs, and do they have a chapter or a book in mind? Here the answer is equally clear. The authors of the two compositions – the paragraphs by my definition of the term – present us with whole and complete statements; they have no need to link these compositions to any that stand fore or aft. Aturfarnbag's question is introduced by the simple statement, "Several questions asked of...." The composition in the Bavli is complete, all the information we need to understand the entire exposition being set forth within the boundaries of the composition itself. But this observation on the two kinds of writing of course begs the question, since, in both cases, free-standing paragraphs do come to us in books (or chapters), and both were intended to. That unproved premise stands at the head of all that follows.

Then what, in theory, joins paragraphs into a chapter (or chapters into a book, there is no interesting difference)? The first and most common medium is, the intent to prove a point, to formulate a sustained argument in behalf of a proposition; that lends cogency to all components of a chapter or a book, that is to say, precisely the same theory of cogent discourse that unites our sentences into a paragraph (composition) serves also to unite paragraphs into chapters and into a book. But that medium of forming large aggregates of cogent and sustained discourse does not pertain here. In the case of our rivayat, that is self-evident, as a glance at Chapter Three will confirm. There is no interest in organizing the little units of question-and-answer by large-scale topic or problem; if we were to take any question-and-answer and place it elsewhere in the document, we should understand the colloquy precisely as well, and in precisely the same way, as we do when it is set where it now is. What that means is, there is no interest in making a larger case, forming a more ambitious argument, establishing a more general proposition, that dictates where things should be or how they should hold together.

What about the Bavli? Here, the data prove somewhat more complicated, but, as a matter of fact, the same result apparently emerges:

4. A. *R. Assi didn't go to the house of study. Coming across R. Zira, he asked him, "So what did they say today in the schoolhouse?"*
   B. *He said to him, "I didn't go either. R. Abin went, and he said that the whole crew agrees with R. Yohanan, And even though R. Simeon b. Laqish screamed like a crane, 'and when she has left, she may be another man's wife' (Deut. 24:2) [so marriage and divorce are governed by the same law, as Simeon b. Laqish maintains], nobody paid any attention to him."*
   C. *He said to him, "So is R. Abin so reliable?"*
   D. *He said, "Certainly is, because the report came as fresh as a fish jumping from the sea into a frying pan."*
   E. *Said R. Nahman bar Isaac, "I know this story in the name not of R. Abin b. R. Hiyya or R. Abin bar Kahana, but R. Abin without further patronymic."*
   F. *Yeah, so what difference does it make?*
   G. *In the possibility of contrasting two statements made by the same authority.*
5. A. Raba asked this question of R. Nahman: **[44B]** "Can a prepubescent girl appoint an agent to accept a writ of divorce from her husband? *Is she comparable to her father's hand or her father's courtyard?...*
   J. *"Not at all, the formulation is flawed, and this is the sense of the matter:* **A minor girl who said, 'Receive my writ of divorce for me' – it is not a valid writ of divorce until it**

reaches her hand [M. Git. 6:3A-B] – then if it were a prepubescent girl, lo, this would in fact be a valid writ of divorce. Under what circumstances? If she has no father. But if she had a father, and **if the girl's father said to him, 'Go and receive my daughter's writ of divorce in her behalf,' if he [the husband] wanted to retract, he may not retract [M. Git. 6:3E-F]."**

6. A. It has been stated:
   B. A minor who was betrothed without her father's knowledge and consent –
   C. said Samuel, "She nonetheless requires a writ of divorce and also the exercise of the right of refusal."
   D. Said Qarna, "Well, there's something going on here: If a writ of divorce, why the right of refusal? If the right of refusal, why a writ of divorce?"
   E. *They said to him, "But Mar Uqba and his court are at Kafri [so let's go ask]." Then they changed their minds and sent the question to Rab. He said to them, "By God, she nonetheless requires a writ of divorce and also the exercise of the right of refusal. But may there be mercy [from heaven] that the son of Abba bar Abba [Samuel's father] should say so."*...

No. 4 does not lead us into No. 5, and No. 5 and No. 4 could change places with no loss in sense, no increment in coherence; the two do not cohere. The same is to be said of No. 5 and No. 6. Here, the pursuit of a generally coherent theme leads to a quite distinct problematic; the issue is a different issue, and if No. 6 changed places with No. 5, we could understand each "paragraph" or composition just as well as we now do. Is that to suggest that the Bavli compares with the Rivayat before us as a sequence of free-standing compositions, arranged any which way?

Nothing could be further from the truth, and, when we understand how and why Nos. 4-6 are set forth where they are, we shall grasp the principle of cogent discourse – the coherence of large aggregates of well-formulated paragraphs – that governs in the Bavli. Then the comparison between the two documents will yield a more useful insight. I present in abbreviated form the entire composite in which our composition finds its place, citing only the operative language that suffices to indicate what each composite in the larger composite is supposed to contribute.

III.1 A. **A man betroths his daughter when she is a girl on his own or through his agent:**
   B. *There we have learned in the Mishnah:* **A betrothed girl – she and her father receive her writ of divorce. Said R. Judah, "Two hands together do not make acquisition simultaneously. But her father receives her writ of divorce alone. And any girl who is not able to keep watch over her writ of divorce cannot be divorced"** [M. Git. 6:2G-K].

III.2 A. *And said R. Yosé bar Hanina, "What is the operative consideration behind R. Yohanan's account of the position of rabbis? In the matter of the writ of* divorce, she reverts thereby to the domain of her father, so either she or her father may receive the writ; *but as to a betrothal,* in which case she removes herself from the domain of her father, her father but not she receives the token of divorce."

III.3 A. *Reason supports the response of R. Yohanan [the declaration made against her will], since the language is used,* which is not the case with respect to tokens of betrothal [which only the father can receive]. *But may one say that that represents a refutation of the position of R. Simeon b. Laqish ["As is the dispute with respect to writs of divorced, so there is a dispute with respect to betrothals"]?*

III.4 A. *R. Assi didn't go to the house of study. Coming across R. Zira, he asked him, "So what did they say today in the schoolhouse?"*

III.5 A. *Raba asked this question of R. Nahman:* **[44B]** *"Can a prepubescent girl appoint an agent to accept a writ of divorce from her husband? Is she comparable to her father's hand or her father's courtyard?"*

III.6 A. *It has been stated:*
 B. A minor who was betrothed without her father's knowledge and consent –
 C. said Samuel, "She nonetheless requires a writ of divorce and also the exercise of the right of refusal."

III.7 A. Said R. Nahman, "But that is the case [that she requires a writ of divorce] only if they negotiated the betrothal afterward with the father."
 B. Ulla said, "Even the right of refusal is not required."

III.8 A. *It has been stated:*
 B. If the man who betrothed a minor without her father's knowledge and consent died, and she fell to the lot of the surviving brothers for levirate marriage –

III.9 A. *Two men were drinking wine under the willows in Babylonia. One of them took a cup of wine, gave it to the other, and said, "Let your daughter be betrothed to my son."*
 B. *Said Rabina, "Even in the view of him who said, 'We take account of the possibility that the father was reconciled,'* **[45B]** *we certainly don't say, 'We take account of the possibility that the son consented'"* [so there is nothing of which to take account here, the boy's father having no right to do what he did].

III.10 A. *There was a man who in the marketplace betrothed a minor with a bunch of vegetables. Said Rabina, "Even in the view of him who said, 'We take account of the possibility that the father was reconciled,' that is the case only if the act was done* in a respectful way and not in a disgraceful way."
 B. "Well, then," said R. Aha of Difti to Rabina, "What yields the judgment that he has acted in the disgraceful way? The vegetables, the marketplace?"

III.11 A. *There was someone who said, "She should marry one of my relatives."*
 B *She said, "She should marry one of my relatives."*
 C. *While they were eating and drinking at the betrothal party, his relative went up to a loft and betrothed her.*
 D. *Said Abbayye, "'The remnant of Israel shall not do iniquity nor speak lies' (Zeph. 3:13)* [and the father does not consent]."

The Pahlavi Rivayat of Aturfarnbag and the Bavli: Description and Comparison   81

    E.   Raba said, "It is an established assumption that someone will not go to the trouble of making a banquet and then waste it. [The meal was prepared to celebrate the wife's relative's betrothal and is not going to be lost, so as Abbayye maintains, the father didn't consent.]"

    F.   *So what's the practical difference?*

    G.   *A case in which he went to no trouble and expense with a banquet.*

III.12 A.   If the daughter [of an Israelite] became betrothed with her father's knowledge and consent [to a priest], and her father went overseas and the girl went and got married [consummating the marriage] –

    B.   said Rab, "She may continue to eat food in the status of priestly rations [which marriage to the priest confers upon her] until her father comes home and protests against the consummation of the marriage."

    C.   R. Assi said, "She may not eat food in the status of priestly rations, lest her father come and protest the consummation of the marriage, and it will retroactively come about that a nonpriest is eating priestly rations."

III.13 A.   If she became betrothed with her father's knowledge and consent and she consummated the marriage without, and her father is here at hand –

    B.   R. Huna said, "She may not eat food in the status of priestly rations."

    C.   R. Jeremiah bar Abba said, "She may eat food in the status of priestly rations."

III.14 A.   If she accepted tokens of betrothal without her father's knowledge and consent and consummated the marriage without her father's knowledge and consent, and her father is here at hand –

    B.   R. Huna said, "She may eat food in the status of priestly rations."

    C.   R. Jeremiah bar Abba said, "She may not eat food in the status of priestly rations."

III.15 A.   *It has been stated:*

    B.   A minor who accepted tokens of betrothal without her father's knowledge and consent –

    C.   said Rab, "Either she or her father has the power to repudiate the betrothal."

    D.   And R. Assi said, "Her father can but she can't."

Now what is happening here? The entire composite commences with the citation of a sentence of the Mishnah, and everything that is collected here serves in some way to clarify that sentence, its relationship to other Mishnah sentences, the rules that derive from, the cases that depend on, the issues that emerge from, those sentences. So we have a composite made up of compositions, and each of the compositions serves the purpose of clarifying the Mishnah sentence before us in one of the several ways just now enumerated. III.1-2+3, 4 work on the intersection of two Mishnah rules, and the relevance is reinforced in the exposition at No. 3, where our Mishnah rule is cited in evidence on the dispute generated by the intersection. Nos. 5, 6-7, 8 raise further theoretical problems, yielding the usual cases, Nos. 9-11. Nos. 12-15 introduce a set of further theoretical problems, all an extended thematic appendix, appropriately joined because of the basic issue of our Mishnah paragraph.

Now can we explain the context and particular position of our colloquy? Of course we can. It forms a step in the exposition of a Mishnah rule and its principle, a rather well-crafted composite in which problems of exposition, theory, and concrete practice are systematically set forth. Could our entry, No. 5, trade places with No. 2? Hardly. And it would find itself out of line, also, if it were to situate itself later on. So while the relationship between discrete units, for example, Nos. 4, 5, and 6, hardly conforms to an ironclad rule of logical sequence, sets of such units, for example, the exposition of the Mishnah rule in relationship to other Mishnah rules, the theoretical problem that underlies the rule, the composite of cases that illustrate aspects thereof – none of these sets could have changed places with the others without vastly recasting the sense and consequence of our huge composite.

Aturfarnbag, or whoever compiled his responsa, had no reason to seek an order that imparted cogency to his 147 paragraphs; his intent was to set forth practical questions and concrete answers. He assumed (so I supposed) that people would work their way through the whole, or that they would look for their particular question and its answer; it made no difference. For him the point of the compilation lay in what was compiled, and the purpose of the compositions that were compiled was to convey accurate information on practical questions. Then, in writing down the great tradition, he quite reasonably supposed, the great tradition is made up of a massive set of rules and principles, laws and theology, to be taken over, mastered, and obeyed and believed. The tradition comprised revealed truth. The task of the great sage was to preserve and hand on that truth.

Do we find in the corpus of Judaism a statement that can express Aturfarnbag's conception of the work? Of course we do, the opening line of tractate Avot, ca. 250:

> Moses received the Torah at Sinai and handed it on to Joshua, Joshua to elders, and elders to prophets. And prophets handed it on to the men of the great assembly. They said three things: Be prudent in judgment. Raise up many disciples. Make a fence for the Torah.

Now, were we to examine the remainder of this chapter and to inspect, in particular, what is attributed to the successive masters, what should we find? Here is a brief sample that makes the point clear:

> **1:6** ...Set up a master for yourself. And get yourself a companion disciple. And give everybody the benefit of the doubt.

1:7 ...Keep away from a bad neighbor. And don't get involved with a bad person. And don't give up hope of retribution.

1:8 ...Don't make yourself like one of those who advocate before judges [while you yourself are judging a case]. And when the litigants stand before you, regard them as guilty. But when they leave you, regard them as acquitted (when they have accepted your judgment).

1:9 ...Examine the witnesses with great care. And watch what you say, lest they learn from what you say how to lie.

I have omitted the names to which the sayings are attributed. What is left? Incoherence, since if we change the order of what is before us and set the sayings out in some other order, we should affect nothing of the sense and meaning at all. All we have is a sequence of sayings, set in no rational sequence whatsoever. What then holds the whole together? Let us now consider the names:

1:6 Joshua ben Perahyah and Nittai the Arbelite received [the Torah] from them. Joshua ben Perahyah says...

1:7 Nittai the Arbelite says...

1:8A Judah ben Tabbai and Simeon ben Shetah received [the Torah] from them.

1:8B Judah ben Tabbai says...

1:9 Simeon ben Shetah says...

The point is obvious: The list is made up of a set of names, and the structure is defined by the pairs. What holds the whole together is the coherence of the names, meaning, the pairs (there are in fact five of them) and their order. Nothing depends on the substance of what is said; that yields only information: good counsel for the upright disciple or judge, in general.

Now what if we were composing a set of statements providing good counsel to such a class of persons? Then, it must follow, we should produce something that, as to the matter of the logic of coherent discourse, would appear no different from Aturfarnbag's sequence: this, then that, then the next thing. Both compositors – the one of a sequence of rules of conduct, the other of a sequence of legal, ritual, and theological truths – bear comparison at their point of coherence; both prove coherent in general, since the document in which they make their appearance admirably holds them together. Both sets of sayings stand, each on its own, because all of the sayings serve the same purpose, and the matter of order or sequence plays no part in the presentation of their sense. In all instances, what makes the sayings persuasive is the document in which they stand, the authority that is claimed for it: in the case of the sayings of tractate Avot, God through Moses, Joshua, the masters and disciples from Sinai onward. Aturfarnbag establishes his authority in the opening line as well, and that authority imparts coherence to the whole: "Several questions asked of aerpat Aturfarnbag son of Farokhuzat, leader of the faithful" – and those last words suffice, "leader of the faith."

I have left to the end the comparison of the topical program, because neither document may be said to follow such a program, but for different reasons. When we briefly examined the rivayat of Aturfarnbag, we noted that he covers this and that, in no compelling order; and we may simply now stipulate that his topics derive from the entire repertoire of interests of the community and its priests, whatever those interests may have been. To put matters in a simple and affirmative way: for a document made up of responsa – questions and answers – the topical program is dictated by the concerns of the community of the faithful and its priests. What lends coherence to the questions and answers – in whatever order they appear – is the mind of the community that sees each of them separately and all of them together in the framework of the social order that that community embodies. Coherence derives from the social order, extrinsic to the writing and definitive of the purpose of the writing. Once more in simple language: The reason that Aturfarnbag writes his questions and answers is the same reason that makes those questions and answers cohere, and that is, the interest of the audience for the writing: those who will value the book, preserve it, and hand it on, also are those who will see in the book a transparent cogency that, to outsiders, is invisible.

The topical program of the Bavli derives from the Mishnah, and the Bavli forms a document the order and structure of which follows the topics of that other, prior writing. The Bavli is organized topically, because the Mishnah is organized topically, and the Bavli is framed as a commentary to, and expansion of, the Mishnah. The Mishnah is a six-part code of descriptive rules; the six divisions are: (1) agricultural rules; (2) laws governing appointed seasons, for example, Sabbaths and festivals; (3) laws on the transfer of women and property along with women from one man (father) to another (husband); (4) the system of civil and criminal law (corresponding to what we today should regard as "the legal system"); (5) laws for the conduct of the cult and the Temple; and (6) laws on the preservation of cultic purity both in the Temple and under certain domestic circumstances, with special reference to the table and bed. The Bavli takes up tractates in the second through fifth divisions. I see no necessary order in the topics of the divisions, or of their tractates, that dictates why one division precedes or follows some other, or why one tractate some other. But within the tractates, as I have shown elsewhere, the order of the chapters follows the logic of the division of the topic of the tractate into its necessarily sequential components.[4]

The Mishnah is a book of lists, and the lists are compared and contrasted. All things thus are classified, and, through comparison and contrast, shown to form an orderly and hierarchical world. For the inner structure set forth by a logic of hierarchical classification alone could sustain the system of ordering all things in proper place and under the proper rule. The like belongs with the like and conforms to the rule governing the like, the unlike goes over to the opposite and conforms to the opposite rule. When we make lists of the like, we also know the rule governing all the items on those lists, respectively. We know that and one other thing, namely, the opposite rule, governing all items sufficiently like to belong on those lists, but sufficiently unlike to be placed on other lists. And, as we noted in our brief example, the Bavli organizes itself around the exposition of these lists and the inner cogency that holds each list together and distinguishes it from all others.[5] The topical program of the Mishnah is the topical program of the Bavli. The Mishnah is about the life of Israel, the Bavli is about the Mishnah.

The upshot may be stated very simply: The Rivayat's topical program is defined by the social order that produces the writer, the writing, and the book and its preservation, a practical and concrete document that addresses real people in a real predicament. The Bavli draws its topical program from a prior writing – a tradition, as a matter of fact – and it never, ever finds programmatic guidance only in the social order in which its sages make their lives. Both writings form works of tradition in the fullest sense of the word: each draws upon received truth, each proposes to hand on that truth, and each sets forth the particular and distinctive contribution of its author or authorship. But while the Rivayat emerges from and refers back to the everyday and the here and now, the Talmud speaks to a different world altogether: the world of mind.[6]

---

[4]See my *History of the Mishnaic Law* (Leiden, 1974-1987: E.J. Brill) in forty-three volumes, where for each tractate I explain why the several subdivisions follow the order that they do and (ordinarily) can follow no other order while retaining the same sense.

[5]We shall return to this matter in the concluding chapter.

[6]A perfectly reasonable objection is: Why choose the Bavli, rather than the more congruent and more contemporary responsa literature? For are there no collections of questions and answers, response precisely in the form and of the character of the Rivayat? Indeed there are, and they derive from the same time, the ninth century and beyond. The letter of Sherira, to which I made reference in Chapter One, is an exact counterpart to this Rivayat as well as to the other. Then what justifies my comparing the Rivayat to the Talmud, rather than to the Iggeret

form, which it more surely resembles. A rereading of Chapter One provides the fully spelled-out answer: the Rivayat was written for the purpose for which the Bavli was written, which was, to write down the tradition. The manner in which the writing was carried out compares to the counterpart writings in Judaism; but the context and purpose of the writing demand comparison to the counterpart of the Bavli – nothing less. Were I to have chosen for comparison the ninth- and tenth-century responsa literature of Judaism and the Rivayats under study here, I should have diminished, in the choice of analogical writings, the far weightier place of the Rivayats in their context than the responsa in theirs. Once we set out to investigate how Zoroastrian priests wrote down their great tradition in comparison with how the Judaic sages wrote theirs, we have to choose for comparison statements of the respective great traditions. And the rest follows.

5

Episodic Comparisons: The Family

Traditions attain greatness, as the Judaic and Zoroastrian ones did for a long time to come, when they find ways of saying some few things not only in a great many ways, but also in a vast variety of circumstances. The power of a system is in its simplicity, on the one side, and capacity for exegetical diversity, on the other: out of many things, one thing, out of one thing, many things. It is, therefore, at circumstantial comparison, if episodic and not systematic,[1] that the comparison of documents becomes indicative. In both instances, priests and sages determined to produce writings that would shape the future of the societies that they valued; their writing was addressed to a broad and general world, and the issues they addressed concerned, or at least were meant to concern, how these societies were to take shape. That meant, identifying situations that would recur perpetually, addressing problems that (so they knew for sure) would require recapitulating the principles of the faith in age succeeding age.

In the nature of things, what would persist would emerge in the here and now of family and home, on the one side, and the enduring social order, on the other. Neither group of writers could imagine the end of the social order to which they meant to speak; that possibility (dying out by reason of disinterest, or the extermination of entire populations, to take the two extremes) never entered their mind. That is why they addressed what they knew would live – more or less – forever. And so

---

[1]For reasons spelled out earlier, systemic description, whether legal or theological, demands a properly capacious frame of reference: the whole of the two systems, fully exposed, not just documents that form mere parts. By that criterion, the Bavli forms a systemic statement, since it is whole and complete, but our two rivayats do not make a pretense at presenting the whole picture.

long as home and family, society and community, would thrive, so they would require the persistence, also, of the great tradition – and also (by the way) recreate in age succeeding age that ongoing audience for their writing. I take for granted the authors of the Talmud and Aturfarnbag wrote their books not only for one time, but all time; that is the point of writing down a great tradition. Then, it follows, they shaped their writing in such a way that it would enjoy perpetual relevance.

How better to do so than deal not with the changing circumstance of the moment but only in the language of, and in conversation with, eternal truths, governing matters of faith and practice that persisted out of the dim past and would be replicated over the furthest horizon? And that is why, when we wish to compare the writings, it is wise to consider not only problems of a formal character – how people wrote in general – but problems of a substantive, or material, social consequence as well, for instance, the conduct of the life of families, on the one side, and families in community, that is, society in general, on the other. That the priests and sages of the two communities made the right decision is shown by the simple fact that, over all, we can understand the problems I have selected and make sense (in their context at least) of their solution. So episodic comparison bears its message about documentary comparison, even though not part of the systemic comparison that, in due course, will replace this initial and preliminary probe of matters.

Accordingly we progress from the form of writing viewed in general terms – rhetoric, logic of coherent discourse, and topic – to the form of the writing when both sides propose to talk about the same problem, details of material culture writ small. That is a much more concrete form of comparison, therefore more suggestive. Now we read the writing not only as a general specimen of how "our sages of blessed memory" or the priests of the good religion expressed their ideas and preserved their traditions, but as a specimen of a very particular writing, for a purpose, with intended consequences, addressing a particular kind of reader or hearer. So, when the respective authors – Aturfarnbag, the sages who wrote the Bavli – formulate their respective statements in concrete terms, and when, as it happens, they go over the same issues and come to the same, or intersecting, or at least concentric conclusions, then a new analytical perspective shapes our view. For now we have to ask, how do the documents compare at the level of such exquisite detail that – read from the view of what, actually, is said – a sentence from the one may be lifted up and dropped down into the other? Then, but only then, do the initial proposals come to their test in very concrete and (therefore) probative detail.

The comparison of topical programs leads to some of the numerous points at which the Rivayat and the Bavli intersect. Just as, for

Episodic Comparisons: The Family

documentary comparison, we found it necessary to select indicative traits in accord with a program pertinent equally to both writings (and, in theory, any writing), so when we wish to see how both books speak to the same question and solve the same substantive problem, we require simple criteria that apply throughout. Since they proposed to write down great traditions, of hoary antiquity, for the future none could then foresee but all believed with perfect faith their books would define, both sets of writers thought about the social order of their respective communities. The issues are concrete, but not trivial; the comparisons simple, but still indicative of the character of the writings that accomplished a single goal but in two quite distinct, and distinctive, kinds of writing.

Like any other theorists addressing that problem, and like any other administrators of group life (as both the Zoroastrian priests and the Judaic sages were), the Judaic sages and Zoroastrian priests therefore had to deal with three dimensions of the life of the community they proposed to shape and also enrich through the provision in writing of the great tradition. By community in this context I mean, the distinctive group, bound by a common ideology (theology) as well as by bonds of genealogy past and future that the writers proposed to address, into whose care the writers planned to commit their books. The community envisaged, in both cases, by definition was required to take up in common – as must any community that falls under the definition just now offered – issues deriving from the nature of the social order realized by these persons living in common and together: [1] the family, the smallest whole unit of the social order; [2] the shared civil order; [3] relationships with the "other" or outsider, that is, with the world beyond. Any writing that purports to deal with how people are to live together as a group will find something to say (if only in theory) about those three dimensions of that shared life. We have examined a sufficient sample of the Bavli and our Rivayat to know that, of course, they do. So what we wish to learn is simple: How, when they address the same problem (not merely deal with the same topic) do our authors formulate their statements?

I. Exercising the Right of Refusal

A minor girl may be assigned by her father to a man as wife, but, when she comes of age (generally: puberty) both Talmudic and Zoroastrian law accords her the right to confirm or nullify the marriage. The issue is, what is the status of the relationship during the girl's minority? And what is her status should she exercise the right of refusal and decide to leave the relationship altogether? The issue is, does she revert to the father's control, so that he can marry her off again (Bavli) or does she revert to his control so he can assign her guardianship to someone else (Rivayat)? Specifically, once he has given her away, has the father any further rights over the daughter, or is she now an independent woman (both)?

XII

Question
1. When a man gives a three-year-old daughter to a man in wifehood; and that daughter attains to majority, and says: "I do not consent to marry this man," with whom will the guardianship rest? If that man says: "Unless thou wilt be my wife, I will not give thee to anyone under guardianship," can that daughter secure a guardian? If she marries, will her status be of an independent woman or not?

Reply
2. As I understand: the wifehood cannot take place; the guardianship shall have been given; and if her father will not withdraw the guardianship during the length of his life, the guardianship will rest with him to whom he will give after the father; and if he says, "If thou will not be my wife, I will not give thee to thy husband," he is rightful; if the husband is agreeable to cause the menstruation month to pass in marriage and the spouse be not agreeable, the sin of the menstruation month originates with the spouse.

Aturfarnbag's formulation of the problem rests on the fact that no woman can remain without a guardian; if the woman's guardian died without appointing another in his place, or without appointing her as her own guardian, she becomes the ward of the community, who finds a guardian for her. Now in our case, the father gives the daughter at the age of three years in marriage; she gets the husband as guardian. If she comes of age after the father's death and becomes independent, she would have the right to reject her husband as guardian, but then she has to have some other guardian in his place (Anklesaria, pp. 38-39). So, while the father as guardian may give her in marriage, the girl being forbidden to marry without his consent, the father also may appoint another person as the daughter's guardian during his lifetime and he can also revoke the guardianship if she agrees. Now the husband would take over as guardian.

Here is the Mishnah's and Talmud's treatment of the same matter. The issue is framed differently. But the basic principle is the same, namely, the girl married off prior to puberty has the right, at puberty, to

Episodic Comparisons: The Family

dissolve the relationship. The Mishnah's concern is, what kind of prior relationship may be dissolved, for the Mishnah knows two stages in which a woman is designated for a particular man, betrothal and the fully consummated marriage. Here the dispute is, may a girl upon reaching puberty leave a fully consummated marriage?

Mishnah-tractate Yebamot 13:1

A. The House of Shammai say, "Only girls who are [merely] betrothed exercise the right of refusal."

B. And the House of Hillel say, "Those who are betrothed and those who are married."

C. The House of Shammai say, "[The right of refusal is exercised] against the husband, but not against the levir" [the deceased childless husband's surviving brother, with whom the girl has entered into levirate marriage, as dictated by Deut. 25:5-10].

D. And the House of Hillel say, "Against the husband and against the levir."

E. The House of Shammai say, "[It must be exercised only] in his presence."

F. And the House of Hillel say, "In his presence and not in his presence."

G. The House of Shammai say, "[It must be exercised] in a court."

H. And the House of Hillel say, "In a court and not in a court."

I. Said the House of Hillel to the House of Shammai, "She may exercise the right of refusal while she is a minor, even four or five times."

J. Replied to them the House of Shammai, "Israelite girls are not to be tossed around like so much ownerless property.

K. "But: She exercises the right of refusal and waits until she reaches maturity, or she exercises the right of refusal and remarries [forthwith]."

I.1 A. [The House of Shammai say, "Only girls who are [merely] betrothed exercise the right of refusal":] Said R. Judah said Samuel, *"What is the operative consideration in the mind of the House of Shammai?* It is because a stipulation may not be attached to a marriage, so if a girl who is married should exercise the right of refusal, *people will come to maintain that* a stipulation may be attached to a marriage.

B. "If the girl had entered the marriage canopy but not had sexual relations, *however, what is to be said?*

C. "It is because a stipulation may not be attached to entry into the marriage canopy.

D. "If the father had already handed over the daughter to the agent of the husband, *however, what is to be said?*

E. "Rabbis made no such distinction [as to the phases of the marriage procedure].

F. *"What is the operative consideration in the mind of the House of Hillel?*

G. "People in general are informed that the marriage of a minor is only on the strength of rabbis' authority."

I.2 A. Rabbah and R. Joseph both say, "The operative consideration in the mind of the House of Shammai is that a man does not treat an act of sexual relations on his part as one of mere fornication.
B. "If the girl had entered the marriage canopy but not had sexual relations, *however, what is to be said?*
C. "It is because the husband doesn't want his marriage canopy to involve a forbidden act.
D. "If the father had already handed over the daughter to the agent of the husband, *however, what is to be said?*
E. "Rabbis made no such distinction [as to the phases of the marriage procedure].
F. "What is the operative consideration in the mind of the House of Hillel?
G. "Since the process involves a betrothal and a marriage contract, people are never going to say that an act of sexual relations on his part is one of mere fornication."

I.3 A. R. Pappa said, "The operative consideration in the mind of the House of Shammai is on account of the usufruct [of the plucking property that belongs to the minor].
B. "And the operative consideration in the mind of the House of Hillel also is on account of the usufruct [of the plucking property that belongs to the minor].
C. "The operative consideration in the mind of the House of Shammai is on account of the usufruct: For if you say that a married girl has the right of refusal, her husband will grab the fruit and eat it up, since she may leave him any time.
D. "The House of Hillel? To the contrary, if you say that she may exercise the right of refusal, he is going to improve the property, thinking that, if not, her relatives will advise her and take her from him."

I.4 A. Raba said, "This is the operative consideration of the House of Shammai: A man will not go to the trouble of making a banquet and then lose all he has spent.
B. "And the House of Hillel? Both parties are glad to be married to one another, so that they may be known as married."

The issue is a vital one: What is the status of the marriage of the prepubescent girl? The House of Shammai treat it as an ordinary marriage, once the marriage has been consummated, and they will want a writ of divorce, not merely a public declaration of refusal. The further explanations of what is at stake present no surprises and speak for themselves. The contrast between the Bavli's presentation of the rule of the prepubescent marriage and the Rivayat's hardly requires extensive explanation. Aturfarnbag gives us the rule, the Mishnah provides a dispute and the Bavli, an explanation of the issues that inhere in the dispute (with the proviso that all parties know that the law follows the position of the House of Hillel).

Now if we set the statements side by side, we see reasonable justification for comparing the passages in the shared problem. But dealing with the dissolution of the prepubescent marriage, each party has its distinctive considerations, which render further comparison

Episodic Comparisons: The Family 93

somewhat puzzling. The issue of guardianship does not intersect with the issue of the status of the marriage that may or may not be dissolved. To be sure, our sages of blessed memory know the issue of the future standing of the girl who has exercised the right of refusal, and this is discussed in later passages of the present chapter of the Mishnah and Talmud. But the details of the presentation serve to distinguish the one from the other treatment of the common issue. At the same time, we may legitimately point to an obvious point of difference. In presenting the same subject, the two documents differ in a fundamental way. Aturfarnbag provides information: question and answer. Had he chosen to present his ideas in the form of the Mishnah, he could readily have done so, for example:

> When a man gives a three-year-old daughter to a man in wifehood; and that daughter attains to majority, and says: "I do not consent to marry this man," the guardianship shall have been given; and if her father will not withdraw the guardianship during the length of his life, the guardianship will rest with him to whom he will give after the father; and if he says, "If thou will not be my wife, I will not give thee to thy husband," he is rightful; if the husband is agreeable to cause the menstruation month to pass in marriage and the spouse be not agreeable, the sin of the menstruation month originates with the spouse.

All I have done is restate the language before us from question-and-answer to declarative sentence to come up with a statement that, with the required changes, could have taken up a comfortable residence in the Mishnah; or it could have stood in the Talmud as a proposition awaiting analysis, for example:

> Rabbah said, "When a man gives a three year old daughter to a man in wifehood; and that daughter attains to majority, and says: 'I do not consent to marry this man,' she has not got the right [the marriage is valid despite her wishes]. Under what circumstance? If the marriage was consummated. But if she was only betrothed, she has the right."

Someone then has to tell us that Rabbah has taken the position of the House of Shammai, and that problem will have to be resolved in one of the various ways available for that purpose.

So, except for "Rabbah said," and its ubiquitous counterparts throughout the Bavli,[2] I find nothing that distinguishes the question-and-answer form from the propositional statement of the law. Where the Bavli differs is at the point that the Bavli takes over the Mishnah

---

[2] Why a document that allows no claim of authorship should be made up of individually assigned statements, while one that speaks for a single writer should so seldom cite prior named authorities or even specific books, has already been addressed. That remains a suggestive paradox produced by this comparison.

paragraph and conducts its analysis. Here, our interest not in the rule but its theory or premise or underlying principle does carry us far from the stated concerns of Aturfarnbag, who rarely tells us more than the rule. So while, making provision for obvious differences, we can treat Aturfarnbag's work as analogous to that of Judah the Patriarch, to whom authorship of the Mishnah is attributed, it most certainly is not analogous to that of the authors of the Talmud.

II. When Equal Shares in an Inheritance Have Been Guaranteed

At issue for both legal systems is a prenuptial agreement, assuring the wife that her children will take equal shares of his estate. Is the husband bound by that agreement, or may he give more to one and less to another? Further, if a daughter marries during the husband's lifetime, is her status changed in respect to that original agreement? The issue is phrased fairly clearly in our Rivayat, the answer being: the agreement is firm.

LXII

Question
1. There is a man who makes an agreement with his wife and says: "The children who are born of thee are made co-partners and joint owners"; and thereafter, to the children who are born of that wife; can that man give a greater share of his property to some one of the children, and less to some one? The father hands over to the husband the daughter who is born of that wife; is a share of the property hers after the father or not?

Reply
2. An equal share belongs to sons and daughters, and one cannot do otherwise; if the daughter takes a husband when her father is alive, even then the share goes to her by way of justice and lawfulness.

The two important points, which could have been stated as a legal proposition, contain no ambiguity: the agreement stands firm, even if the daughter marries while the father is alive. The framing of the issue in the Mishnah and Talmud focuses upon a different problem, namely, a conventional stipulation that is left unarticulated. If the husband made no commitment regarding the wife's offspring in the union, nonetheless, the stipulation that is routine is held to prevail. The topic is the same, but the problematic quite different. To show that with clarity, I cite somewhat more of the abstract than before:

Mishnah-tractate Ketubot 4:10

A. [If] he did not write for her, *"Male children which you will have with me will inherit the proceeds of your marriage contract, in addition to their share with their other brothers,"*

B. he nonetheless is liable [to pay over the proceeds of the marriage contract to the woman's sons],

C. for this is [in all events] an unstated condition imposed by the court.

I.1 A. [If he did not write for her, *"Male children which you will have with me will inherit the proceeds of your marriage contract, in addition to their share with their other brothers,"* he nonetheless is liable to pay over the proceeds of the marriage contract to the woman's sons, for this is in all events an unstated condition imposed by the court:] Said R. Yohanan in the name of R. Simeon b. Yohai, "How come sages ordained the clause in the marriage contract covering 'male children'? It is so that a man should be encouraged to provide for his daughter as much as for his son [since her male sons would inherit her estate]."

B. *So is there a parallel to a case in which the All-Merciful has said that the son is to inherit and the daughter not, but rabbis come along and ordain that the daughter also inherit?*

C. *This, too, derives from the Torah, for it is written, "Take you wives and beget sons and daughters, and take wives for your sons and give your daughters to husbands" (Jer. 29:6) – now as to the counsel to marry off one's sons, that is understandable, since it is within the father's power to do just that, but as to giving the daughters, does he have the power to do that [since the man goes looking for the woman, not the reverse]? Lo, in this statement we are informed that a father has to provide for his daughter clothing and a trousseau and has to provide a dowry, so that people will come looking for her and marry her.*

D. *To what proportion of his assets?*

E. *Both Abbayye and Raba say, "To a tenth of his assets."*

I.2 A. *So might one say that the sons will inherit what the mother got from her father, but not what she is getting from her husband [the marriage settlement and excess]?*

B. *If so, then the father, too, will refrain from handing over a sizable dowry to his daughter.*

C. *Then might one say that in a case in which the father wrote over assets to the daughter, the husband must add the cited clause, but where the father has not written over any dowry, the husband does not have to write over the stated clause?*

D. *Rabbis made no such distinction.*

E. *Then why should not a daughter of a woman who had no sons among sons of other wives not also inherit a share in the father's estate?*

F. *Rabbis regard the marriage settlement in the category of an inheritance.*

G. *Then why not invoke that clause, at any rate, for a daughter of a woman who had no sons among other daughters of other equally sonless wives, that she should inherit [among the other daughters]?*

H. *Rabbis made no such distinction.*

	I.	Then why isn't the marriage settlement recoverable by the sons from movables as well?
	J.	The rabbis treat the clause covering additional dowry as equivalent to the basic sum of the marriage settlement [which cannot be collected from the movables of the estate].
	K.	Then why not permit distraint or property that was sold or mortgaged [so that the sons can collect what is coming to them from such property, as much as their mother can in recovering her marriage contract]?
	L.	The operative language is **will inherit** [and an inheritance cannot be recovered from sold or mortgaged property].
	M.	Then is it possible to recover the excess even if there was no surplus in the basic estate, over what is needed for the payment of the marriage settlements, of a least a denar [to see that all sons inherit at least something]?
	N.	Rabbis did not make an ordinance that would effect the nullification of the Torah's law of inheritance....
I.3	A.	R. Yemar the Elder asked R. Nahman, "If the wife sold her marriage settlement to her husband, does the marriage settlement clause covering the male children continue to prevail, or does that clause not prevail?"
	B.	Raba said to him, "So raise the question in the case of a woman who forgave her marriage contract altogether?"
	C.	He said to him, "No, I'm raising the question as to a case in which she sold it. For even though one may then allege that it was the need for ready cash that forced her to make the sale, one might claim that she is in the position of someone who got hit a hundred times with a hammer [but then conceded willingly, so the sale is treated in an ordinary way]. Would I then have to ask about the case of a woman who just forgave the marriage contract willingly? [Surely the same answer would apply anyhow.]"
	D.	Said Raba, "It is obvious to me that if the wife sold her marriage settlement to third parties, the marriage settlement clause covering the male children does continue to prevail. How come? Because it was the need for ready cash that forced her to make the sale. And as to a woman who forgave her marriage contract altogether, the marriage settlement clause covering the male children does not continue to prevail. How come? Because she wanted to give up her claim."
	E.	But then Raba raised this question: "If the wife sold her marriage settlement to her husband, is she in the status of one who sells it to others, or is she in the status of one who forgives the husband the requirement of paying it off?"
	F.	After he raised this question, he went and solved it: " If the wife sold her marriage settlement to her husband, she is in the status of one who sells it to others."
	G.	Objected R. Idi bar Abin, "**And if she should die, the heirs of either one of the husbands do not inherit her marriage settlement [M. Yeb. 10:1M].** And we considered the matter in the following terms: What's her marriage settlement doing here? And said R. Pappa, 'Reference is made here to the clause in the marriage settlement covering male children' [that is, her sons are entitled to receive the payment of her marriage contract from the father's estate when he dies, even if she should die first and the father remarried and had

Episodic Comparisons: The Family 97

      more sons with the second wife; they get shares in the father's estate but also the marriage settlement of the mother; but here, they lose that claim (Slotki)]. *Now why should this be the case [that her children are so deprived]? Couldn't one argue here, too, 'She was overcome by lust [and that's why she remarried, but, having acted under compulsion, she does not deprive her children of their rights in her marriage settlement]?"*

H.   *In that case, loss of the marriage settlement is an extrajudicial penalty that rabbis imposed on her.*

It is clear that the rule as stated by the Mishnah expresses the same fundamental policy as in the Rivayat, namely, the wife's expectations in regard to the disposition of the husband's estate are to be honored, whether circumstances change (the Rivayat) or the expectations are not even articulated (Bavli). Not only so, but when we come to the Talmud, we find an explanation for the Mishnah's rule that draws us still closer to the Rivayat's principle. Sound social policy, both systems maintain, requires that daughters as much as sons be provided for in a fair way (Yohanan).

But the generative problematic, which defines the Talmud's exegetical concern, hardly derives from the details of the law. The somewhat protracted abstract shows that fact with great clarity. And here is where the distinctive character of the Talmud emerges. The Talmud's problem is not legal but hermeneutical, not exegetical but philosophical. Aturfarnbag solves a problem of law by giving a decision of justice. The Talmud asks a different question, one that derives from an intellectual, not a practical, concern. What the Talmud wants to know is how the law of the Mishnah can set aside the law of the Torah, which, after all, makes no provision for the very consideration that the Mishnah deems to take priority: even if unstated, the stipulation holds! That is the point of I.1B, which shapes the discussion, and which provokes a suitable reply at C. The secondary development at No. 2 serves only to clarify the effects of the Mishnah's rule. A further point of interest is at No. 3, which gives us a case that has only general bearing upon the rule of the Mishnah and its exegesis at Nos. 1-2. If a Pahlavi writer wished to translate this story into a case involving a question and an answer, he presumably could have done so, but the story has its own point and hardly enriches our understanding of the role. The question at No. 4 brings us still closer to the style of our Rivayat, since, lacking the attribution, it could have stood in the Pahlavi compilation. The upshot remains the same, and both documents make the same general point.

III. Disposing of an Inheritance of Thievery

How a family disposes of an inheritance that has been amassed through the father's sinfulness presents a problem to the framers of the rules for both communities. Aturfarnbag's question is framed in his circumstance, use of the money for ceremonies for the father's soul or for the souls of those who inherit the wealth, the Talmud's addresses their problem: how to right the wrong done by the father.

CXLI

Question

1. Can the man who obtains from his father wealth which is accumulated with unrighteousness, enjoy that wealth, and make a provision for duty and good deeds or not? And if he performs out of it ceremonies for his own soul and even that of his father, will they reach their souls or not?

Reply

2. For all the wealth which the father had accumulated before the coming forth of the child, I cannot understand his child to be a sharer in his sins or good deeds; and then when it comes into the possession and authority of the child, he shall return, whatever he knows as having been obtained from the thief or the robber; a half or one third, just as the Dasturs may direct, and he shall restore the rest, that which is worthy of him; and he shall make provision according to religious usage, just as may be very helpful, for the expiation of the sins of his father; as to that of which he does not know anything, as he himself is authorized to keep the wealth in his possession, it is good that he shall, in all respects perform ceremonies, votive-offerings, and other works of merit for the soul of his father, for making the atonement of the sins of his father and by way of good deeds even for the sake of the soul of his father, so that he may expiate the sins and impurities, and the indebtedness of his father; for the expiation of sin is the most compulsory work of merit, whereby glory and radiance are increased.

The child is in no way responsible for what the father has done, but the child has nonetheless to seek to restore part of what is known to have been stolen, as he is instructed to do. But as to what is not known to have been stolen, he can keep it and do good with it, for both himself and his father's soul. The key then is knowledge and intentionality. If one knows something has been stolen, he cannot keep it but must restore it in the proper manner; if he does not know that an object has been stolen, then mere suspicion is null; one does good with what he has.

10:1A-C

A. He who steals [food] and feeds [what he stole] to his children, or left it to them –
B. they are exempt from making restitution.
C. But if it remained something which could serve as security [for example, subject to a mortgage, that is, real estate], they are liable to make restitution.

The Mishnah's distinction is a different one. If what has been stolen is movable or intangible and has been consumed, the beneficiaries are exempt from all further obligation. The reason has yet to be explained; the operative consideration is whether or not title is retained by the victims of the theft or has passed to the thief. As to the heirs, the rule is unambiguous. If they cannot restore what they have received from the father's wrongful action, they are not responsible. But if it is a matter of real property, that has to be restored. The rule is then simpler and does not invoke the consideration of intentionality; and the disposition of the property also is not subjected to extraneous considerations, for example, doing good with it. What is the heirs' is theirs, and what should not be theirs is restored. But the Talmud immediately adds the issue of intentionality – now with reference to the victim.

I.1 A. Said R. Hisda, "If one stole something [such as an animal], and, before the owner had despaired of getting it back [at which point the thief acquires title to the object], someone else came along and ate up what he stole, the owner has the choice of collecting the payment from the one or the other." *How come? The reason is that, for so long as the owner did not despair of getting the thing back, the stolen object is still in the title of the original owner.*

Our problem is tangential to the Mishnah's rule and immediately revises the discussion by introducing a distinct problem. That problem then is referred back to our Mishnah rule for solution.

B. *But have we not learned in the Mishnah:* **He who steals [food] and feeds [what he stole] to his children, or left it to them – they are exempt from making restitution. But if it was something which is subject to a mortgage [that is, real estate], they are liable to make restitution?** *Does this not contradict the position of R. Hisda?*
C. R. Hisda will say to you, "When that is set forth as a Tannaite rule, it pertains to the situation that prevails after the original owner has despaired of getting the thing back [and so title has passed to the thief]."

In the following, we introduce a distinct consideration. If someone loses an object, he retains title to it so long as he hopes to recover it. But if he despairs of recovering the object, then by that act of despair he expresses the intentionality of giving up title to the object, which then becomes abandoned property and enters the domain of whoever seizes the same object. That consideration is introduced at II.1.B, C; now we want to know the governing analogy, and our discussion veers off into an analytical direction that leads us away from the issue at hand.

II.1   A.   **Or left it to them – they are exempt from making restitution:**
      B.   Said R. Ammi bar Hama, "That is to say, the domain of the heir is equivalent to the domain of the purchaser [and if after despairing of getting the object back, at which point the object was subject to the robber's title, the robber died, the article would remain with the heirs, just as would an article that was purchased]."
      C.   And Raba said, "The domain of the heir is not equivalent to the domain of the purchaser, *for with what sort of a case do we deal? It is one in which the food was eaten after the father died.*"
      D.   *But since it is said,* **But if it remained something which could serve as security [for example, subject to a mortgage, that is, real estate], they are liable to make restitution,** *it should follow that, in the opening clause, we deal with a case in which the stolen object is still available [and has not yet been consumed].*
      E.   Raba may say to you, "This is the sense of the statement: If their father had left them **something which could serve as security [for example, subject to a mortgage, that is, real estate], they are liable to make restitution.**"
      F.   *But lo, Rabbi repeated as the Tannaite formulation to R. Simeon, his son,* "The meaning is not literally, **something which could serve as security [for example, subject to a mortgage, that is, real estate],** but rather, even a cow that could be used for ploughing, or an ass that could be used for driving, they are liable to make restitution, on account of the honor that is owing to their father."
      G.   Rather, said Raba, "When I die, R. Oshaia will come out to meet me, for I interpret the Mishnah's in accord with his view. For it has been taught on Tannaite authority by R. Oshaia: He who steals [food] and feeds [what he stole] to his children, or left it to them – they are exempt from making restitution. If he left it to them as an inheritance, then if the stolen object is available, they are liable to restore it, but if not, they are exempt. But if it remained something which could serve as security [for example, subject to a mortgage, that is, real estate], they are liable to make restitution."...

We come now to another way of phrasing the question. It is forbidden to lend money on interest, which is treated as an act of thievery. What happens if the children inherit the proceeds of interest or usury? This question raises once more, in different form, the problem with which we commenced, linking still more tightly the issue of the correct analogy of the domain of the heir – is it or is it not like the domain of the purchaser – to the problem before us: restoring stolen property. The power of the Talmud to move from case to abstract principle to a fresh case finds renewal in the explicit case that follows, where the case is the same and the abstract principle is also the same:

4.   A.   *R. Adda bar Ahba repeated the statement of R. Ammi bar Hamma in connection with the following:* "**If the father died and left money gained on interest to his children, even if the heirs know that it was money paid as interest, the children do not have to return the money collected as interest. [But if the father had left them a cow, field, cloak, or any sort of object for which he bore responsibility for replacement, should the object be lost, they are liable to return such an object for the honor of their father]** [T. B.M. 5:25-6]. Said R. Ammi bar Hama, 'That is to say, the domain of the heir is equivalent to the domain of the purchaser [and if after despairing of getting the object back, at which point the object was subject to the robber's title, the robber died, the article would remain with the heirs, just as would an article that was purchased].' Raba said, 'I shall say to you, the domain of the heir is not equivalent to the domain of the purchaser. But this case is exceptional, for Scripture has said, "Do not take usury of him or increase but fear your God that your brother may live with you" (Lev. 25:36), *meaning, return the money to him so that he may live with you. The man himself is the one whom the All-Merciful has placed under admonition, his children are not so admonished.*'"

    B.   *One who repeats the dispute in connection with the cited Tannaite formulation external to the Mishnah all the more so would maintain that it pertains to the Mishnah passage itself. But one who repeats it in connection with the Mishnah passage would maintain that in regard to the cited Tannaite formulation external to the Mishnah R. Ammi bar Hamma would repeat the passage along the same lines as did Raba.*

Now we make a distinction Aturfarnbag does not introduce, between adult and minor heirs, thus asking about the status of those who do or do not bear responsibility for making restitution:

5.   A.   *Our rabbis have taught on Tannaite authority:*
    B.   **He who steals something and feeds it to his children – they are exempt from having to pay restitution. If he left it before them [as an inheritance], the adult heirs are obligated to pay restitution. The minors are exempt from having to pay restitution. If the adults say, "We are not familiar with the dealings of our father with you," they would also be exempt from having to pay restitution** [T. B.Q. 10:21D-E].

6.   A.   *Well, then, merely because they say,* **"We are not familiar with the dealings of our father with you,"** *are they going to be exempt from having to pay restitution? [That's ridiculous.]*
    B.   *Said Raba, "This is the sense of the passage:* If the adults say, 'We know full well the dealings that our father had with you, and we therefore know for sure that there was no balance in your favor,' they are exempt from having to pay restitution."

7.   A.   *Our rabbis have further taught on Tannaite authority:*

	B.	He who steals something and feeds it to his children – the latter are exempt from having to pay restitution. If he left it before them as an inheritance and they consumed it, whether adult or minor, they are liable.
8.	A.	*How come the minors are liable? They are in no worse a situation than if they had deliberately done damage [and they would not then have had to pay restitution]!*
	B.	*Said R. Pappa, "This is the sense of the passage:* If he left it before them as an inheritance and it has not yet been consumed, then whether adult or minor, they have to pay restitution."...
9.	A.	*Our rabbis have taught on Tannaite authority:*
	B.	"He shall restore the misappropriated object which he violently took away" (Lev. 5:23) – what is the sense of "which he violently took away"? If it is like what he violently took away, he shall restore it; [if not, then it is the value that he must pay.] In this connection sages have said: He who steals something and feeds it to his children – the latter are exempt from having to pay restitution. If he left it before them as an inheritance and they consumed it, whether adult or minor, they are liable.
	C.	In the name of Sumekhos they have said, "The adults are liable, the minors, exempt."

As before, what we find are intersecting discussions, a shared problem, common principles, but modes of analyzing the problem and identifying operative principles quite awry.

Clearly the two codes have introduced the same operative consideration, that of intentionality, but each negotiates matters in its own way. Aturfarnbag concerns himself with the intentionality of the heir to the stolen property; if he knows it is stolen, he has to restore it. But that of course is the very point at which the Mishnah's case commences: we know as fact that the food was stolen. The children have eaten it. Now do they have to return the stolen food or its value? Not at all. Why not? Because the intentionality of the victim of the theft is such that he has relinquished, by his despair of recovering his food, title to the stolen property. So while intentionality comes into play, it is for a different consideration altogether from the one operative in the Zoroastrian law.

And yet, once more, we have to say, had Aturfarnbag had the advantage of a talmud to make his rules dense and suggestive, the first thing that talmud would have said is, well isn't it obvious that if the property is known to have been stolen, it has to be returned? If it is not returned, then the heir becomes a thief; if it is returned, then what's the problem? And the answer could well have been, what might you otherwise have imagined? That if the heir knew it was stolen, he has under all circumstances to return it? Not at all. If the food is no longer available, no restitution is required – the heirs having no part in the theft and having eaten the food in good faith; if the stolen property of course

Episodic Comparisons: The Family

can be returned, it is to be returned. So, in all, the diverse expressions of somewhat awry cases turn out to conceal a community of viewpoint, despite the rather different consideration – the original owner's despair and the transfer of title on that account – that animates the Bavli's thinking.

A second point of remark concerns the Talmud's capacity to restate the case law in a sufficiently abstract manner to draw into the discussion quite distinct principles, for example, the matter of correct analogies: is the domain of the heir equivalent to that of a purchaser or is that not the case (II.1). Now that consideration is not essential for the solution of the problem before us, but it can be taken up in the setting of that same solution, and that is why it is introduced. The point then is, the Bavli will want to restate the case in abstract principle, then extend that same abstract principle to further cases, through the analysis of analogy and contrast. The upshot is, the Bavli will aim at an ever wider, and abstract, range of discourse; Aturfarnbag's, like the Mishnah's formulation, remains bound to the case at hand. The Bavli has a destination beyond the case; the Mishnah, and the Zoroastrian responsa writer, do not. That will become abundantly clear when we have concluded our comparisons and, in Chapter Nine, determined to answer the larger question: so what?

6

Episodic Comparisons: The Social Order

Sometimes the author of the Rivayat and the authorship[1] of the Talmud say the same thing, but what they say proves so banal that we need not devote much attention to analyzing the point in common. All comparison proves is that wise people say obvious things. Issues facing both documents' writers raise fundamental questions, which yield no interesting points of comparison, and problems of detail, which do. An example is the following, to which the Talmud can readily provide an equivalently commonplace counterpart:

CXXIV

Question
    1.   A man is passing along a road; enemies approach him: can he fight or not?

Reply
    2.   Unless he indubitably knows it to be rightful, he cannot.

With all due regard to the weight of the issue ("just war" indeed!), the point is trivial. If Aturfarnbag had been favored by a talmud, the first question would have been in Aramaic, *peshita* – "obviously!" It would have been followed by *mahu detema*, "what might you otherwise have said?" and then, an inventive exegete would have turned a commonplace into an important observation. But, with or without a talmud, the self-serving quality of the answer – assuring the faithful that when they fight, it is right, and that enemies are enemies – scarcely conceals its banality. That a random sample of legal writings not only in the Talmud but

---

[1] The anonymous collectivity of writers who bear collective responsibility for the document.

pretty much in any writing of the same sort endorses the same empty wisdom proves only that, at the abstract edge of wisdom, platitudes flourish. It is only in small details – what you eat for breakfast, how your words take effect and how you exercise the power of everyday speech – that the two systems speak of what really counts: the things people ordinarily do control for themselves. And there the messages become serious, specific, and indicative. The first covers the very matter of defining the boundaries of the two communities; here the differences in treating the same topic – eating nonbelievers' food – reveal systemic differences, which do not concern us in this study, but also documentary ones, which do.

I. Relations to the Outside World

Every account of a social order owes insiders a theory of how to relate to outsiders, and none in recorded time so vastly overspread the universe of its discourse as to see no need in theory to define the other. But to one theory of the social order the issue plays itself out in a vast tissue of endless detail, so that regulations of relationships to the other turn out to define the inner life of society, while to another theory, matters are routine and lacking consequence. The Bavli, carrying forward the interests of the Mishnah, puts forth a dense web of rules, together with deep thought on the issues inherent in them, to cover the outside world; the Rivayat makes a simple, factual statement, which contains its entire message. The substance of the rules varies only slightly; for Israel, the other worships idols, and therefore his food is taboo; for Zoroastrian Iran, the other fails to observe the menstrual taboo, so his food is taboo, too. The one finds theology, the other, sexuality, intrinsically related to food, at which point social differentiation takes place. Not eating what the outsider produces – wine in particular, other edibles in general – is what designates the outsider as other; and eating what "we" produce makes us us. What marks the outsider – wrong faith, yielding sins of commission, idolatry, or omission, failure to observe the menstrual taboo – then accounts for the alterity of the other.

We should not, therefore, find striking the difference between the laconic way in which Aturfarnbag makes his statement; it is all that has to be said, and, when we examine the Talmudic counterpart, with its prolix and elaborate restatement, we shall in the end know more than Aturfarnbag tells us in fifty words or less.

CXXV

Question
1. Can we purchase wine and other eatables from the Christians or not?

Reply
2. We cannot purchase but during helplessness, for they do not abstain from the menstrual impurity which they hold as lawful.

While I cannot claim to understand quite how Anklesaria has formulated the English counterpart to the Pahlavi, the sense is clear: no, because they do not abstain. Obviously, "our sages of blessed memory" concur that the wine and some other edibles of gentiles will be prohibited; at issue for us is how the Bavli sets forth these prohibitions.

The Mishnah, elucidated by the Bavli, has a great deal to say on the same topic, which occupies a considerably larger place and receives a far denser discussion, in detail and in generative principle, than the rather routine observation just now cited. When I spoke of documentary comparison, I had in mind the difference between scarcely thirty words on the one side, and thousands on the other; the difference between a single, sufficient rule, which for Aturfarnbag says what is to be said, on the one side, and an elaborate structure, with many stages and floors of distinctions, a full account of reasoning, and a rich secondary expansion in cases, on the other. I do not think we can account for the documentary difference by appeal to the theory that what to the Zoroastrian was inconsequential to the Judaic sage made a great difference; I do not think that is so. On the surface, the rule that Zoroastrians may not use Christian wine or food covers an area of everyday life that is bounded by frontiers of precisely the same dimensions as the range of the workday world covered by the Judaic rules, which are more numerous and more complex at every stage. So the difference in the documents yields not a judgment as to practical weight or formidable consequence, but another matter altogether. To state matters at the outset, the Israelite sages ask the matter of gentile food and cooking to bear a far greater burden of systemic meaning, even while the rules are not appreciably different in their effect upon the everyday life from the Zoroastrian ones. So the systemic character and message, not the practical consequence, accounts for the vastly more elaborate statement that follows.

To facilitate my presentation, I have sharply abbreviated the discussion, highlighting only what is of special interest to a picture of the way in which the tradition on gentiles' food is set forth. The entire issue is clear at the outset: idolatry, pure and simple; anything that has been used or that has been left over from what has been used or dedicated for use for an idol's service is forbidden.

Mishnah-tractate Abodah Zarah 2:3-5

A. [29B] These things belonging to gentiles are prohibited, and the prohibition affecting them extends to deriving any benefit from them at all:
B. (1) wine, (2) vinegar of gentiles which to begin with was wine, (3) Hadrianic earthenware, and (4) hides pierced at the heart.
C. Rabban Simeon B. Gamaliel says, "When the tear in the hide is round, it is prohibited. [If it is] straight, it is permitted."
D. "Meat which is being brought in to an idol is permitted.
E. "But that which comes out is prohibited,
F. "because it is like *sacrifices of the dead* (Ps. 106:28)," the words of R. Aqiba.
G. With those who are going to an idolatrous pilgrimage it is prohibited to do business.
H. With those that are coming back it is permitted.

Clearly, sages take many more words to say what Aturfarnbag has told his faithful about their gentiles. But they raise a variety of issues that pertain to food, making distinctions of no interest to the Zoroastrian counterpart: not using but at least trading in a product is considered, so there are distinctions that extend beyond eating to other kinds of transactions. But that seems to me to inhere in the matter: if the concern is uncleanness, then, if one can avoid contracting the uncleanness, there can be no objection to trading in what one cannot eat. But if the concern is one of the relationship of the object to idolatry, then the intrinsic character of the object, not only its function (serving as food, serving as an object of trade) is going to form a consideration and yield distinctions. Now let us see how the Talmud wants the faithful to understand these taboos.

Since the Talmud's first point of interest always requires showing how a rule of the Mishnah rests on a verse of Scripture, we cannot find surprising the initial exercise, presented in somewhat abbreviated form:

I.1 A. **Wine:**
B. *What is the source in Scripture for this prohibition?*
C. Said Rabbah bar Abbuha, "Said Scripture, 'Who did eat the fat of their sacrifices and drink the wine of their drink-offering' (Deut. 32:38) – just as it is forbidden to derive benefit from the sacrifice, so it is also forbidden to derive benefit from wine used for a libation."
D. *And as to the prohibition of the sacrificial meat itself, what is the source in Scripture for this prohibition?*
E. "They joined themselves also to Baal of Peor and ate the sacrifices of the dead" (Ps. 106:28) – just as it is forbidden to derive benefit from whatever belongs to the dead, so it is also forbidden to derive benefit from whatever pertains to pagan sacrifices.

The second point of interest focuses on Mishnah exegesis as well. The faithful have in the Mishnah what is not merely informative but

Episodic Comparisons: The Social Order

persuasive by reason of its formal perfection as well as the sponsoring authority. So the document cannot repeat itself or say what is banal, and that has to be shown at every pertinent turning. Here the question is raised at B.

II.1　A.　**Vinegar of gentiles which to begin with was wine:**
　　　B.　*So what's new! Merely because the wine has turned to vinegar, does the prohibition affecting it disappear?*
　　　C.　Said R. Ashi, *"The rule comes to inform us that* if our vinegar is left in the keeping of a gentile, it does not require a seal within a seal [but a single seal suffices to indicate that the gentile has not opened the jar and made a libation of the contents]. *If the operative consideration is concern that he not offer a libation of the jug's contents to idols, that is not generally done with vinegar; and if the operative consideration is that he might exchange the vinegar for his own, since there is a seal, he will not take the trouble to falsify it."*

II.2　A.　Said R. Ilaa, "We have repeated as an authoritative rule: Wine that has been boiled, which belongs to gentiles, that to begin with was raw wine [belonging to a gentile], is forbidden."
　　　B.　*So what's new! Merely because the wine has been boiled, does the prohibition affecting it disappear?*

When I composed a Talmudic counterpart to the formal convention followed by Aturfarnbag, I had in mind something like the following:

II.4　A.　Both Rabbah and R. Joseph say, "Mixed wine is not subject to the prohibition on grounds of wine that has been left uncovered, and boiled wine is not subject to the consideration if it's serving as libation wine."

Here is yet another way in which the same mode of discourse is formulated, namely, as a case; Aturfarnbag would have found it easy to recast the following by leaving out the names and formulating the issue in a simple way: "is boiled wine...?"

II.5　A.　*R. Yannai bar Ishmael was sick. R. Ishmael b. Zerud and rabbis came to call on him. They went into session and raised this question:* Is boiled wine subject to the prohibition on account of being left uncovered, or is it not subject to the prohibition on account of being left uncovered?
　　　B.　Said to them R. Ishmael b. Zerud, "This is what R. Simeon b. Laqish said in the name of a major authority, and who is that? It is R. Hiyya: 'Boiled wine is not subject to the prohibition on account of being left uncovered.'"
　　　C.　*They said to him,* "May we rely upon this formulation?"
　　　D.　*Gestured R. Yannai b. R. Ishmael,* "Rely on me and on my shoulders."

Another characteristic trait of the Talmud is constant citation of the example of the saints; here the sages' actions form as valid a source of the law as a statement of the Mishnah or of Scripture. That is why their actions are recorded as part of the tradition and offered as a model, not only for virtue, but also for right action in the smallest matter.

II.6 A. *Samuel and Ablat were in session. Boiled wine was brought for them, and Ablat desisted.*
  B. *Samuel said to him, "Lo, they have said: Boiled wine is not subject to prohibition on the count of serving as libation wine."*
II.7 A. *The servant girl of R. Hiyya found boiled wine that had been left uncovered. She came before R. Hiyya, who said to her, "Lo, they have said: Boiled wine is not subject to prohibition on the count of having been left uncovered."*
II.8 A. *The servant of R. Adda bar Ahba found diluted wine that had been left uncovered. He said to him, "Lo, they have said: Diluted wine is not subject to prohibition on the count of having been left uncovered."*

Enough of the discussion of this Mishnah statement has been given to provide an ample account of how the Talmud treats the topic of common interest. Let us proceed to the regulation of social relationships consequent upon the principle of separation from idolatry, therefore also from idolators, that motivates the law. Two further, highly particular traits of our Talmud come to the fore.

First of all, the document records not only the great deeds of sages but also arguments controverting their opinions, as at C below; then the exposition of the processes of reasoning, including the introduction of a hypothesis and its evidence, countered by refutation and a contrary hypothesis, forms a central and characteristic trait of the great tradition in Talmudic form. The second point of note, at No. 2, is that the tradition extends to other, prior authoritative compilations besides the Mishnah; the Tosefta, a compilation of statements attributed to the same authorities as the Mishnah, is cited as equally authoritative. So, too, sayings are marked with a sign that they enjoy the status of sayings that occur in the Mishnah, being situated in the process of oral formulation and oral transmission of authoritative rules by being given the mark, "Tannaite," in one of several forms, here, "our rabbis have taught on Tannaite authority," my rendition of TNW RBNN.

What has been said thus far leaves the impression that the primary consideration behind the rules on gentile food derives from idolatry. But that is not the case, There is, in fact, a separate and equally important social policy effected through the food taboo, and that is, to separate Israelites from gentiles. That is a consideration that I do not find in Aturfarnbag's writing, even though he gives ample evidence of widespread apostasy. He evidently has in hand no tradition that means to separate Zoroastrians from others except so far as outsiders are unclean. By contrast, we shall now see that the Mishnah, as read by the Talmud, is explicit in setting forth as a matter of social policy, even when idolatry is no consideration, the separation of Israelites from gentiles. A tradition deriving from a group living as a minority, even in a territory it regards as God's gift to that group alone, presents its contrast with one deriving from a group that has, for many long centuries, formed the governing majority of its country.

2:6

A. And what are things of gentiles which are prohibited, but the prohibition of which does not extend to deriving benefit from them?
B. (1) Milk drawn by a gentile without an Israelite's watching him; (2) their bread; and (3) their oil –
C. (Rabbi and his court permitted their oil) –
D. (4) stewed and pickled [vegetables] into which it is customary to put wine and vinegar; (5) minced fish; (6) brine without *kilkit*-fish floating in it; (7) *hileq*-fish; (8) drops of asafoetida; and (9) sal-conditum –
E. lo, these are prohibited, but the prohibition affecting them does not extend to deriving benefit from them.

The concluding list goes on to things prohibited not by reason of use in the cult, on the one side, and things which are entirely permitted, on the other. The basic idea is that what a gentile has cooked is prohibited. The reason is not the consideration of idolatry but rather dietary laws, for example, food which may be unclean in accord with the Levitical rules. And the role of gentiles in the dietary laws in general – which, after all, with some effort they could have observed for Israelite guests – is explained in a simple way, as we shall now see in a typically contentious presentation:

II.1 A. Their bread:
B. Said R. Kahana said R. Yohanan, "Their bread was never declared by a court to be permitted [though Judah the Patriarch's court permitted Israelites to use their oil]."
C. *Does that statement then contain the inference that there is an authority who permits it?*
D. *Indeed it does, for when R. Dimi came,* he said, "One time Rabbi [Judah the Patriarch] went out into the field, and a gentile brought before him a loaf of bread that had been baked in a large oven from a seah of flour. Said Rabbi, 'What a beautiful loaf of bread! How come sages declared it forbidden!'"
E. "How come sages declared it forbidden"! It was because of the possibility of intermarriage.
F. Rather: "'How come rabbis declared it forbidden in a field [where there is no possibility of socializing and hence of intermarriage]?' So people supposed that Rabbi had declared their bread to be permitted. But that is not the case. Rabbi did not declare their bread to be permitted."

	G.	R. Joseph, and some say, R. Samuel bar Judah, said, "That was not the story. But they have said, 'One time Rabbi [Judah the Patriarch] went to a certain place, and he saw that the disciples were having trouble getting bread. Rabbi said, "Is there no baker here?" People supposed that he meant a gentile baker, but that is not what he had said, but rather, an Israelite baker.'"
	H.	Said R. Helbo, "Even in the view of the one who has said that what he had in mind was a gentile baker, that would have been the rule only if there were no Israelite baker. But in a locale in which there is an Israelite baker, the baking of a gentile would not have been permitted."
	I.	Said R. Yohanan, "Even in the view of the one who has said that what he had in mind was a gentile baker, that would have been the rule only if it were in the field. But if it was a transaction in town, then the gentile baker's products would have been permitted, on account of the consideration of intermarriage."
II.2	A.	Aibu would bite and eat bread baked by gentiles [only at] the boundaries of the fields.
	B.	Raba – and there are those who say, R. Nahman bar Isaac – said to them, "Do not have any dealings with him, because he eats bread baked by Aramaeans."

Even though I have severely curtailed the Talmud's extensive discussion of the theme shared with the Zoroastrian document, readers have an ample picture of how differently the document makes its statement from Aturfarnbag's simple and laconic statement.

It would not be unfair to observe that the Zoroastrian priest takes for granted a simple statement suffices, while the Talmudic rabbis leave nothing to imagination or to change. But it is equally apropos to point out that while Aturfarnbag's statement is simple, so, too, is his analysis of the issue, and however run-on and even tedious sages' treatment of the same subject certainly is, they discern a range of issues and problems that make the topic a very formidable one. Aturfarnbag lays his stress elsewhere – apostasy, for instance. Not only so, but, as we have now seen several times, the Bavli's sages have their own idea of what it means to write down a great tradition, and of what that great tradition is composed.

If I had to explain why the very thick layer of theory undergirds a rather simple rule about gentile food and cooking on the Judaic, but not on the Zoroastrian, side, I should point to the ongoing Israelite obsession with marking out the boundaries and building high walls at the outer fringes of the Israelite community, and that is in particular in connection with maintaining the sanctity of the community through endogamy. When sages explicitly introduce the consideration of intermarriage, our minds go back to Ezra's initial concern with the same matter, expressed in the vivid concern in the Torah compilation that Ezra made out of the priestly, the Deuteronomic, and other ancient codes and traditions (written or otherwise). The entire story of the formation and election of Israel is intertwined with the descent, from a single couple, Abraham and Sarah, then Isaac and Rebecca, then Jacob and Leah and Rachel, of all Israel. And that is meant to bear the message of endogamy. The upshot is that for the Talmudic sages the stakes are much higher, though Aturfarnbag would have no reason to concede that the law's practical implications run any less deep for his community than for the Talmud's. The upshot is, as I said at the outset, the differences between the two documents' treatment of the same point prove systemic. Here on the Talmudic side, the writing down of the great tradition proved traditional in a substantive, not only a formal, sense.

II. Oaths Imposed on Children in Connection with the Father's Estate's Debts

We turn from relations between the group and outsiders to those within the group, between generations. Here we revert to a theme already introduced, the situation of the heirs of a wicked father, but the issues are not merely public and civil: correct procedure in the community at large; not merely moral and ethical: a private decision on what is to be done or not done with stolen goods. In the problem at hand, a father takes a loan and dies without repaying it. The wife and children deny the loan. Both traditions solve the problem in the same way, by imposing an oath on the heirs that they know nothing of the matter and deny it. The oath is owing by the heirs to the estate; it then frees them from any further obligation. Here is the Zoroastrian version:

CHILDREN TAKE AN OATH THAT THEY DID NOT KNOW OF A LOAN CLAIMED AGAINST THE PARENTS' ESTATE

LXVI

Question

1. There is a man who gives a loan to a man; that man departs from this world; he has a wife and children in this family; the widow does not return the loan taken from the man; when she departs from this world, and there are sons and daughters in the family, and the man asks the return of the loan from a son; and the son is perverse and says, "I do not know it"; the man who is this creditor says, "Swear that thy father did not take this loan from me, and I and other heirs of my father have neither to return nor give this property to thee; their returning or giving is not lawful"; the man who took the loan says, "Let us you and I so undergo the ordeal";

"I and other heirs of my father have no knowledge of this event" – what is the advice?

Reply

2. As I understand: then he shall certainly undertake the ordeal, saying, "My father and mother did not take this loan from thee, O Man! And we who are the heirs of our father and mother have not to return this loan to thee."

The Talmud introduces exactly the same issue at M. Ketubot 7:7E, below, but has the oath taken by heirs of an estate with the consequence that they have the power to collect an amount owing. Now they allege that they have proof of the loan but no proof of payment, F. The basic principle – appeal to the oath – is the same; the sole point of difference is, who takes the oath and with what consequence. That the imposition of the oath in this case is anomalous is announced at the outset of the Bavli's exposition of the larger passage of which this item forms a part, which finds scriptural evidence for the principle at hand, the oath itself:

Mishnah-tractate Ketubot 7:7

A. Just as they have said [M. Ket. 9:7], (1) A woman who impairs her marriage settlement collects only by taking an oath,

B. [and] (2) [if] a single witness testifies that it has been collected, she collects it only by taking an oath;

C. [and] (3) she collects from indentured property and from property belonging to the estate only by taking an oath;

D. [and] (4) she who collects her marriage settlement not in her husband's presence collects it only by taking an oath,

E. so (5) heirs of an estate collect [debts owing to the deceased] only through an oath:

F. "(1) We swear that Father gave us no instructions [in this matter], (2) Father said nothing to us about it, and (3) we did not find among his bonds evidence that this bond had been paid off."

G. R. Yohanan b. Beroqah says, "Even if the son was born after the death of the father, lo, this one must take an oath before he collects [what is owing to the estate]."

H. Said Rabban Simeon b. Gamaliel, "If there are witnesses that the father had stated when he was dying, 'This bond has not yet been paid off,' [the son] may collect [the debt] without taking an oath."

I.1 A. All those who are subjected to oaths which are [required] in the Torah take [said] oaths and do not pay [the claim against them]:

B. *How do we know this on the basis of Scripture?*

C. "[The oath of the Lord shall be between them both, to see whether he has not put his hand unto his neighbor's goods.] And the owner thereof shall accept it and he shall not pay" (Ex. 22:10). [The owner accepts the oath, and the bailee does not have to pay (Silverstone).]

D. So the person who would have to pay has to takes the oath [so that he does not have to pay].

Episodic Comparisons: The Social Order

XIII.1 A. ...so (5) heirs of an estate collect [debts owing to the deceased] only through an oath: "(1) We swear that Father gave us no instructions [in this matter], (2) Father said nothing to us about it, and (3) we did not find among his bonds evidence that this bond had been paid off." R. Yohanan b. Beroqah says, "Even if the son was born after the death of the father, lo, this one must take an oath before he collects [what is owing to the estate]." Said Rabban Simeon b. Gamaliel, "If there are witnesses that the father had stated when he was dying, 'This bond has not yet been paid off,' [the son] may collect [the debt] without taking an oath":

B. *From whom is the debt collected? Should we say from the borrower? The father could have gotten back his money without an oath, and should they have to take an oath? Rather, it means,* And so also orphans cannot collect payment from orphans without taking an oath.

C. *And both Rab and Samuel say,* "This rule pertains only if the lender died in the lifetime of the borrower. But if the borrower died in the lifetime of the lender, the lender is already obligated to take an oath to the children of the borrower, and someone may not then leave as an inheritance to his children the requirement to take an oath."...

XIII.4 A. *R. Nahman came to Sura and went to see R. Hisda and Rabbah b. R. Huna. They said to him,* "Will the master come and uproot this rule of Rab and Samuel [that someone may not bequeath the requirement to take an oath to his son]?"

B. *He said to them,* "Have I gone to the trouble of coming this vast distance merely to uproot this rule of Rab and Samuel [that someone may not bequeath the requirement to take an oath to his son]?"

C. "So then give us this: Don't add to it [and apply it only to the case of which they spoke]."

D. "For instance?"

E. "For instance what R. Pappa said, 'He who impairs his bond and died – his oaths may take the oath of heirs and collect on the strength of the bond.'" [The bondholder admitted having collected part, so has to take an oath to get the rest; if he dies, his oaths can swear the oath of heirs, and here we do not apply the ruling of Rab and Samuel about not bequeathing the right to take an oath and collect (Silverstone).]

XIII.5 A. *A certain man who died left a guarantor [for the loan, who, upon the man's death, became surety for the loan; the burrower died as well, so the creditor has to take an oath to collect; then the creditor died, and his heirs claim the money from the guarantor of the loan]. R. Pappa considered ruling,* "In a case of this kind the principle, don't add to it [and apply it only to the case of which they spoke] applies."

B. *Said R. Huna b. R. Joshua to R. Pappa,* "Will the guarantor of the loan not go after the orphans [to collect what is owing]?" [So the heirs of the creditor, if permitted to taken an oath and claim the loan from the guarantor, will ultimately be depriving the debtor's heirs because of the oath, and to such a case the ruling of Rab and Samuel applies.]

XIII.6 A. *A certain man died and left as his heir only a brother.* [The borrower had died, leaving children; the lender's brother claims the debt from the borrower's children.] *Rammi bar Hamma considered ruling,* "In a case of

		this kind, too, the principle, don't add to it [and apply it only to the case of which they spoke] applies."
	B.	Said to him Raba, "What difference does it make to me whether the claim is, 'My father did not leave me orders,' or, 'My brother did not leave me orders.'" [There is none, and the lender cannot bequeath such an oath to his sons, so also to his brother.]
XIII.7	A.	Said R. Hama, "Now that the decided law has not been stated either in accord with Rab and Samuel or in accord with R. Eleazar, a judge who rules in accord with Rab and Samuel has done a valid deed, and who rules in accord with R. Eleazar has done a valid deed."

Enough of the Bavli's treatment of this theme has been given for one point to emerge. The very basis of the rule is challenged at XIII.1, with the result that severe limitations are imposed upon the conception that an oath is required, or imposed, at all. How can the requirement to take an oath be bequeathed to one's children? So, once more, a simple principle of law, that debts can be exacted, or avoided, through the intervention of an oath, yields complexities, such that the rule is transformed beyond recognition. That is the point of No. 4. No. 5 shows us how, nonetheless, the revision leaves in place the social benefit intended by the basic rule: to provide for the guarantee of capital that has been put forth as a loan. Here we contrast a simple rule covering a simple case with an interest in formulating principles that extend over many cases, take account of a variety of conflicting interests – the children's, the estate's, the borrower's, the lender's, the stability and security of financial transactions, the whole guaranteed in the end by supernatural intervention to penalize him who takes a false oath.

III. Can One Transfer Ownership of What Has Not Yet Come into Existence?

Now we come to an exceptionally striking confluence: not only is the detail, but the principle that generates the problem, the same on both sides. At issue in religious systems that assign to the faithful the power of effective speech is the relationship between words and things, between what one says and the status, as to permissibility of otherwise, of objects out there. Since both Zoroastrian and Judaic traditions recognize the validity of vows and accord to believers the power through vows to transform the status of things, both the priests and the sages had to speculate on theoretical questions concerning vows with intensely concrete consequences for those who took them. And here, as a matter of fact, the intersection is nearly verbatim.

In the present instance, we deal with two distinct questions that meet in a problem of high abstraction: Can one take a vow (Zoroastrianism) or by a statement transfer title of ownership (Judaism) to something not

Episodic Comparisons: The Social Order 117

now in existence? The first question concerns the effect of a vow upon what is intangible at this time but will become tangible, for example, an object one will make, a meal one will cook. The second, a deeper, perennial philosophical issue, concerns the reality of the potential. Framed in neutral terms, can I dispose of an oak, when only the acorn is in hand? Is what is potential classified, because of what will come about inevitably and inexorably, as what is actual? Or do we distinguish the here and the now from what might come about? Left as an abstract question, the issue of the potential and the actual could not have come up in either the Talmud or the Rivayat, neither of which knows how to frame philosophical questions in a philosophical way. But stated in concrete terms, both writings prove highly qualified to analyze philosophical problems.

The Rivayat states matters in language that with only slight revision could have appeared in the Mishnah. If one takes a vow to dedicate for someone else whatever actions of merit that he may carry out in the future, is this a valid act of dedication? Aturfarnbag's answer is virtually identical to language that we can find in the Talmud, if we translated the question into the status of "property that has not come to his possession," which is difficult to distinguish from "something that has not yet come into the world." Not only so, but the Talmud knows the problem of whether one can transfer title to something that has not yet come into the world (an unborn baby) or of something that has not yet come into one's possession (a crop in the sowing stage).

LXXIV

Question
1. Whoever makes a solemn vow with this sort of colloquy: "I have dedicated to such and such person all acts and good deeds which I may perform from this day onward," what is your opinion of this case: this as to whether they will have been dedicated by him or not?

Reply
2. If he declares as "dedicated" that property which has not come to his possession, it will not have been dedicated; and if he speaks of that good deed which has not become his, he shall not have dedicated in the same manner; if he speaks of that property which has not come to his possession, or of that good deed and property which have not together come to his possession, if a fear, or a difficulty, or a trouble, or depressing thought, or a defect has not come, such as that which is said in detail in the ordeal section of the Husparam, if he speaks of one who is worthy; then when that property

came to his possession, or that good deed came to achievement, then he shall have been dedicated, in the same manner, to him to whom they are dedicated, if even now that worthiness has not elapsed; it can be dedicated for that one fear of fears, when one dedicates anything to worthy persons for fear of the wicked existence; if he says, "I will dedicate a good deed, not for any earthly gain, but for the friendship of the soul of a person who is worthy, it will be his to whom he said, "I will dedicate," when he has performed it; and it will not be the less, of him who performed it; it will come to him in the same manner as if he had performed it for the sake of his own soul; since he declared that colloquy, "I will dedicate," for the love of righteousness, he advances this in the path of a soul, even this munificence which he advances with a good deed will be such as his who performs a worship, without earthly reward and gain, for the souls of persons; then, the recitation by him of what is in the oath ordeal has gone by, which brings out the least preparation of this kind, then he shall recite the words of Rasnu, those which the Avesta has demonstrated, those which he can verily consider, such as one says: (Av.) "Here is such utility," so is this regulation for defense, (Av.) or, "Here is its information unto me," so I have information of it by proof, (Av.) or, "I do not know of it," or I have not that by knowledge, if by non-recitation of it, I am a sinner who misuses a trust; then, I do not know of any formula to explain that he has to take effectively in reckoning those words which it is not according to the law for him to speak, and to decide the matter.

3. It is instituted that if there has been such a man, a man who, on account of fear, speaks in the presence of judges: "This man had smitten me," the judge understands that he spoke on account of fear, he shall release him on the highway.

4. They shall leave the decision of this, as to for what reason that man spoke in dedicating that good deed, to the Yazats who ordain; they can decide; otherwise, since the judges of this world cannot effectively return to the real holder the property which is invisible, which is known to have been in the keeping of one who carried it away with force, therefore, as an invisible good deed becomes requisite by declaration, he has to atone for the false oath; the punishment of the atonement is evident as determined; they shall not mitigate

the penalty of that which is indubitable and that which is doubtful, and they shall adjudicate the material person and property; they shall leave the judgment of the soul and the good deed to Him who knows; it is even due to His power that the righteous is inculpated by that over which he has no power.

Aturfarnbag's answer leaves nothing in ambiguity: one has not got control of what is not now in the world or subject to one's possession. When he rapidly qualifies matters, it is to make an obvious point, one that is irrelevant to the question. Once the deed has been done, it does indeed go to the credit of the person for whom he has dedicated it. What makes the difference is the motive. If one does the act for the sake of his own soul, it serves for the other. The exposition leads on at Nos. 3, 4 to related matters; the main point throughout is that we take account not only of the dedication of what does not exist but also the intentionality of the person who makes that statement. Then, if the intentionality is valid, the statement before the fact takes effect; if the intentionality is invalid – coercion having led to the pledge, for instance – then the act later on is not classified by the initial language.

To state matters simply, the Zoroastrian priest's statement takes account of three considerations, not two: [1] the power of a person to make such an affective statement; [2] the distinction between what is potential and what is actual; [3] the character of the intentionality that has brought about making the statement. The person with the right attitude and intention indeed can make such a statement stick.

Now to the Talmud's discussion of the same matter. It is stated in the very same context as the Zoroastrian, namely, vow taking. The issue is not spelled out in the Mishnah but is invoked as soon as we propose to interpret the Mishnah, at I.1.B: May a person sanctify something that is not yet in existence? The act of sanctification is a statement that a person makes concerning an object that he owns that it is donated to the Temple, for example, for sale with the proceeds to go to the upkeep of the altar and the building. Can he make such a statement concerning what is not now in existence? That is an exact parallel, controlling for the differences in systemic detail, to the problem that interests Aturfarnbag.

M. Nedarim 11:4
A. [If she said,] "Qonam if I work for Father," or, "For your father," or, "for your brother," he cannot annul that vow.
B. [If she said, "Qonam if I work for you," he need not annul [that vow, which is null to begin with].
C. R. Aqiba says, "Let him annul it."

120   *The Pahlavi Rivayat of Aturfarnbag and the Talmud*

> D. "lest she place a burden upon him more than is appropriate for him."
> E. R. Yohanan b. Nuri says, "Let him annul it, lest he divorce her, and she be prohibited from returning to him."

I.1 A. Said Samuel, "The decided law is in accord with the position of R. Yohanan b. Nuri."
B. *Is that to imply that Samuel takes the view:* A person may sanctify something that is not yet in existence? *And by way of objection:* **He who sanctifies to the Temple the fruits of his wife's labor [her wages], [85B] lo, this woman [continues to] work and eat [maintain herself]. And as to the excess – R. Meir says, "It is consecrated." R. Yohanan Hassandlar says, "It is unconsecrated" [M. Ket. 5:4].** And said Samuel, "The decided law accords with the position of R. Yohanan Hassandlar," *which proves that [in his view here]* a person may not sanctify something that is not yet in existence. *And, moreover, should you say that, when he said,* "The decided law accords with the position of R. Yohanan Hassandlar," *it was only with reference to the excess [but not other wages that she would receive in the future],* then he should have said, "The decided law in respect to the excess accords with the position of R. Yohanan Hassandlar," *or, otherwise,* "The decided law accords with the position of the initial, anonymous authority," *or, otherwise,* "The decided law accords with R. Aqiba."

The issue that interests us enters through a side door, the implication of Samuel's statement being that he takes the position that is specified, even though, in another setting, it is clear that he takes the opposite view. So we harmonize the two positions assigned to Samuel, rather than analyze the issue before us. What this tells us about how the Judaic sages thought it important to set forth the great tradition is clear: part of the power of the tradition lies in its formal perfection; not only does the Mishnah not repeat itself or tell us obvious things, but the authorities of the Mishnah and those in charge of its exegesis are perfectly consistent in all their positions.

The process of harmonization, however, permits us to state why a vow may indeed affect what has not yet come into existence, even though, in general, we do not treat as substantive what does not yet exist. It is because in general one has the power to affect by a vow a variety of future actions and events. Just as someone can take a vow not to derive benefit from what belongs to his neighbor – which is one of the key points that makes vowing attractive – so one can take a vow concerning other matters that may or may not come about in the future. But that distinction does not help; it depends upon a flawed analogy.

> C. *Rather, said R. Joseph,* "The case *of qonam vows is exceptional,* since someone thereby prohibits himself from enjoying his neighbor's

Episodic Comparisons: The Social Order   121

produce, so he can also prohibit himself from deriving benefit from what is not then in existence."

D. *Said to him Abbayye, "Well, there is no problem understanding that a person may prohibit his own deriving benefit from the produce of another party, for lo, a person my prohibit another party from deriving benefit from his own produce. But can he also forbid another party's deriving benefit from what does not then exist, since in any event he cannot prohibit another party from deriving benefit from that other party's own produce?"* [Freedman, *Nedarim*, ad loc.: The analogy is thus defective, since in both cases cited by Joseph, the one who takes the vow controls one element of the vow, namely, the person himself; but as to a woman who prohibits her earnings to her husband, neither her husband nor her future earnings are subject to her control at the moment at which she takes the vow.]

We have now completed our analysis of the problem that has led to the introduction of the issue of interest to us; we shall now solve the problem of consistency in another way altogether. But the same point recurs: if one retains power over what is to be in the future, his vow is valid; if not, it is invalid. So we sidestep the issue of potentiality and actuality altogether by resolving matters in favor of what is actual.

E. Rather, said R. Huna b. R. Joshua, "It is a case in which she says, 'Let the work of my hands be sanctified in respect to what they will produce.' In this case, the vow is valid even after she is divorced, *since her hands are already in being."*

F. *But if she made such a statement, are the hands consecrated? Surely the hands are subject to the husband's lien!*

G. It is a case in which she said, "When he divorces me...."

H. *But now, in any event, she has not been divorced, so how do you know that such a statement, if she made it, would prove effective anyhow?*

I. **[86A]** *Said R. Ilaa, "[So why not?]* If someone said to his fellow, 'Lo, this field that I am selling to you, when I buy it back from you, will be consecrated,' *is it not consecrated [from that later point]?"*

J. *Objected R. Jeremiah, "But are the cases really comparable? In that case, the man has the power to consecrate the field, but in this case, the woman has not got the power to secure her own divorce! So the cases are hardly parallel. Rather, the point of comparability is to a case in which* one says to his fellow, 'This field that I have sold to you, when I shall buy it back from you, will be consecrated,' *in which case the field is certainly not consecrated."*

K. *Objected R. Pappa, "But are the cases comparable? There [in the case of the field that has been sold],* both the field and the produce belong to the buyer, but here, the wife's person remains in her own domain. *Rather, the point of comparability is to a case in which* one says to his fellow, 'This field that I have mortgaged to you, when I shall redeem it from you, will be sanctified,' *in which case the field is certainly consecrated."*

L. *Objected R. Shisha b. R. Idi, "But are the cases properly compared? In that case, the man has the power to redeem the field, but in this case, does* the woman have the power to arrange her own divorce? Rather, the point of comparability is to a case in which one who says to his fellow, 'This field that I have mortgaged to you for ten years, when I shall redeem it from you, will be consecrated,' in which case it is consecrated."

M. Objected R. Ashi, "But are the cases properly compared? In that case, the man has the power to redeem the field after ten years, but in this case, the woman will never have the power to arrange her own divorce."

N. [86B] Rather, said R. Ashi, "Oaths that use the language qonam are exceptional, for they effect the sanctification of the body itself. And it is in accord with Raba, for said Raba, 'Sanctification of cattle [mortgaged for a liability] or of leaven and the freeing of a slave remove these things from subjection to the mortgage that may have previously pertained to them.'" [Slotki, Ketubot 59A: Similarly here, the consecration cancels the husband's claim on the body or work of his wife; hence the validity of her consecration.]

O. But then why say, lest he divorce her, and she be prohibited from returning to him?

P. Repeat the passage as, moreover, lest he divorce her, and she be prohibited from returning to him."

The problem that interests us remains tangential to the Talmudic analysis. Still, it is clear, both the priest and the sage have introduced the same problem, taking account of roughly parallel considerations in producing the same answer: all depends on the attitude of the one who vows, when that person has power over that concerning which he takes the vow.

IV. Some Preliminary Generalizations

Where the two compilations deal with the same thing and even make the same general point about public policy – the provision of a share of the father's estate for the daughter, the inviolability of a prenuptial agreement with the wife, the return of stolen goods, the status of a vow concerning something not then in existence – they differ in a predictable way. The Rivayat is better compared to the Mishnah than the Talmud, for it now appears to us to constitute a compilation of rules that – to be sure – with different conventions of organization and rhetoric in play, could have found a comfortable spot for themselves in the Mishnah. The Mishnah organizes its materials thematically, within classifications of shared taxonomic traits; the Rivayat prefers a different mode of organization than the topical one (it is not my task to explain that principle).

And yet, if we were comparing the Rivayat to the other Talmud, the one of the Land of Israel, we should find a perfectly comfortable comparison between Aturfarnbag's program and that of the authors of the earlier Talmud: spell out needed, ad hoc information. For that is mostly what the writers of the prior Talmud did do. In the final chapter,

Episodic Comparisons: The Social Order 123

we shall see that the sages who produced the other, prior Talmud, the one of the Land of Israel, would have found themselves entirely at home with Aturfarnbag's definition of what is to be done, and his contemporary Judaic sages in what was Babylonia but would become Iraq likewise concurred that providing information – now in the form of questions and answers – defined the work of sagacity: justice specific to the case, general to the society.

How then does the Bavli differ even when going over the same concrete episode in the life of home and family? It is the exposure of a layer of analytical thought, the exegesis of rules, the imposition of a hermeneutical program that reshapes the Mishnah and makes something denser of it, that differentiates the Talmud from the Rivayat of Aturfarnbag. But, after all, that is the point: The Talmud, not the Mishnah, forms the statement of the great tradition. So at the very point at which the Talmud differs from the Mishnah, it also, as a matter of fact, differs from the Rivayat.

Where the rules run parallel, the presentation does not, and the difference in the presentation proves not merely stylistic – stylistic differences have struck me as trivial and readily ironed over – but in the deepest, most penetrating and substantive sense, hermeneutical. The Judaic sages, in a word, framed their statement of the great tradition so as to expose the hermeneutical program they wished to set forth. Only when the two documents present us with authentic parallels of viewpoint may we make that statement without further qualification. Saying the same thing, the Judaic sages set forth a message quite different from that of the Pahlavi tradition. And, as we now see with considerable clarity, that message bears a sense and a meaning not to be found on the surface of things. It is now our task to take up another Rivayat and to find out whether the differences now identified prove fixed or particular to Aturfarnbag's responsa.

Part Two

THE PAHLAVI RIVAYAT ACCOMPANYING THE DADESTAN I DENIG AND THE TALMUD

7

The Pahlavi Rivayat Accompanying the Dadestan i Denig Compared to the Bavli

Comparison requires attention to not only how a tradition is written down and what is said in it, but also the identification of the authority who speaks in the written-down version. "Our sages of blessed memory" who wrote the Talmud would have found nothing surprising in Aturfarnbag's repertoire of questions and answers, and they would have taken for granted the character of his authority, which was no different from theirs: learning and the power of reasoning, the whole deriving its authority from revealed tradition. Aturfarnbag received questions because he knew what he was talking about, provided answers because he mastered the rules of right reasoning, and had mastered the tradition. Every line of his rivayat places him into that same category of authority that sages occupied, the master of tradition and right reason. That is why we could analyze his conclusions and (in some measure) the reasoning behind them, or observe the anomaly (from the Bavli's perspective) of a statement of facts and conclusions without the anticipated, intervening layer of reasoning.

But what would our sages have made of a tradition – also associated with the household of the same priestly family that gave us so much else – formulated in the name of one who speaks as if with authority of tradition, not solely citing "as it was written" or "as it was said" or implicitly drawing upon tradition, but who quoted the exact words of Ohrmazd spoken to Zoroaster himself and revealed in no prior writing! That claim of authorship and authority – verbatim revelation of God to the prophet, now reported for the first time – finds no counterpart in the Bavli or any other rabbinic document. But that is what we find throughout this rivayat. Here is a version of the great tradition that contrasts stunningly with the Bavli's mode of expression:

The Omniscience of Ohrmazd

This chapter: Zoroaster asked Ohrmazd: "Are you wise and omniscient?"

And Ohrmazd said: "I am wise and omniscient."

And Zoroaster said: "Of what nature is your wisdom?"

Ohrmazd said: "My wisdom is such that if they take all the milk of every (living) thing into one cup, then I know how to tell one by one separately from whose breast (the milk comes); and if they let all the water which is in the world (flow) into one place, I know how to tell one by one separate(ly) from which spring (the water comes); and if they compress (together) finely all the plants which are in all the world, I know how to put them back one by one into their own place."[1]

Yet another colloquy will provide more of the flavor of these colloquies, since what we have is much more than set-piece speeches, which can readily be translated into theological propositions, for instance, Ohrmazd is wise and omniscient; his wisdom is beyond measure; one may as well sing a hymn as form a "conversation" out of the foregoing; and the Bavli could have made the same statement without straining its authors' ability to formulate appropriately a theological conception, for example, "the Holy One, blessed be He, is wise and omniscient, as it is said...." When, however, we find an authentic conversation, not merely a set-piece speech, in which Zoroaster participates as a thoughtful, feeling personality, and God responds in the same way, we move beyond the range of the Bavli's authors' imagination of what writing can convey.

Here Zoroaster weeps, and Ohrmazd comforts him and explains his fate in a reassuring manner, the whole bespeaking a powerful pen, able to capture and convey deep emotions: "You created the wind, you created the water, you created the clay (of the earth), you created the fire, you created everything, behold, seek for me a means whereby I may be saved from death":

Zoroaster Asks Immortality of Ohrmazd

This also (is) revealed, Zoroaster said to Ohrmazd: "When you go away (to Heaven)" and I also go away, when shall I return to the bodily state?

Ohrmazd said: "In the assembly of Isadwaster."

---

[1] All translations are by A.V. Williams, *The Pahlavi Rivayat Accompanying the Dadestan i Denig* (Copenhagen, 1990: The Royal Danish Academy of Sciences and Letters through Munksgaard).

This also (is) revealed, the souls of the righteous will thus arrive together with one another, friend and brother and father and son and kinsman and wife and husband. If they are wicked, then they will not arrive in the end.

When Zoroaster came before Ohrmazd he wept and said: "O Ohrmazd, make me immortal!"

Ohrmazd said: "It cannot be done, for (if so) the Tur Bradres the karb whom Ahriman created for the purpose of killing you, he (also) will become immortal, and there will be no resurrection of the dead or Future Body, in which the poor have hope."

Zoroaster, weeping, replied: "You created the wind, you created the water, you created the clay (of the earth), you created the fire, you created everything, behold, seek for me a means whereby I may be saved from death."

And then Ohrmazd bestowed omniscient wisdom upon Zoroaster.

Zoroaster saw everything which was and is and shall be of this place of the material world, and that also of the spiritual world and that also of every person.

And he saw the place of him who was immortal, and who had no children, and (such persons) appeared to him sad and sorrowful.

And he saw the place of him who was mortal, and who had children, and he appeared full of peace and joy.

And then he said to Ohrmazd: "Transience, then, seems better to me than everlasting life and childlessness."

Ohrmazd said: "Good, and you have listened well and seen, O Zoroaster, that if you have pure-hearted children, then it seems better to me than if you are eternal and (yet) you have no child. Take a wife, so that you will have children, for whoever, by sinfulness, has no wife will not reach Heaven."

Men should teach and learn that which is (revealed) in the Avesta and the Zan and that (also) which they see with their eyes and hear with their ears; for from their teaching (there will be) knowledge and from their learning there will be confidence [?] and gentleness, and from knowledge and gentleness there will be worthiness of (going) to Paradise and Garodman and of beholding Ohrmazd and of the love of the amahraspands.

I state very simply the Bavli contains great writing, but knows no "Zoroaster" – that is, Moses our lord.

The radical and surprising character of the confrontation of Zoroaster and Ohrmazd, the exchange as if between equals, the conception that Zoroaster interrogates Ohrmazd and is given a reasoned answer – these tell us that a ninth-century author has placed himself into a position that no counterpart in seventh-century Babylonian Israel could have imagined for himself. And yet, they, too, clearly maintained, their writing down of the great tradition formed a component of the one whole Torah revealed by God to Moses at Sinai, so what they had to communicate enjoyed the standing of truth from God. But it was a tradition engraven in a different medium, a truth preserved in another kind of speech. The reason, I think, is that for "our sages of blessed memory," a different mode of encounter between God and man, not the encounter of revelation that takes the form of conversation and resorts to articulated speech, was in mind. Before we pursue the contrast, let us improve our acquaintance with the Pahlavi Rivayat Accompanying the Dadestan i Denig.

This document comes to us in the first-class edition and translation and commentary of A.V. Williams,[2] whose description and translation are followed throughout. All that follows is made possible by his interest in not only philology but also the religious system of the writing. Given the differences of which we already are aware, we must ask, on what basis to begin with do we set such a writing alongside the Bavli? What draws our interest to this text is that like the Bavli, it is anonymous; like the Bavli, it has, in Williams's words, "no title, author's name, or date of its own, and we identify it only with the textual tradition in which it has been preserved."[3] But the same may be said of other documents, to which a comparison with the Bavli would hardly demand attention. More to the point, the question answers itself when we point to the provenience of the writing: here is another way of writing down a great tradition. The document indubitably forms part of that larger trove of writings produced at one time by one family as a sustained and deliberate effort to preserve the ancient truth for time to come. For the Pahlavi Rivayat Accompanying the Dadestan i Denig is found among the manuscripts associated with the Dadestan i Denig of Manushchihr, high priest of Pars and Kirman, and forms part of that writing down of the great tradition that took place in the ninth century under his sponsorship.[4] So the document falls well within the framework of our interests.

Although we began with what strikingly differs from the Bavli's fundamental trait, we should not ignore a large component of writing

---

[2]A.V. Williams, *The Pahlavi Rivayat Accompanying the Dadestan i Denig* (Copenhagen, 1990: The Royal Danish Academy of Sciences and Letters through Munksgaard). I. *Transliteration, Transcription, and Glossary*. II. *Translation, Commentary, and Pahlavi Text*. Dr. Williams was kind enough to give me his translation on computer disc, to make it easier to cite his work, and that is only one mark of his superlative collegiality, for which I am grateful. References are to his volume and page.
[3]Williams, 1:7.
[4]Williams, 1:8: "[It] is placed in the manuscripts with works by authors from one well-known family of learned priests and it is likely that a member of the family might have compiled this Rivayat."

that the Bavli's authors would have found analogous to their own. That is the part of this rivayat made up of questions and answers, whether or legal or theological character. In general, most of the chapters "are in some ways answers either to a question, explicit or implied, or to a predicament." It is "neither speculative, philosophical, nor in any narrow sense theological; it is pedagogical, for here, above all, the doctrines of purity, righteousness, and just, meritorious action are extolled to the reader by every available means. Clearly, the voice is that of a priest."[5] Then the colloquy between Zoroaster and God is the priest's recording of the received tradition, as much as the Mishnah represents Judah the Patriarch's allegation of having preserved in fixed and readily memorized form – thus published in an odd way – the received tradition.

Closer to the trait of the Bavli still, this rivayat contains numerous citations of prior, authoritative writings. So the work is traditional in another sense parallel to the Bavli: received authoritative writings are the sources for much that is said, so Williams: "Much of the material appears to come directly from a knowledge of the Pahlavi versions of the Avesta with the Zand, either oral or written." Williams comments:

> [The text] was addressed to Zoroastrians living in Muslim Iran, at a time of great insecurity for those who adhered to the older religion. The text was intended not only to impart information, whether practical, ritual, or theological, to the community; rather it intends to preach solidarity and faithfulness in the community.[6]

In this context, Williams cites de Menasce's comment:

> The documents of this type do not generally insist on what, in a faith, is the most current and the most actual. Interest is turned more on what is in danger of being forgotten and on what is the object of controversy. Thus one will not find a balanced and complete account.

Whether or not the same may be said of specific passages of the Bavli, the highly contentious and argumentative character of the Bavli's unique writing (as distinct from kinds of writing it shares with other documents, for example, the Mishnah, not only cited but imitated in authoritative formulations of law) points to the same intentionality.

Further, just as the Mishnah and the Bavli constitute systemic statements, making some few points in a great many ways, so the same characterizes this rivayat. Williams discovered in his analysis of the document a systematic effort to make a systematic statement. For, he

---

[5]Williams, 1:9.
[6]Williams, 1:10.

holds, the work rests on a solid theological foundation, specifically, stemming from, in Williams language,

> the duality of worldly existence in the material state of the world – the state of opposition and strife of the hostile and heterogeneous forces of Ahriman against the creations of Ohrmazd. This duality is perceived in all aspects of life, personal, public, and spiritual, and [the rivayat] deals with a range of oppositions. Each chapter...has one or more of these dualities as its explicit theme. In most cases the text attempts to resolve the duality, either explicitly, in doctrinal or ritual presections from orthodox tradition, or more allusively, in legendary narrative, cosmological symbolism, or religious mythology.

Thus, while the document covers a great many subjects, and while the arrangement of the document yields no obvious plan governed by topics, in fact, Williams shows, the Pahlavi Rivayat Accompanying the Dadestan i Denig manages in many ways to make a single encompassing point.

Williams points to the dualities of trade – wholesome but contrasted with greed, resolved by giving of charity; menstrual relations are wholesome, menstruation is heavily polluting, the problem resolved by a code of controls regulating such relations. Here is the language:

Trading and Acquisition of Wealth

> This (question): how should trading take place so that there will be no sin in it? When (a trader) buys for four drachms a single piece of clothing, worth four drachms, and he takes it to another town, and (in) the place where he takes it it is worth ten drachms, he sells it for ten drachms, and takes out of it wages and daily sustenance for himself and his horse, and he gives away what remains (of it) as a righteous gift, it is a (work of) great merit.

Marriage

> When a man marries, and he has made a contract of marriage with the young woman's guardian, (if he acts) generously, there is the merit of righteousness. If her menstrual cycle is completed (without menstruation), then every time the merit (is) 300. There was an authority who said: "once (only) the merit (is) 300." If she becomes pregnant, the merit (is) 300.

All things then are held to moderation. One may make a profit, but the profit is fixed. One may enjoy sexual relations, in moderation. Too much becomes a vice; and too little is no virtue either. Here, Williams finds, writ small is the large principle of dualism. From our perspective, the consequence is, both documents not only collect and present information but make statements, and the statements, in each case, emerge in masses of details; if we know how to read the details, we can readily construct the main point throughout, and that is the intent of the writer. So behind the obvious differences, we find one kind of document, the systemic, highly systematic kind.

Among the points of emphasis in the rivayat before us, can we find any that "our sages of blessed memory" would have identified as their own? We indeed locate at least two fundamental principles that the Talmud would have known as its own, righteousness joined with practical observance. The Talmud would also have concurred that there is retribution or reward for one's actions, wisdom is the highest virtue of humanity, and the resurrection of the dead is a principle of the Mishnah and a given for the Talmud as well. So all of the five main "religious resolutions" identified by Williams in general work well with the points of interest and conviction of the Bavli. These, in Williams's words, are "righteousness, practical observance, retribution and reward, wisdom, eschatological hope."[7] All of these themes are marshaled in such a way as to strengthen the faithful against the "hardship which was imposed upon the Zoroastrian community by Islam."

But of course the writings take leave of one another when specific theological facts intervene. For "our sages of blessed memory" had to work out their ideas about righteousness rewarded and sin punished within the tensions generated by the conception of an All-Powerful God of monotheism, while the Pahlavi Rivayat before us could readily negotiate conflict by appeal to a thoroughgoing, theological, and cosmological dualism. This was absorbed into the theological structure that saw the world under attack from other forms of evil. The religious imperative of the document derives from righteousness and eschatological hope: "Both types of resolution put the evils of the day into a greater perspective, for example, that of a cosmic struggle, and at the same time urge the strengthening of a religious commitment. The practical, social result of righteousness in all its forms (ritual, moral, spiritual) is to protect the community from hostile, indeed all, outside influence."[8]

While the dualism before us came from a much earlier time, it certainly corresponded in theology to the social experience of a hostile world that the faithful encountered. For, as with Aturfarnbag's rivayat, this one refers time and again to the ever-present apostasy that tore the community down and led to fears of its survival. For one instance, if one sells a slave to a nonbeliever (that is, a Muslim), then all the sins the slave commits are assigned to the blame of the one that sold him:

> If they have made him an infidel, thereafter all the sins which he has committed on account of evil religion, including that of his own self

---
[7]Williams, 1:12.
[8]Williams, 1:15.

being taken into evil religion, then (the sins) become such as if he who sold him and he who bought him had committed them with their own hands.

In this passage, as in the many we noted in Aturfarnbag's writing, with the destruction of marriages and families through conversion to Islam, the theologians appealed to the world the faithful knew in winning credence for their theological system and structure. A believer who lost his children to the new faith knew full well that Gods contended, a good and an evil one, and all that can be done to strengthen the power of light is demanded. The counterpart conviction of the Bavli's framers, corresponding in the realm of theory to the facts of everyday life, remains to be identified.

Rather, let us turn to the description of the document itself: how it makes its statement. For the analysis of selected passages, let us turn first to a well-balanced colloquy, question-and-answer style:

Bodily Effects of Sins and Good Deeds

And this also he asked of Ohrmazd: "If a man commits a sin (through) all (his) bodily members, then to which of his members does the evil first come?"

Ohrmazd said: "Because in the human body the organ of the tongue (is) the most valuable, then it first comes to the tongue."

And this also he asked: "Then where does it come?"

And Ohrmazd said to him: "Then it comes to the heart, and then it comes to his stomach. And spoilt and ugly children are born of him, because he sins and does not perform good deeds."

If people do good deeds, to which of their members does the goodness first come?

Ohrmazd said: "It comes first to the tongue, because the tongue has been created better than all the (other) organs, and then it comes to his heart, and then it comes to his stomach, and then it comes to his whole body. And well instructed, dutiful, law abiding and sociable children will be born of him, because he does good deeds and does not sin."[9]

We again note that "he" is Zoroaster, and Ohrmazd then instructs him through a dialogue.[10] So what we have is a colloquy between God and the prophet. This form once more yields a symmetry that allows the text to convey "the dualism of the teaching. By juxtaposing the results of good and wicked actions, the redactor presents the principle of divine retribution not as Ohrmazd's reward and punishment but rather as truths of universal law." Williams once more reminds us that the medium of the document, in this case, its forms, conveys its message.

---

[9]Williams, 2:7.
[10]William, 2:122; Chapter Three, n. 1.

The enumeration form – working through elements of a fixed list, which may or may not be enumerated but always are systematically ordered – characterizes the Mishnah and the Talmud, but most of the other documents of the canon of the Dual Torah as well. The reason is that the authors of compositions, as much as the compilers of documents, worked through that highly conventional form. In the case before us, the text is carefully expounded, point by point: the punishment of sin begins with the mouth, then the heart, the stomach, and so on; reward likewise begins with the mouth, proceeds to the heart, and so on, all in careful balance. The same pattern occurs in the following, at Chapter Six:

On Covenant Breaking

Zoroaster asked Ohrmazd: "How many kinds of covenant breaking are there?"

Ohrmazd said: "Six kinds."

This also (is) revealed: "Whoever (is) a covenant breaker with someone, (the retribution for) that (is) very swift: it will come upon him then within nine years."

This also (is) revealed: "If a man commits (this) sin and evil (he is) a covenant breaker and it comes upon the children who are born to him after the committing of the sin and evil."

As with the Mishnah, the mnemonic uses of the enumeration are obvious.

The purpose of the well-crafted formulary speech is to convey a moral and a theological message. The former brings us closer to the Mishnah and the Bavli. The focus of the work on morality is set forth in Chapter Ten, as follows:

On Truthfulness and Charity

This chapter: Zoroaster asked Ohrmazd: "Which (is) the one virtue that is best for mankind?"

Ohrmazd said: "Truthful speech (is) best, because in truthful speech (there is) good in the world and good life and salvation in Paradise; and as regards your descendants and progeny, by doing good deeds it will be better for their families, and your soul will indeed be blessed." For him who is condemned as regards (material) wealth for the sake of truth, it is better for him than for one who is condemned as regards the soul for falsehood, because it is possible to amass wealth again, but when (people have) died, (their) souls pass on. Then there is no remedy for it.

For (it is) revealed that no friend (will be) a friend to him, no brother (will be) a brother to him, no father (will help) him as a son; and even if their good deeds are more than that by which they will be righteous, when they have gone from the material world, they cannot give (that merit) one to another.

This chapter: charity is a merit so great and valuable and renowned that the coming of the yazads and good men and the goodness of Ohrmazd and the amahraspands are greater in the material world (coming) from the houses of the charitable. If charity is performed righteously to good and worthy men, (it is) goodness for the worthy; herbads and disciples will resort to the houses of the charitable who are righteous.

(In) every good action of theirs which they perform in the houses of the charitable, it will be as though the charitable person who is righteously charitable shall have performed it with his own hands.

As regards the charitable who (are) sinful in their charity, who (give to) very bad and undutiful men, thieves and robbers come to (their) houses. From that house (comes) affliction for Ohrmazd and the other yazads; the evil which those wicked ones think and speak and do in that house will be just as though the charitable man who (is) sinful shall have performed it with his own hands.

This also (is) revealed in the religion, that Ohrmazd said to Zoroaster: "He who performs charity knowingly and discriminately (is) like me, I who am Ohrmazd. And he who performs charity ignorantly and without understanding and indiscriminately (is like) Ahriman."

This also (is) revealed in the religion, that when two men are disputing and one says: "Since I apply discrimination in giving, unless I know well his goodness and character and skill, until (then) I do not give him anything"; when he speaks so with those words, he will go to Hell.

(The other) one says: "I do not recognize righteous or wicked, but he who undertakes from me (to perform) good deeds so that he praises righteousness and afflicts the demons and I do not know of any sinfulness of his, then in (a case of) doubtfulness, I consider him a good man, and I give him food and clothing"; when he speaks so with those words he will reach Paradise.

This also (is) revealed in the Avesta that he who gives something to a righteous man will reach Paradise. And he who gives something to a sinner, and does not know that he is sinful, when he comes to know that he is sinful, then he must take it [i.e., the gift] back; if he has to produce a witness [i.e., to prove his claim] that: "I did not give this thing to you," and he produces (a witness), whatever harm he [i.e., the sinful man] is able to do, (even if) he does this, let him not take possession of the property.

This also (is) revealed in the religion, that charity is so miraculous that when one gives property to a good man, then immediately the sound of his words reaches Ohrmazd the Lord, and they give him [i.e., the man who is charitable] reward and recompense.

The colloquy between Zoroaster and Ohrmazd proves a rather conventional form for the transmission of a moral teaching; a named sage would have served as well (if, in context, without the same power of persuasion). If I had to choose the counterpart to "truthful speech," it would have to be "study of the Torah." Once we make that substitution, the following would hardly have surprised Zoroaster:

The Sayings of the Fathers
Tractate Abot Chapter Two

2:1 Rabbi says: "What is the straight path which a person should choose for himself? Whatever is an ornament to the one who follows it, and an ornament in the view of others. Be meticulous in a small religious duty as in a large one, for you do not know what sort of reward is coming for any of the various religious duties. And reckon with the loss [required] in carrying out a religious duty against the reward for doing it; and the reward for committing a transgression against the loss for doing it. And keep your eye on three things, so you will not come into the clutches of transgression. Know what is above you. An eye which sees, and an ear which hears, and all your actions are written down in a book."

The form, omitting the attribution of the colloquy, is the same: a general question, standing at the head of an answer so phrased as to cover a variety of situations: one virtue applying everywhere.

But that omission is of course critical. The counterpart for the Mishnah and the Bavli to the colloquy of Zoroaster and Ohrmazd is the relationship between master and disciple. The same types of messages are conveyed through a completely different relationship. Contrast the passive Zoroaster with the active disciples, but compare, too, Ohrmazd and Yohanan ben Zakkai. For he stands in the tradition of Sinai, along with other masters, along with other disciples. Here is a much thicker tradition indeed than one that begins with Ohrmazd and ends with Zoroaster, leaving the ages to copy the words and hand them on, with no role in the colloquy except a passive one:

Tractate Abot Chapter Two

2:8A Rabban Yohanan ben Zakkai received [the Torah] from Hillel and Shammai. He would say: "If you have learned much Torah, do not puff yourself up on that account, for it was for that purpose that you were created."

He had five disciples, and these are they: Rabbi Eliezer ben Hyrcanus, Rabbi Joshua ben Hananiah, Rabbi Yosé the Priest, Rabbi Simeon ben Nethanel, and Rabbi Eleazar ben Arakh.

2:9A He said to them: "Go and see what is the straight path to which someone should stick."

2:9B Rabbi Eliezer says: "A generous spirit." Rabbi Joshua says: "A good friend." Rabbi Yosé says: "A good neighbor." Rabbi Simeon says: "Foresight." Rabbi Eleazar says: "Goodwill."

2:9C He said to them: "I prefer the opinion of Rabbi Eleazar ben Arakh, because in what he says is included everything you say."

2:9D He said to them: "Go out and see what is the bad road, which someone should avoid." Rabbi Eliezer says: "Envy." Rabbi Joshua says: "A bad friend." Rabbi Yosé says: "A bad neighbor." Rabbi Simeon says: "A loan." (All the same is a loan owed to a human being and a loan owed to the Omnipresent, the blessed, as it is said, The wicked borrows and does not pay back, but the righteous person deals graciously and hands over [what is owed].) Ps. 37:21.

2:9E Rabbi Eleazar says: "Ill will."

2:9F He said to them: "I prefer the opinion of Rabbi Eleazar been Arakh, because in what he says is included everything you say."

Now we see a repertoire of differences, which may be summarized in five points: [1] Contending propositions respond to the general question. [2] Reasons are given in behalf of each. [3] The process of tradition involves the active participation of the sage and disciple. [4] The tradition expands, with each generation taking up a place in the process. [5] The process is one of contention, argument, and conflict of principles, there to be sorted out and worked through to a conclusion through a process of analytical argument (the giving of reasons) on the one side, but authority (the sage decides) on the other. When, at the end, we shall draw our conclusions about the character of the Bavli highlighted by contrasts with the Mishnah, the Talmud of the Land of Israel, and the Pahlavi books, we shall underscore these traits as definitive of the Bavli and distinctive to it. But it is now clear that the beginnings of the matter lie in the representation of tractate Abot, when we see that tractate in the context of the Pahlavi Rivayat at hand: wisdom comes from Ohrmazd to Zoroaster, from God to Moses and thence the sages and their disciples; and the utensils for the formation and transmission of wisdom are conventional: deep question, eloquent response, covering all manner of concrete circumstances, the principles of being. But in the middle, in the process of representation and presentation, the differences prove formidable.

Another point of intersection is in this rivayat's interest in what we should have to classify as medical matters:

Incantations for Fever

Praise to the Creator Ohrmazd, to all the yazads, to all the yazads of the spiritual and physical worlds.

The incantation for fever: surahi visra amnao karosi vasa ahras ahras.

And for injury of mother and daughter, the coming in the name of that person (is to be) for three times [i.e., days].

If there is fever on the fourth (day), make the knot in straw which remains on the wall.

And three knots are to be tied in the middle of it, according to one rule three knots (three knots according to one rule), and two according to one (other) rule; and if there is fasting, three knots are tied on the middle, and one according to one rule, if a man, upon his arm, if a woman, upon her arm.

Breathe the incantation and spell for the sake of resistance the baj of Ardwahisht is taken. This incantation is to be repeated seven times, or eleven times, or twenty-one times; the incantation (is) this: kokaro aca karo.

Water from the spring which was dry [lit. "closed"] came from the mountain at the order of the valiant Fredon. (He) covered the bodily wound [?] of a horse[?], and he dressed "the bodily wound[?] of a horse[?]" and he held nine battle-axes in his hand.

It is simple to find counterparts in the Bavli, long stretches of incantations and forms of healing for specified ailments. Here is a sample, drawn from Bavli Gittin 68b-69b, severely abbreviated, which shows that the foregoing finds a counterpart in the Bavli, not only in form but in the type of healings that are set forth:

11. A. *For blood rushing to the head, the remedy is to take shurbina cedar and willow and moist myrtle and olive leaves and poplar and rosemary and cynodon and boil them all together. The patient should put three hundred cups on one side of his head and three hundred on the other. Or he should take white roses with all the leaves on one side and boil them and pour sixty cups over each side of his head....*

    D. *For night blindness one takes a string made of white hair and ties with it one of his own legs to the leg of a dog, and children should rattle potsherds behind him, saying, "Old dog, stupid cock." He should take seven pieces of raw meat from seven houses and put them on the doorpost and let the dog eat them in the rubbish dump of the town. Then he should untie the string and they should say, "Blindness of Mr. So-and-so, son of Mrs. Such-and-such," and they should blow into the dog's eye.*

    E. *For blindness by day one takes seven milts from the innards of animals and roasts them in the sherd of a bloodletter, and while sitting inside the house, someone else should sit outside, and the blind man should say to him, "Give me something to eat," and the other, with sight, answers, "Take and eat," and after he has eaten, he should break the sherd. Otherwise the blindness will come back.*

    F. *To stop a nose bleed one brings a priest by the name of Levi and writes Levi backward, or anybody and writes, "I Pappi Shila bar Sumki" backward; or writes, "The taste of the bucket in water of silver, the taste of the bucket in water of blemish." Or take root of clover and the rope of an old bed and papyrus and saffron and the red part of a palm branch and burn them all together and take a fleece of wool and weave two threads and steep them in vinegar and roll them in the ashes and put them in his nostrils. Or look for a watercourse running east to west and stand over it and pick up some clay with his right hand from under his left leg, and with his left hand from under his right leg, and twine two threads of wool and rub them in the clay and put them in his nostrils. Or sit under a gutter pipe while they* bring water and pour it over him saying, "As these waters stop, so may the blood of Mr. So-and-so, son of Mrs. Such-and-such, stop."...

L. For toothache: Rabbah b. R. Huna said, "He should take the top of a garlic with one stalk only and grind it with oil and salt and put it on his thumbnail on the side where the tooth aches and put a rim of dough around it, and take care that it doesn't touch his flesh, since it can cause leprosy....

O. For a gira fever he takes an arrow of Lilith and places it, point up, and pours water on it and drinks it. Or he can take water a dog has lapped at night, but make sure it wasn't exposed. For drinking water that has been exposed, take an anpak of undiluted wine....

QQ. For external fever take three sacks of date stones and three stacks of adra cedar and boil each separately, sitting between them, and put them in two basins, and bring a table and set them on it and bend first over one and then over the other until thoroughly warmed, and then bathe himself in them and drinking them afterward, he drinks only of the water of the adra cedar but not of the date stones, since they cause barrenness....

SS. For internal fever take seven handfuls of beet from seven beds and boil them with the dirt and eat them and drink adra leaves in beer *[70A]* or grapes from a vine trailing on a palm tree in water.

Apart from the predictable resort to named authorities, the style is pretty much the same: a combination of incantations and use of materia medica, specific to various ailments.

If, to conclude, we ask our systematic questions about rhetorical form, principles of logical coherence, and topical program, we find that the Mishnah and the Bavli intersect with this rivayat in some of the specific forms that governed the writing of compositions, such as the example just now given. But so far as the Bavli is made up of large composites, organized around a prior text, and the rivayat at hand is made up of completed compositions set forth as free-standing chapters, not linked to a prior text or to one another, the two documents are organized in accord with utterly unrelated theories. The rivayat is held together in its way, the Bavli in its way, and the bindings are not to be compared. What is lacking is that middle range of coherence afforded by linking discrete compositions and even large-scale composites to Mishnah chapters characteristic of the Bavli.

By contrast, here is the topical order of a random sequence of chapters in the Williams's rivayat:

2. Cooked and uncooked food; fire and water
3. Bodily effects of sins and good deeds
4. On forbearance
5. Old age
6. On covenant breaking
7. The man of good religion and the margarzan

Or, again, these:

17. Performance of worship
18. The value of fire
19. Carrying out the dead
20. Making offerings
21. The killing of good and evil creatures
22. The omniscience of Ohrmazd
23. The fate of the souls of the righteous and the wicked
24. The affliction of the wicked after death

Now we should have no difficulty in explaining why some of the chapters stand side by side with others of them, for instance, Nos. 2 and 3, 17-18, or 23-24. But there is no clear rhyme or reason for the layout of these groups; no effort is invented in forming transitions from group to group, or even item to item (for example, Nos. 4, 5, 6). So some chapters cohere with other chapters, but no large-scale principles of composition that are visible to the naked eye explain the layout of the whole. But we always know the reason for the layout of the Bavli's smallest and largest compositions and the composites as well.

The upshot is that, at some points, a shared rhetorical convention links the two writings. But the paramount rhetorical characteristics of the Bavli are in no way comparable to those of the rivayat. Then again, compositions in both documents appeal to that logic of the syllogistic coherence of propositions to link sentence to sentence; in that regard, the rivayat forms a model of propositional discourse; in Williams's translation, I did not find a single counterpart to the Bavli's very commonplace logic of fixed association of sentences through common linkage not to one another but only to a prior text. Where the documents differ radically, however, is in their responses to specific propositions. The topical program of the one rarely corresponds to that of the other, and the propositions of the entries that do correspond yield only contrasts, to which we now turn.

8

Episodic Comparisons

I. The Transmission of Uncleanness

Comparison of episodes at which the two documents – the Rivayat Accompanying Datestan i Denig and the Bavli (inclusive of the Mishnah) – address the same question and even say the same thing by the nature of this inquiry on the face of it cannot claim to accomplish the required, systematic task. For the Rivayat forms only a part of a much larger set of writings, and its rules testify to only one component of a complete legal and theological system. The severely limited range of comparison, to be sure, is not because, even at their most arcane, the two writings do not cover the same ground in the same way. The contrary is the fact. Anyone familiar with the Judaic law of uncleanness will find himself at home in a statement such as the following, concerning the transmission of uncleanness through being affected by the motion of, without direct contact with, the source of uncleanness:

> If they are carrying a dead (body) over a bridge of wood or of stone, if it trembles, if everyone who is standing on the bridge (is standing) still, (they are) not polluted, but if anyone keeps going he will indeed be polluted.

The principle here is that the corpse uncleanness is conveyed through motion, but not at rest; the criterion (who has to be moving) is, the person who is a candidate for contamination.

Let me paraphrase the Iranian rule. If a corpse is carried across the bridge, and if others are moving on it, too, if the bridge trembles under the weight of the corpse, then all other persons on the bridge are made unclean, the movement of the bridge transmitting the corpse uncleanness to third parties if they, too, are moving. But if they are not moving, then the uncleanness is null. It then follows that [1] if the bridge is firm and does not shift, [2] and if occupants of the bridge also do not move, then others standing on the bridge are unaffected. The upshot is simple. Corpse uncleanness is transmitted through the motion of an object that bears its weight.

In the following the same principle of the physics of the transmission of uncleanness pertains, though it works itself out somewhat differently. The datum is the category of uncleanness described at Lev. 15, called in Hebrew the *Zab*, a person afflicted with flux uncleanness. Such a person transmits uncleanness to objects that bear his weight, even though not touching those objects – just as the corpse does in the Zoroastrian case – if the other party also is in motion by reason of the same cause, the movement of the ship or the raft or the beast.

Mishnah-tractate Zabim 3:1

A. The Zab and the clean person who sat in a ship or on a raft,
B. or who rode [together] on a beast,
C. even though their clothes do not touch –
D. lo, these are unclean with midras uncleanness.
E. [If] they sat on a plank, or on a bench, or on a bed frame, and on the beam,
F. when they are infirm –
G. [if] they climbed up on a tree which was shaky,
H. on a branch which was shaky on a firm tree –
I. [if they climbed up] on an Egyptian ladder when it is not fastened with a nail,
J. on the bridge,
K. and on the beam,
L. and on the door,
M. when they are not fastened with clay –
N. they are unclean.
O. R. Judah declares clean.

At Eff. we come to precisely the case before us: the *Zab* and the clean person are on the same plank, bench, bed frame or beam or tree or ladder or bridge; if these are shaky, then the clean person is made unclean. Why? Because the uncleanness of the *Zab* is transmitted to the clean person through the motion of the infirm bridge or other object. And that is the exact counterpart to the Zoroastrian detail, if the persons on the bridge are moving, too. The point of difference proves equally obvious: for the Mishnaic law, it is the bridge that is moving, for the Zoroastrian, the afflicted parties. For the one, the uncleanness is transmitted by the movement of the weight-bearing component of the tableau, for the other, the movement of the candidate for uncleanness. In the following, we find the same principle:

M. Negaim 13:7

A. The unclean [person] stands under the tree, and the clean person passes –

B. he is unclean.
C. The clean person stands under the tree, and the unclean passes –
D. he is clean.
E. If he stood, he is unclean.
F. And so with the stone which is afflicted with plague – he is clean.
G. And if he put it down, lo, this one is unclean.

Now if the unclean person is at rest (put the corpse down on the bridge) and the clean person walks by (add: and overshadows it, in line with Num. 19), then the clean person contracts uncleanness. The opposite is also the rule: if the uncleanness is in motion and the clean person or object at rest, then the clean person or object remains clean. So the distinction recurs, and makes the same difference, but, for the Judaic system, in reverse. The point of this arcane exercise should not be missed: we can readily identify, even in the most remote and hermetic chapters of the law of uncleanness of Iran and Israel, more than a few points of intersection, where the same principles and the same cases generate decisions that are either the same or the opposite: a fine problem for comparison and contrast indeed. And, I am sure readers will agree to stipulate, a search through the ninth-century documents (all the more so prior ones) will yield countless points of parallel and even intersection.[1] But until we have formed a theory of the whole, each system compared in its entirety to the other, these details remain inert facts, generating nothing beyond themselves. That is why, for the present purpose, a clear view of what we wish to find out has always to remain in plain sight. It is to compare the two traditions when they go over the same theme and reach comparable conclusions, a comparison that, once more, shows us how the documents differ where they are alike.

II. Master-Disciple Relationships

Certainly the two systems' orbits come close in their address to the relationship prized by each, that is, the one upon which the formulation and transmission of the great tradition ultimately depends: the

---

[1] A systematic comparison of the two systems' purity rules, encompassing the entirety of their respective canons (on the side of the Mishnah and Talmuds, Leviticus and Numbers and the Tosefta, for instance) would certainly yield a hypothesis on how the entirety of the two systems compare. One can work from details to the whole – and has to. Nonetheless, episodic intersection such as what is before us leaves open too many variables to allow for the forming of hypothesis on the comparison and contrast of the systems at hand. A fine preliminary effort in just the right direction is in A.V. Williams, "Zoroastrian and Jewish Purity Laws. Reflections on the Viability of a Sociological Interpretation," to be published in a future volume of *Irano-Judaica*.

relationship between master and disciple. That is how God's word has come down in both traditions. The myth of the Oral Torah, beginning with Moses at Sinai, rests upon that relationship; the claim of the ninth-century priests to set down the great tradition depends upon it as well.

In the Judaic case, it is through the chain of master-disciple relationships, extending forward from Sinai, that the tradition is formulated and transmitted. In the Zoroastrian case, in the two rivayat writings before us and also in the Pursishniha, the literary form – question, answer – and much of the contents as well presuppose the relationship of master and disciple, the one answering, the other asking questions. And in both cases, the model derives from the original moment of revelation: God instructing Moses at Sinai, Ohrmazd instructing Zoroaster. The Bavli's presentation – functioning as counterpart to the colloquy language utilized by our rivayat, is as follows:

Bavli Erubin 54B-55A

43. A. *Our rabbis have taught on Tannaite authority:*
    B. What is the order of Mishnah teaching? Moses learned it from the mouth of the All-Powerful. Aaron came in, and Moses repeated his chapter to him and Aaron went forth and sat at the left hand of Moses. His sons came in and Moses repeated their chapter to them, and his sons went forth. Eleazar sat at the right of Moses, and Itamar at the left of Aaron.
    C. R. Judah says, "At all times Aaron was at the right hand of Moses."
    D. Then the elders entered, and Moses repeated for them their Mishnah chapter. The elders went out. Then the whole people came in, and Moses repeated for them their Mishnah chapter. So it came about that Aaron repeated the lesson four times, his sons three times, the elders two times, and all the people once.
    E. Then Moses went out, and Aaron repeated his chapter for them. Aaron went out. His sons repeated their chapter. His sons went out. The elders repeated their chapter. So it turned out that everybody repeated the same chapter four times....
44. A. *So why shouldn't everybody learn directly from Moses?*
    B. It was so as to pay honor to Aaron and his sons and honor to the elders.
    C. *Then why not have Aaron go in and learn from Moses, then his sons may go in and learn from Aaron, then the elders may go in and learn from his sons, and these in the end will teach all Israel?*
    D. Since Moses had learned from the mouth of the All-Powerful, the matter would work out better that way.

What we see here is characteristic of the Bavli: presentation of the fact, then systematic analysis of that fact.

Not only in myth, but also in law, the master-disciple relationship proves of critical interest to both traditions. For instance, the merit of a disciple accrues to the master; not only so, but if the disciple then teaches other disciples, "the merit of teaching the disciple to teach other disciples shall verily be unto the teacher. Unto those who shall so practice it, just as it is. Even those which the other teacher performs, it is just as if they perform [i.e., that which the disciple performs goes over to the teacher, and that which goes over to the disciple from other persons does not go over to the teacher].[2] In the Judaic counterpart, the teacher enters into the status of the father and deserves the respect owing to the disciple's father by the disciple; and takes precedence over the father. The principle is the same, the details, diverse.

In that context, we compare rules of conduct delivered by masters to disciples. The form is essentially the same: an instruction by a named master to a disciple, consisting in both case of a long set of rules of proper attitude and action. I find the "counsels of Adurbad" and those of the Judaic sages in tractate Avot to serve the same purpose and to take the same form. For the sake of brevity, I give only the initial part of Adurbad's counsels, also abbreviating the repertoire in tractate Avot:

Chapter Sixty-Two
Counsels of Adurbad, Son of Mansarspand,
from the Sayings of his Teacher Mihr Ohrmazd

There was a disciple of Adurbad of immortal soul, son of Mannsarspand; he was with Adurbad for a long time.

And this indeed he said to Adurbad: "Instruct me, so that when I go forth from the presence of the teacher instruction of my soul can then (proceed) better on account of that."

Adurbad said: "Be certain (in faith) in the yazads. Keep your thought, speech and action honest and true. Neither think nor speak nor do any sin whatsoever, and may you be blessed."

And the disciple said: "O teacher, I am not perfect in this, give me special instruction, so that I shall practice it and I shall be blessed."

Adurbad said: "Consider the twenty-two precepts of Mihr Ohrmazd, my teacher; understand all (of them), put them into practice and may you be blessed!"

The disciple said: "If you consider me as worthy, please tell (me the precepts), so that I may understand and practice (accordingly)."

Adurbad said in reply: "The precepts (are) these three kinds of generosity, fourth truthfulness, fifth virtuousness, sixth diligence, seventh intercession, eighth trustworthiness, ninth peace seeking, tenth law abidingness, eleventh union, twelfth laying down of weapons, thirteenth moderation, fourteenth lowliness, fifteenth humility, sixteenth modesty, seventeenth pleasantness, eighteenth completeness (of mind),

---

[2]Jamaspasa and Humbach, *Pursishniha*, pp. 29-31.

nineteenth patience, twentieth love for people, twenty-first contentedness, twenty-second oneness (of mind).

"The best generosity: first, he who is not asked but gives; second, he who is asked (and) gives immediately; third, he who is asked and fixes a time and does (his giving) on time. He (is) best, who, when he gives, who entertains no hope as regards that (receiver of his generosity, thinking): 'He will give (it) back to me'; he does not give for the sake of acquiring trade, nor for the sake of covetousness....

"Twenty-second, oneness is (as regards) those two pathways which (are) revealed in religion that the way was created in two branches, and one is righteous and one is sinful; you should avoid the sinful one and stand upon the righteous one, never go out of that way and do not turn away, and you will neither think nor speak nor do anything sinful whatsoever."

The disciple said: "Master teacher, may you be blessed!" for from the instruction which was given by the teacher to the world (he was) blessed. In particular the words of this instruction to us (are) indeed a means of providing much help and growth, and even if by (his) wisdom and by (his) diligence he does not resemble us, then if we and all men put (something) of this instruction into practice (all) will be blessed through the will, strength, power, beneficence, and mercifulness of the yazads.

What we have is a catalogue of virtues, systematically expounded as a handbook for the good life. I fail to see any material differences, in the chosen form of transmitting a tradition on good attitude and action, from the mode of tractate Avot, in the following (also abbreviated) reprise:

Tractate Avot Chapter Three
Chapter Four

4:1   Ben Zoma says, "Who is a sage? He who learns from everybody, as it is said, From all my teachers I have gotten understanding (Ps. 119:99). Who is strong? He who overcomes his desire, as it is said, He who is slow to anger is better than the mighty, and he who rules his spirit than he who takes a city (Prov. 16:32). Who is rich? He who is happy in what he has, as it is said, When you eat the labor of your hands, happy will you be, and it will go well with you (Ps. 128:2). (Happy will you be – in this world, and it will go well with you – in the world to come.) Who is honored? He who honors everybody, as it is said, For those who honor me I shall honor, and they who despise me will be treated as of no account (1 Sam. 2:30)."

4:16   R. Jacob says, "This world is like an antechamber before the world to come. Get ready in the antechamber, so you can go into the great hall."

4:17   He would say, "Better is a single moment spent in penitence and good deeds in this world than the whole of the world to come. And better is a single moment of inner peace in the world to come than the whole of a lifetime spent in this world."

Episodic Comparisons 149

4:22B He would say, "Those who are born are [destined] to die, and those who die are [destined] for resurrection. And the living are [destined] to be judged – so as to know, to make known, and to confirm that (1) he is God, (2) he is the one who forms, (3) he is the one who creates, (4) he is the one who understands, (5) he is the one who judges, (6) he is the one who gives evidence, (7) he is the one who brings suit, (8) and he is the one who is going to make the ultimate judgment.

4:22C "Blessed be he, for before him are no (1) guile, (2) forgetfulness, (3) respect for persons, or (4) bribe-taking, for everything is his. And know that everything is subject to reckoning. And do not let your evil impulse persuade you that Sheol is a place of refuge for you. For (1) despite your wishes were you formed, (2) despite your wishes were you born, (3) despite your wishes do you live, (4) despite your wishes do you die, and (5) despite your wishes are you going to give a full accounting before the King of kings of kings, the Holy One blessed be He."

In both cases an important component of the master-disciple relationship is the transmission of wisdom on proper conduct. In both instances, the master is named, and in both cases, a liturgy is tacked on to the end of the catalogue of virtuous attitudes and behavior. To be sure, this kind of writing would have presented no surprise to sages and disciples who flourished from the remotest times of writing onward; Sumerian, Akkadian, Egyptian, not to mention Greek and Roman, writers recorded the same kind of advice, and even much the same advice (recommendations of arrogance are vastly outnumbered in the literature by the counsel of humility, but, to be sure, praise of masters' humility is outweighed in volume by complaints about their arrogance). But in the Zoroastrian and Judaic writings, the master-disciple relationship finds definition in not only generalizations but detailed rules, and that is what makes the comparison particular to the two cases and distinctive as well.

III. Father-Son or Master-Disciple Relationships

The comparison of the relationship of father to son and master to disciple comes to expression in this rivayat in the revelation by Ohrmazd to Zoroaster on the rule – parallel in the two relationships – governing law suits between persons of said classifications. The tradition tells the judge how to adjudicate a case in which each party presents evidence of the same weight as that of the other. In that case, the judge is to favor the master or the father, who has nurtured him. Indeed, the father, and, by extension, the master, owns the earnings of the son or disciple and the merit of his good deeds, as though the father of the master had done those deeds himself:

Chapter Twenty-Nine
The Privileges of Seniority

This also (is) revealed, Ohrmazd said to Zoroaster: "If a father is engaged in a lawsuit with his son, or a herbad with his pupil, or a father-in-law with his son-in-law, and if the father (has) one witness on his side, and the son one witness on his, make the decision in favour of the father, and entrust the property (at stake) to the father, for this reason that the good that the father does for his son, the son can never re-pay that goodness. He has nurtured him from childhood and immaturity until that (time) when he becomes an adult. Indeed according to this saying: 'Until a son is 15 years old his nurture (comes) from his father,' then also so long as he [i.e., the father] (is) alive the (son's) earnings belong to the father, and all the good deeds which the son does will thus belong to the father as if he had done them with his own hands."

What attracts our attention is two facts, first, the reason – the father has nurtured the son, and the master is in the status of the father and so is deemed to have nurtured him, too – and second the consequence, the father or master owns the son's earnings and merits. We find the same issue worked out along intersecting lines in the following:

Mishnah-tractate Baba Mesia 2:11

A. [If one has to choose between seeking] what he has lost and what his father has lost,
B. his own takes precedence.
C. [If he has to choose between seeking] what he has lost and what his master has lost,
D. his own takes precedence.
E [If he has to choose between seeking] what his father has lost and what his master has lost, that of his master takes precedence.
G. For his father brought him into this world.
H. But his master, who has taught him wisdom, will bring him into the life of the world to come.
I. But if his father is a sage, that of his father takes precedence.
J. [If] his father and his master were carrying heavy burdens, he removes that of his master, and afterward removes that of his father.
K. [If] his father and his master were taken captive,
L he ransoms his master, and afterward he ransoms his father.
M. But if his father is a sage, he ransoms his father, and afterward he ransoms his master.

The issue is framed in different terms, of course, since it is the son who has the decision to make, not the judge. And the son has to give priority to his own interest, for a reason that the Talmud will immediately want to uncover. At issue is when he (not the judge) has to choose between his father and his master. The answer, however, would have interested the author of our rivayat, since the Mishnah rule carries forward the same

Episodic Comparisons 151

principle as the Zoroastrian one: the master enters into the status of the father. The Mishnah cannot imagine that the master or father will take over the property or the merit of good deeds of the son.

But the framer of the Bavli wants to know why the son's interests take priority, and that is, I assume, in light of the commandment to honor father and mother. The answer follows:

I.1   A.   What is the scriptural source of this rule ["**his own takes precedence**"]?
       B.   Said R. Judah said Rab, "Said Scripture, 'Except that there shall be no poor among you' (Deut. 15:4). Your own takes precedence over anybody else's."
       C.   But said R. Judah said Rab, "Whoever treats himself in such a way will end up in such a condition [of poverty]."

II.1   A.   **[If] his father and his master were carrying heavy burdens, he removes that of his master, and afterward removes that of his father.**
       B.   Our rabbis have taught on Tannaite authority:
       C.   "**The master of which they have spoken is the one who taught him wisdom, not the master who taught him Scripture or Mishnah**," the words of R. Meir.
       D.   R. Judah says, "It is anyone from whom he has gained the greater part of his learning."
       E.   R. Yosé says, "Even someone who has enlightened his eyes in his repetition of a single Mishnah paragraph – lo, this is his master" [T. B.M. 2:30D-F].
       F.   Said Raba, "For example, R. Sehorah, who explained to me the meaning of the words that stand for a certain utensil [at M. Kel. 13:2]."

II.2   A.   Samuel tore his garment as a mark of mourning for one of the rabbis, who had merely taught him the meaning of the phrase, **one of the keys goes into the duct as far as the armpit and the other opens the door directly [M. Tam. 3:6E].**

II.3   A.   Said Ulla, "Disciples of sages who are located in Babylonia stand up in respect to one another and tear their garments in mourning for one another.
       B.   "But as to returning a lost object, in a case in which there is a choice between his father [and his master], he goes first of all in search of his master only when it is his principal teacher."

The Bavli's initial contribution, as is commonly the case, links the Mishnah's rule to a source in the Written Torah. The proof is such as to eliminate possibility that the father or master owns the son's or disciple's property. The Talmud's next step is to enrich the discussion through the qualification produced by Tosefta's supplement: defining the master who counts. Here we recall the rivayat's distinction between a disciple who does not teach others and the one who does; the master gets credit for the good deeds of the disciple who teaches others. We find ourselves moving in the reverse direction: the identification of the master who enjoys the status that is subject to discussion here. No. 3 pursues the same matter.

IV. Husband-Wife Relationships: The Wife's Perfect Obedience

The Zoroastrian code finds it possible to say in a few words precisely what the wife owes the husband, which is perfect and unquestioning obedience to his will in all matters; and anyhow, she shouldn't torment him. Between the ritual ideal, on the one side, and the concession to the everyday, on the other, presumably lies what can be expected. On the Judaic side, the same thing is spelled out in more concrete ways, the Mishnah being a far more detailed document than the two rivayats before us (or the Pursishniha, for that matter):

Chapter Thirty-Nine
Wife and Husband

This (question): how should a wife behave towards her husband?

The wife of *padixsay* (status) should consult her husband three times every day saying: "What do you require when I think and speak and act, for I do not know what is required when I think and speak and act, tell (me), so that I will think and speak and act as you require?" Then she must do everything that the righteous husband tells her, and she should refrain from tormenting and afflicting her husband.

The concrete obligations of the woman to the man in Judaism convey the same attitude, but because of their specificity, place some (few) limits on the husband's caprice:

Mishnah-tractate Ketubot 5:5

A. These are the kinds of labor which a woman performs for her husband:
B. she (1) grinds flour, (2) bakes bread, (3) does laundry, (4) prepares meals, (5) gives suck to her child, (6) makes the bed, (7) works in wool.
C. [If] she brought with her a single slave girl, she does not (1) grind, (2) bake bread, or (3) do laundry.
D. [If she brought] two, she does not (4) prepare meals and does (5) not feed her child.
E. [If she brought] three, she does not (6) make the bed for him and does not (7) work in wool.
F. If she brought four, she sits on a throne.
G. R. Eliezer says, "Even if she brought him a hundred slave girls, he forces her to work in wool,
H. "for idleness leads to unchastity."
I. Rabban Simeon b. Gamaliel says, "Also: He who prohibits his wife by a vow from performing any labor puts her away and pays off her marriage contract. For idleness leads to boredom."

Episodic Comparisons

The Bavli's reading of the rule follows, in abbreviated form. The traits we have found characteristic recur here.

I.1   A.   **Grinds flour:**
       B.   *Under what circumstances [can we imagine that a woman would grind flour, which involves moving heavy machinery]?*
       C.   *Read:* taking charge of the grinding.
       D.   And if you prefer: grinding with a hand mill.

I.2   A.   *Our Mishnah paragraph is not in accord with R. Hiyya, for R. Hiyya set forth the following Tannaite rule:*
       B.   [Marrying] a woman is only for her beauty, only for children.
       C.   *And R. Hiyya set forth the following Tannaite rule:*
       D.   A wife is for wearing women's ornaments.
       E.   *And R. Hiyya set forth the following Tannaite rule:*
       F.   He who wants his wife to be attractive should dress her in linen clothes. He who wants his daughter to have a bright skin should feed her young chicken and give her plenty of milk to drink as she comes toward her first period.

II.1   A.   **Gives suck to her child:**
       B.   *May one say that this does not accord with the position of the House of Shammai? For it has been taught on Tannaite authority:*
       C.   If she took a vow not to give suck to her child,
       D.   the House of Shammai say, "She pulls her teats from the child's mouth."
       E.   And the House of Hillel say, "He can force her to give suck to her child."
       F.   If she was divorced, however, they do not force her to give suck to him.
       G.   If her son recognized her as his mother, they give her a wage, and she gives suck to him, because of the danger to the child's life. The husband cannot force his wife to give suck to the child of his fellow, and the wife cannot force her husband to permit her to give suck to the child of her girlfriend [T. Ket. 5:5A-H].
       H.   *Well, you may even maintain that the House of Shammai stand behind our Mishnah paragraph. Here with what case do we deal? It is a case in which she took the oath and he confirmed it for her. The House of Shammai take the view that* he has put his finger between her teeth [the vow is his fault], *and the House of Hillel maintain that* she put her finger between his teeth....

III.1   A.   **[If] she brought with her a single slave girl, she does not (1) grind, (2) bake bread, or (3) do laundry:**
       B.   *But the rest of the duties she has to do.*
       C.   *But why can't she say to him, "I brought you another woman in my place [for all manner of work, not just for this]"?*
       D.   *Because he can say to her, "That slave girl works for me and for herself, who's going to work for you?"*

IV.1   A.   **[If she brought] two, she does not (4) prepare meals and does (5) not feed her child:**
       B.   *But the rest of the duties she has to do.*

	C.	But why can't she say to him, "I brought you another woman in my place [for all manner of work, not just for this], and she's going to work for me and for her, and the first one will work for you and for herself"?
	D.	Because he can say to her, "So who's going to work for our guests and visitors?"
V.1	A.	**[If she brought] three, she does not (6) make the bed for him and does not (7) work in wool:**
	B.	But the rest of the duties she has to do.
	C.	But why can't she say to him, "I brought you a third one still, to work for our guests and visitors"?
	D.	Because he can say to her, "The bigger the household, the more numerous the guests and the visitors."
	E.	*If so, then even if she brought in four, you could have the same colloquy!*
	F.	*If there are four, since they are that many, they help one another.*

This drastically abbreviated presentation of the Bavli's analysis points in an obvious direction, which we may discern by noting that what is of special interest to us in the Bavli is not the rule, but the mode of representing it. Here, clearly, we come to the principal point of difference between this Rivayat and the Bavli, when the two writings intersect. To state the difference in a simple way: What should we have found in the Rivayat, had the words, "The wife of *padixsay* (status) should consult her husband three times every day saying: 'What do you require when I think and speak and act, for I do not know what is required when I think and speak and act, tell (me), so that I will think and speak and act as you require,'" been followed by: [1] what is the source [in the Avesta or Gathers] of this rule? or [2] under what circumstances? and [3] this rule is not in accord with the following, known in some other compilation? Then again, if we had the same rule, followed by, "may we say this does not accord with the position of...," followed by a contrary view in some other source, what should the rivayat have looked like? Or if we had, "if the husband said...," and then, "but does she have to do no more?" what shape would the writing have taken? The answer is simple: We should have had something very like the Bavli. And we do not have anything like the Bavli.

Having laid so much stress on the second of the two Talmuds, let me now introduce the first, so that the full point of differentiation between the Iranian and the Judaic formulations of the respective great traditions may be exposed. The difference between the Judaic sages' and the Iranian priests' representation is that, while the Mishnah exhibits a policy on how the great tradition is to be written down that proves in general congruent to that of the two rivayats (and the Pursishniha), the full representation of the tradition by both Talmuds sets the Judaic apart from the Iranian statement. The tradition, for the Zoroastrian priests, consists of rules. For both Talmuds, rules do not suffice, and, as I shall show in the concluding chapter, for the second of the two Talmuds, amplification and extension, such as we shall now see in the Yerushalmi, also do not suffice; there, the very sense of "tradition" undergoes profound reconsideration.

Here is the Yerushalmi's treatment of the same Mishnah paragraph (again severely abbreviated):

[I.A] **The kinds of work which a woman does for her husband –**
[B] **seven basic categories of labor did they enumerate.**
[C] **And the rest did not require enumeration [M. 5:6A-B]** [T. Ket. 5:4A-C].
[II.A] **She feeds her child [M. 5:6B].**
[B] Said R. Haggai, "It says only, 'Her child.' Lo, in a case of twins, she is not [required to suckle both]."
[C] And why does it say, "Her child"?
[D] It is so that she should not nurse her friend's child....
[III.A] **If she brought [with her a single slave girl, etc. (M. 5:6C-F)].** Said R. Samuel bar R. Isaac, "It is not the end of the matter that she actually brought [the slave girls with her]. But even if she was in a position to do so [but did not actually bring them in, the same law applies]."
[B] That is in line with what is taught: **His wife goes up with him, but she does not go down with him [T. Ket. 5:9B].** [She rises in status and perquisites, but does not lose what she already has if she marries down.]
[C] A widow and her children go down but do not go up.
[D] Workers go up but do not go down.
[E] A daughter neither goes up nor goes down.
[F] [Since the Mishnah specifies the work of the several slave girls, M. 5:6C-F, we now ask:] And let her bring a slave girl to do all the work?
[G] Said R. Hiyya bar Judah, "It is for the welfare of the slave girl [who should not be overworked]. [That is why the slave girl has a specified set of tasks, and the mistress of the household must do the rest of them.]"
[H] Said R. Bun, "It is because these sorts of work are menial that they assigned them to the slave girl."
[I] Said R. Judah b. R. Bun, "[The reason sages assigned the remainder of the work to the woman] is that it is not usual for a woman to sit idle in her husband's household."
[J] R. Huna said, "Even if she brought in to the marriage a hundred slave girls, he may force her to perform for him certain tasks best done in private."
[K] What are these tasks best done in private?
[L] She anoints his body with oil, washes his feet, and mixes his cup.
[M] What is the reason? Is it because she is obligated to do these things, or is it because it is not appropriate to make use of a slave girl to do them?
[N] What is the practical difference between these two reasons?
[O] A case in which she brought slave boys into the marriage.

[P] If you say that these are not tasks for which it is appropriate to make use of a slave girl, lo, she has brought slave boys into the marriage [who may do these tasks].

[Q] Accordingly, the reason is only on the count that she is liable to do these things for him.

[R] R. Abudema in Sepphoris raised the question before R. Mana, "Is it not reasonable to suppose that the reason is only on the count of her being liable to do these things for him?"

[S] He said to him, "I, too, maintain that view."

The amplification of the rule in the Yerushalmi involves, first, the introduction of Tosefta's supplement; then a close reading of the language at hand (II.B-D), and the extension of the rule, III.A. There are then some supplementary statements that set forth rules, rather than analysis, III.Dff. Enough of the passage is given so that the point is established that both Talmuds accord to the Mishnah what no one provides for the rule given in the Rivayat. The great traditions differ in one fundamental point: the Mishnah has two Talmuds, the Rivayat has none; and so far as descriptions of the library written in the ninth century afford an accurate account of what is there, there is no talmud for any document in the Zoroastrian corpus, and no document serves any other document as a talmud.

V. Commercial Relationships: True Value

Our final specific comparison of the two traditions as they intersect on the same matter concerns the conception of true value. That theory maintains that an object possesses an intrinsic and inherent value, which is distinct from the price that the market sets on the same object (that is, what an informed buyer and informed seller are willing to pay and to receive for the object to change hands). The notion of true value logically belongs together with the conception of money as an item of barter or meant merely to facilitate barter, because both notions referred to the single underlying conception of the economy as a steady state entity in which people could not increase wealth but only exchange it. Fraud involves not adulteration of a product or misrepresentation of the character or quality of merchandise, such as we should grasp, but simply charging more than something is worth, and that can only mean, than something is worth intrinsically.

The Zoroastrian formulation maintains that if an object has a true value of four, and one sells it elsewhere for ten, he may not retain six; he may keep the four that he paid, plus his expenses and his wages, and the rest of the profit goes to a meritorious purpose. Now the given is that, in that other place, the object has a true value of ten. Then the man is governed by the criterion of the true value set by the place in which he bought the object, not the place in which he sold it.

Trading and Acquisition of Wealth

This (question): how should trading take place so that there will be no sin in it?

When (a trader) buys for four drachms a single piece of clothing, worth four drachms, and he takes it to another town, and (in) the place where he takes it it is worth ten drachms, he sells it for ten drachms, and takes out of it wages and daily sustenance for himself and his horse, and he gives away what remains (of it) as a righteous gift, it is a (work of) great merit.

"True value" then is negotiated in relationship to market value. That is, the "true value" of four, set at the time of purchase, has to be brought into relationship with the true value of ten, which the market has placed on the object in that other place. We take account of the difference between the true value, which is the purchase price where the trader lives, and the market value, by refunding the difference between the market price and the true value in acts of piety.

The Mishnah expresses the identical notion, that an object possesses a true value. But it sets forth the idea in a different context. It speaks of an "overcharge," meaning, what the market has paid for an item that exceeds true value; true value then is a fixed and known value, and "fraud" or overreaching is whatever the market pays over and above that value, which is anything more than 16.667 percent above true value. The difference has to be refunded:

Mishnah-tractate Baba Mesia 4:3

A. Fraud [overreaching] is an overcharge of four pieces of silver out of twenty-four pieces of silver to the sela –
B. one-sixth of the purchase price.
C. For how long is it permitted to retract [in the case of fraud]?
D. So long as it takes to show [the article] to a merchant or a relative [who will know the true value of the object that one has bought].

Fraud here is simply a charge higher than the intrinsic worth of the object permits. That definition rejects the conception of "free" and "market," that redundancy that insists upon the market as the instrument of the rationing of scarce resources. If an object has a true value of twenty-four and the seller pays twenty-eight, he has been defrauded and may retract. Tarfon gave and took, E-K. What is expressed here are, first, the notion of a just price, second, the emphasis upon barter. The reason is that the logic of the one demanded the complementary logic of the other. Once we impute a true value to an object or commodity, we shall also dismiss from consideration all matters of worth extrinsic to the object or commodity; hence money is not an abstract symbol of worthy but itself a commodity, and, further, objects bear true value.

The Talmud's amplification of the matter addresses ambiguities in the Mishnah's rule:

I.1   A.   It has been stated:
      B.   Rab said, "What we have learned to repeat in the Mishnah is, 'a sixth of the purchase price [reckoned at true value]" **[one-sixth of the purchase price]**.
      C.   And Samuel said, "A sixth of the money paid also was taught."
      D.   *Obviously if something worth six was sold for five or seven, all parties concur that we follow the purchase price and if there was overreaching by one-sixth, [the law of fraud is invoked]. Then what is at issue? It would be a case in which something worth five or seven was sold for six.*
      E.   *As to Samuel, who has said that we follow the money paid as well, in both instances there is a valid claim of fraud.*
      F.   *But in the view of Rab, who has said that we follow only the purchase price, then if something worth five went for six, the sale is invalid, but if something worth seven is sold for six [so it is only a seventh of the true value of the purchase price], then the seller is deemed to have renounced part of what is really coming to him.*
      G.   *And Samuel said, "When do we maintain that there is renunciation by the seller or invalidation of the sale? Only if there is not a sixth variation from true value on either side [whether we regard the true purchase price or the money paid (Freedman)], but if there is a sixth of variation on one side, then it is a case of fraud."*

I.2   A.   We have learned in the Mishnah:
      B.   **Fraud [overreaching] is an overcharge of four pieces of silver out of twenty-four pieces of silver to the sela — one-sixth of the purchase price.**
      C.   *Does this not mean that one has sold something worth twenty for twenty-four, so a sixth of the money paid also is covered by the Mishnah's teaching?*
      D.   *No, what it means is that twenty-four coins' worth was sold for twenty, and who was subjected to fraud? It was the seller!*
      E.   Then what about the concluding part of the rule? **For how long is it permitted to retract [in the case of fraud]? So long as it takes to show [the article] to a merchant or a relative.**
      F.   And R. Nahman said, "This refers only to the purchaser, but as to the seller, at any time he may retract."
      G.   *The meaning is that he sold something worth twenty-four for twenty-eight.*

Enough of the Talmud is before us to show how a sustained analysis of the secondary issue raised by Rab and Samuel is set forth. So the simple rule at hand requires amplification and clarification. Had this Rivayat's author wished to address the problem, he could well have given us an entirely factual statement along the same lines; he certainly could have told us how to calculate the overcharge, if his formulation (4/10) had left any point of unclarity. So in comparison, the issue is not where the presentations of the rule differ, rather, it is the mode of discourse, to which, in the final chapter, we shall devote considerable attention.

VI. The Relationship between Zoroaster and God, and between Our Sages of Blessed Memory and God

In addition to the episodic points of intersection, we take note of the more general point of comparison afforded by the fact that both the Zoroastrian priests and the Judaic sages present their ideas as not secular laws but heavenly norms. If, then, we move from details to the main characteristics of the Pahlavi Rivayat Accompanying the Dadestan i Denig in comparison to those of the Talmud, the single most remarkable quality of the Zoroastrian text captures our attention: it is the repeated claim that, in this document, we have the record of conversations between Ohrmazd, the God, and Zoroaster, the prophet. It goes without saying that not a line of the Bavli places God into conversation with a sage, though, not uncommonly, sages do receive instructions from echoes held to speak in behalf of heaven, and these instructions concern legal as much as theological matters.

So, in comparing the documents, now we have to ask ourselves, who is the voice or persona behind this writing, and how does this persona know of what he speaks? He is now either a witness to the colloquy, knowing what Zoroaster asked Ohrmazd and Ohrmazd answered, or he records a revelation out of a long-ago age. In the context of a great tradition, it can only be the latter. In that case, what we are given is the record of ancient revelation, preserved through oral tradition and only now written down. That certainly accords with the Bavli's prevailing theory of the Oral Torah, but with one striking difference: the Bavli takes for granted its framers hold ancient, oral traditions; but it never sets down a direct colloquy between a human being, for example, a sage, and God; never records a conversation between God and man that is not drawn from the written record of the Written Torah (a.k.a. Old Testament).

Indeed, to find a counterpart to the first colloquy, cited in Chapter Eight, on the omniscience of Ohrmazd, we should have to follow Moses into the cleft of the rock. It goes without saying, moreover, that while the Written Torah shows us Moses in conversation with God even on his, Moses', own concerns, to know the character of God, to enter the promised land, the Bavli may contain expansions upon those stories but never presumes to introduce into the tradition fresh stories that correspond to the Torah's and the Prophets' accounts of God's authoritative, revealed statements. And, even more strikingly, while the author of Job would have found himself in familiar territory in Zoroaster's petition for immortality, "It cannot be done...," not a line in the Bavli allows for God to explain himself in such a way. When, by contrast, Moses asks God how, given Aqiba's acumen, Aqiba's reward is to have his flesh weighed out and sold for supper in the marketplace, God tells Moses to shut up before God's ineffable decree. So, it is clear, the two traditions contain radically different kinds of writing, and in the difference, we learn something about the Bavli's silences, as much as in the comparison with Aturfarnbag's rivayat, we learn about the Bavli's speech.

Bavli Menahot 29B

5. A. Said R. Judah said Rab, "At the time that Moses went up on high, he found the Holy One in session, affixing crowns to the letters [of the words of the Torah]. He said to him, 'Lord of the universe, who is stopping you [from regarding the document as perfect without these additional crowns on the letters]?'
   B. "He said to him, 'There is a man who is going to arrive at the end of many generations, and Aqiba b. Joseph is his name, who is going to interpret on the basis of each point of the crowns heaps and heaps of laws.'
   C. "He said to him, 'Lord of the Universe, show him to me.'
   D. "He said to him, 'Turn around.'
   E. "He went and took a seat at the end of eight rows, but he could not grasp what the people were saying. He felt faint. But when the discourse reached a certain matter, and the disciples said, 'My lord, how do you know this?' and he answered, 'It is a law given to Moses from Sinai,' he regained his composure.
   F. "He went and came before the Holy One. He said before him, 'Lord of the Universe, how come you have someone like that and yet you give the Torah through me?'
   G. "He said to him, 'Silence! That is how the thought came to me.'
   H. "He said to him, 'Lord of the Universe, you have shown me his Torah, now show me his reward.'
   I. "He said to him, 'Turn around.'
   J. "He turned around and saw his flesh being weighed out at the butcher stalls in the market.
   K. "He said to him, 'Lord of the Universe, such is Torah, such is the reward?'
   L. "He said to him, 'Silence! That is how the thought came to me.'"

Here we find ourselves at the end point of comparison and differentiation. If I had to point to the fundamental point of difference between the one tradition and the other, at the very point at which the writing down is subject to comparison, it is in this contrast:

Zoroaster, weeping, replied: "You created the wind, you created the water, you created the clay (of the earth), you created the fire, you created everything, behold, seek for me a means whereby I may be saved from death."

And then Ohrmazd bestowed omniscient wisdom upon Zoroaster.

"He went and came before the Holy One. He said before him, 'Lord of the Universe, how come you have someone like that and yet you give the Torah through me?'

"He said to him, 'Silence! That is how the thought came to me.'"

Ohrmazd comforts Zoroaster through wisdom. Ohrmazd is omniscient, and so is Zoroaster. Challenged to account for his decision, the God of our sages of blessed memory gives a different reply altogether. The sage never represents himself as having been given the wisdom of God, only the tradition of Sinai.

But then we have to ask ourselves, precisely what defines that wisdom, if omniscience is not its trait? And that brings us to the final question: Precisely what do the Zoroastrian priests and the Judaic sages know as "tradition," and what is it, in the end, that each party claims to pass forward to the future? Only when we have compared the Bavli with a variety of prior Judaic, as well as Iranian, versions of great traditions shall we find our answer to the question: Of what does the great tradition consist? And it is in that answer that we shall account for the striking differences in the writing down of traditions that separate the Iranian from the Judaic documents in their ultimate phases at the dusk of late antiquity.

Part Three

PERSPECTIVE ON THE GREAT TRADITIONS

9

Ways of Writing Down Great Traditions in Israel and Iran

We have seen three modes of writing down great traditions, all of them variations upon a single one: put the information down in permanent form. All parties concur that the great tradition encompasses rules of conduct and norms of theological truth. None of the framers cared to rely on media other than writing. For instance, we have no record of resort to art or music, drama or dance, which, under other circumstances, have served others for the formation and expression of what was meant to survive the ages. Nor, for more obvious reasons, did either Zoroastrian priests or Judaic sages imagine that in the formation of enduring communities, their rules lived out in the lives of living persons, models of how things must be, their work would be accomplished, even though both groups wrote for precisely that kind of rule-encased community. And, for equally clear cause, neither party conceived that – for a long time to come, at least – politics might form the path to perpetuating the valued truth. It all came down to writing down rules. But once that one way was chosen, variations unfolded, of which, in the data before us, I see three.

I. [1] The Rule Unadorned, [2] the Rule Attached to a Myth, and [3] the Rule Joined to Its Reason: The Three Types of Re-Presenting Great Tradition in Late Antique Iran and Israel

Some authors find it sufficient to give [1] a rule alone, some want [2] a myth to accompany the rule, but one authorship insists that [3] the rule be subordinated to a process of critical analytical reason. As we shall now see, [1] in the first category fall Aturfarnbag's Rivayat, on the one side, and the Mishnah, on the other. In the second we find [2] the other rivayat, the one that accompanies the Datestan i Denig – not to mention on the Israelite side all of the pentateuchal law codes. In the third is only [3] the Bavli, which, as we shall see, so reformulates discourse as to redefine what can be meant by "tradition."

Of the documents we have surveyed, two suffice with [1] the statement of rules alone, Aturfarnbag's Rivayat, which sets forth rules in the form of questions and answers, and the Mishnah, which uses simple declarative sentences, statements of fact, with the same effect. A third document, the Yerushalmi, wants a rule with secondary clarification, and forms a secondary development within this same category. Further, the Pursishniha – called by its editors "a Zoroastrian catechism" – exhibits the same general characteristics: it conveys information through unadorned statements of fact in the form of questions and answers. Its governing form does not greatly vary from Aturfarnbag's:

> Question: Do any of them who stand by the religion of Ohrmazd and Zartuxsht become worthy of Hell or not?
>
> Answer: No. Because everyone who stands by the religion of Ohrmazd and everyone who has worshiped Zartuxsht are all worthy of Paradise....

The laconic style runs on in this way for fifty-eight such exchanges. It requires very little writing skill to produce out of that form a statement of facts, for example, "None of them who stand by the religion of Ohrmazd and Zartusht become worthy of Hell, because everyone who stands by...are all worthy of Paradise." How far does that formulation stand from the following:

Mishnah-tractate Sanhedrin 10:1

A. All Israelites have a share in the world to come,
B. as it is said, "Your people also shall be all righteous; they shall inherit the land forever, the branch of my planting, the work of my hands, that I may be glorified" (Isa. 60:21).
C. And these are the ones who have no portion in the world to come:
D. (1) He who says, the resurrection of the dead is a teaching which does not derive from the Torah, (2) and the Torah does not come from Heaven; and (3) an Epicurean.

In the presentations of theological norms in the two documents I see no consequential difference in form – use of laconic declarations of facts – other than the cited prooftext. Both suffice with simple declarative sentences. Neither demands a myth in situ – in the very context of its presentation, I mean – to validate the information. The principal point is what accompanies these declarations: validation or not. When, by contrast, we find persistent reference to Zoroaster's asking Ohrmazd questions, even though the questions form simple, laconic statements, and the answers likewise, we are in a different frame of reference altogether.

The point of differentiation is clear when we come to the second type of presentation. The joining of rule to myth characterizes [2] the Pahlavi Rivayat Accompanying the Dadestan i Denig, invoking an implicit myth at most of its statements of rules by having Ohrmazd answer Zoroaster's questions. This occurs early on, setting the stage for the governing (but not sole) form of the document:

The Omniscience of Ohrmazd

This chapter: Zoroaster asked Ohrmazd: "Are you wise and omniscient?"

And Ohrmazd said: "I am wise and omniscient."

And Zoroaster said: "Of what nature is your wisdom?"

Ohrmazd said: "My wisdom is such that if they take all the milk of every (living) thing into one cup, then I know how to tell one by one separately from whose breast (the milk comes); and if they let all the water which is in the world (flow) into one place, I know how to tell one by one separate(ly) from which spring (the water comes); and if they compress (together) finely all the plants which are in all the world, I know how to put them back one by one into their own place."[1]

But the same form persists when mere factual information, rules of conduct, for example, is set forth, as in the following:

Bodily Effects of Sins and Good Deeds

And this also he asked of Ohrmazd: "If a man commits a sin (through) all (his) bodily members, then to which of his members does the evil first come?"

Ohrmazd said: "Because in the human body the organ of the tongue (is) the most valuable, then it first comes to the tongue."...

Not all of the pericopes are prefaced by the attributions to God and Zoroaster, but enough of them are to impart to the entire document the character of a writing on the authority of the communication of God to the prophet, one that provides a verbatim record of revelation, and that bears the implicit myth that the information conveyed is revealed.

The third mode of writing down a great tradition belongs only to the Bavli: rules accompanied by analytical reasoning and sustained, dialectical argument. When we see that kind of writing down in comparative context, we realize, as I shall presently explain, that the Bavli has its own, very particular theory of what it means to write down

---

[1]As before, all translations are by A.V. Williams, *The Pahlavi Rivayat Accompanying the Dadestan i Denig* (Copenhagen, 1990: The Royal Danish Academy of Sciences and Letters through Munksgaard).

the great tradition, which is to say, a definition of what constitutes the great tradition that is unique to its own authorship.

II. Myth and Rule in the Rivayats and in the Torah
(Exodus, Leviticus, Deuteronomy)

Before turning to the Bavli in its comparative context, both within Israelite writing and also in the comparison and contrast to the Iranian one, let us quickly note that the theory governing the second of the two Rivayats, the one that insists rules be encased in a myth of origin and authority, would hardly have surprised more than a few of the ancient, classical Israelite writers. Specifically, those ancient Israeli writers whose formulations of traditions – legal rules, theological norms – found their way into the Torah book insist that the traditions were spoken by God to Moses, then written down and preserved as the record of that conversation. These form the counterpart to the colloquies of Ohrmazd and Zoroaster.

The following familiar presentations, standing at the head of important pentateuchal law codes, suffice to make the point:

> In the third month, when the children of Israel had gone forth out of the land of Egypt, the same day they came into the wilderness of Sinai....And Moses went up unto God and the Lord called to him out of the mountain saying, "Thus shall you say to the house of Jacob and tell the children of Israel: 'You have seen what I did to the Egyptians, how I bore you on eagles' wings and brought you unto myself. Now therefore if you will obey me and keep my commandments, then you shall be a peculiar treasure for me above all people, for all the earth is mine; and you shall be to me a kingdom of priests and a holy nation.' These are the words which you shall speak to the children of Israel." And Moses came and called for the elders of the people and laid before them all these words that the Lord commanded him. And all the people answered in unions and said, "All that the Lord has spoken we will do...." And God spoke all these words saying, "I am the Lord your God who brought you out of the land of Egypt, out of the house of bondage....You shall have no other gods before me...."
>
> Ex. 19:1, 2-8, 20:1ff.

> And the Lord spoke to Moses, saying, "Speak to the congregation of the children of Israel and say to them, 'You shall be holy, for I the Lord your God am holy. You shall fear every man his mother and his father and keep my sabbaths, I am the Lord your God....'"
>
> Lev. 19:1-3

> And Moses called all Israel and said to them, "Hear Israel the statutes and judgments which I speak in your hearing today, that you may learn them and keep and do them. The Lord our God made a covenant with us in Horeb. The Lord did not make this covenant with our fathers, but with us, even us, who are all of us here alive this day.

And the Lord talked with you face to face in the mount out of the midst of the fire. I stood between the Lord and you at that time, to show you the word of the Lord, for you were afraid by reason of the fire, and did not go up into the mountain; saying, 'I am the Lord your God who brought you out of the Egypt, out of the house of bondage. You shall have no other gods before me....'"

Deut. 5:1-7

The pentateuchal codes invariably commence with the equivalent to Ohrmazd and Zoroaster, which is, of course, the Lord our God and Moses. In fact, we look in vain in the pentateuchal components for any representation of law that is not encompassed within a myth of God's revelation to Moses, whether elaborate, as in Exodus and Deuteronomy, or simple and merely allusive, as in Leviticus and Numbers; there is no material difference between "The Lord spoke to Moses saying, 'Speak to the congregation of that children of Israel and say to them...,'" and "And this also he asked of Ohrmazd....Ohrmazd said...."

It may fairly be asked, then does the Mishnah not come equipped with its myth of origin at Sinai? The classification of the Mishnah depends upon our view on whether tractate Avot is integral to the document or a post facto apologia. If the former, then the opening paragraphs of the document supply its myth, namely, in the orally formulated and orally transmitted revelation by God to Moses at Sinai, validated in the here and now of master-disciple relationships, with the masters standing in a direct line extending backward from the Mishnah's named authorities to Moses.

Tractate Abot 1:1

Moses received the Torah at Sinai and handed it on to Joshua, Joshua to elders, and elders to prophets. And prophets handed it on to the men of the great assembly. They said three things: Be prudent in judgment. Raise up many disciples. Make a fence for the Torah.

The list of names that commences here ends with Shammai and Hillel, who founded Houses that form a critical element in the attributive structure of the Mishnah, as well as other named figures in the line of tradition, Gamaliel, Simeon b. Gamaliel, and the like, who are the ancestors of Judah the Patriarch, to whom the publication of the Mishnah is credited.

If, therefore, we take the view that tractate Avot is integral to the Mishnah, then the Mishnah presents both rules and a myth that accounts for their origin and authority; if not, then the Mishnah is rapidly joined by such a myth; for our purposes it comes down to the same thing. If we see the Mishnah as free-standing and not encapsulated by a myth of origin and validation, the people who received it saw it otherwise. The main point is not to be missed: The Bavli differs from all these other writings, since it provides the rules with something no one else thought necessary: a vast and profound capsule of critical thought and analysis. No other writing in ancient Israel, and none we have noted in the ninth-century Pahlavi books, suggests that any other authorship considered such a possibility; the Bavli in that context is original and indeed unique. But, when we understand what is at stake, we shall also know the reason why.

III. The Rule and Its Amplification in the Yerushalmi

Any statement regarding the Talmud of Babylonia in the setting of comparison forthwith introduces the other Talmud, the one of the Land of Israel known as the Yerushalmi. The context of comparison begins, after all, not on the other side of the boundary but at home, and the Yerushalmi, heir to the same Mishnah as the Bavli, formed as a commentary and amplification of that document just as is the Bavli, demands comparison with the Bavli. The Yerushalmi and the Bavli form species of a single genus, talmud, meaning, a sustained, analytical commentary to the Mishnah; another, distinct species of that genus, which is the Tosefta, a compilation of supplements, need not detain us here.

Having announced that the Bavli is original and unique, let me spell out the challenge to that statement presented by the Yerushalmi. That writing, too, transcribes the Mishnah together with traditions for posterity. It, too, serves the Mishnah as a protracted restatement. But the Yerushalmi's choices on how to present the Mishnah, when compared with and contrasted to the Bavli's, underline the latter's quite distinctive mode of writing down the great tradition. It differs because, as we shall now see, for the framers of the Yerushalmi, it suffices to present a rule and then to amplify or clarify that same rule. So the Yerushalmi provides us with a variation of the Mishnah's and Aturfarnbag's classification of tradition: rules lacking a substantial myth of origin and authority, but provided with (in this case) a very rich secondary layer of amplification. In the rivayats, here and there, we see the germ of such a counterpart amplification, for example, secondary questions, theoretical problems, sometimes encased in the formulation of the question. So in the Yerushalmi we do not travel far from the Iranian counterparts in the same enterprise.

Because the contrast between the Yerushalmi and the later Talmud, the Bavli, as much as between the Rivayats and the Bavli, yields the conclusion of this study, we require attention to the traits of the Yerushalmi on its own, so let us briefly examine the Yerushalmi's treatment of the same Mishnah passage dealt with in Chapter Three by the Bavli abstract given there. I abbreviate as before.

Yerushalmi Tractate Baba Mesia 1:1

- [A] [7d] Two [in court] lay hold of a cloak –
- [B] this one says, "I found it!" –
- [C] and that one says, "I found it!" –
- [D] this one says, "It's all mine!" –
- [E] and that one says. "It's all mine!" –
- [F] this one takes an oath that he has no less a share of it than half,
- [G] and that one takes an oath that he has no less a share of it than half.
- [H] And they divide it up.
- [I] This one says, "It's all mine!" –
- [J] and that one says, "Half of it is mine!" –
- [K] the one who says, "It's all mine," takes an oath that he has no less a share of it than three parts,
- [L] and the one who says, "Half of it is mine," takes an oath that he has no less a share of it than a fourth part.
- [M] This one then takes three shares, and that one takes the fourth.

- [I.A] [The following is a paraphrase of T. Shebu. 5:3, which is as follows: If the plaintiff was claiming a maneh in the presence of a court, and the defendant denied it, and two witnesses came and gave testimony that he owes him fifty zuz, lo, this one pays (fifty zuz) and is exempt from the requirement of taking an oath. But if there was only a single witness who was giving evidence against him, lo, this one takes an oath covering the whole amount.] It was taught: A man who said to his fellow, "Give me the maneh which you owe me!"
- [B] The other said to him, "It never happened!"
- [C] The lender went and brought witnesses that he owes him fifty zuz....
- [D] [Concerning the foregoing case,] R. Hiyya the Elder said, "The admission by witnesses [that the man owes the money] is tantamount to his own admission [that he owes part of the debt, namely, the fifty zuz which the witnesses say has been lent out of the hundred claimed by the creditor],
- [E] "and consequently, the borrower must take an oath covering the remainder [of what has been claimed by the creditor]."
- [F] R. Yohanan said, "The admission by witnesses is by no means tantamount to his own admission which would produce the consequence that the borrower must taken an oath covering the remainder [and he need not do so]."

All of this is interesting but has no bearing upon our passage. This part of the treatment of the Mishnah passage in fact serves a different Mishnah paragraph altogether, one in Mishnah-tractate Shabuot. In fact, this Talmud composition serves a different Mishnah passage altogether. In the following statement, the reason for its inclusion is introduced:

[G]	Said Rabbi, "The position of R. Hiyya the Elder derives from **Two in court lay hold of a cloak [M. B.M. 1:1A-H]**. Since the man is holding on to half of [the cloak], it is as if he brought witnesses to court that half of it belongs to him.
[H]	"And you then rule that he takes an oath [as at M. 1:1F, G] and retains possession of the half in his hand. Now this case before us is similar to that case. [Possession of the cloak is deemed parallel to having witnesses to ownership thereof.]"
[II.A]	Rabbah bar Mamal and R. Mamal introduced the following issue of Rab into [the present discussion]:
[B]	[Rab] said to [R. Hiyya], "Do they then not hand over an oath [for swearing by] someone suspect of lying [under oath!] [For the debtor of T. Shebu. 5:3, cited above, has alleged that he owes nothing. The witnesses prove that he is a liar. How then can he take an oath covering the remainder, since he is a known perjurer?]"
[C]	He said to him, "Even a statement using the language of an oath [but omitting the operative clauses] they do not hand over to him."
[III.A]	**[With reference to M. 1:1F, G: This one takes an oath that he has no less a share of it than half...,]** how does he then swear? [What sort of language is used here? For the claim is that the man owns not less than half of the cloak. Even if the man owns none of the cloak, he can make that statement without in fact lying under oath, since, indeed, he does not own less than half, for he owns none of it.]
[B]	R. Huna said, "'By an oath! I have a right to it, and I own no less of it than part worth a perutah.' [By using this language, the problem of A is avoided. These are meaningful statements.]"
[IV.A]	[Reverting to I.G,] said R. Yohanan, "If from this matter [that the parallel to M. B.M. 1:1 is decisive], you prove that an oath is required, then it is an oath [at M. B.M. 1:1] which has been ordained as a remedy [by the rabbis]. Each party may take that same oath. Why should they not divide the claimed cloak without taking any oath at all insofar as their actual possession is the equivalent of witnesses to their claim. Accordingly, the case of M. B.M. 1 is not pertinent to the matter under discussion at T. Shebu. 5:3 at all, with the consequence that the claim of Rabbi is not valid.]"

The obvious question to someone who knows the Mishnah will be the relationship between the oath of which M. B.M. 1:1 speaks and the larger theory of oaths at tractate Shebuot, concerning oaths in general. This is what is accomplished at units I, II, and IV, interrupted by the brief interpolation at unit III. The discussion is formally disjointed but substantively coherent. Units V and VI (not given here) then move on, quite systematically, to important ideas of T., with the former analyzed, the latter simply cited for information. A glance back at the treatment of the same Mishnah paragraph by the Bavli shows that we are in a different world altogether. A brief further abstract suffices to show how the two Talmuds radically differ.

Y. 1:2

- [A] Two were riding on a beast,
- [B] or one was riding and one was leading it –
- [C] this one says, "It's all mine!" –
- [D] and that one says, "It's all mine!" –
- [E] this one takes an oath that he has no less a share of it than half,
- [F] and that one takes an oath that he has no less a share of it than half.
- [G] And they divide it.
- [H] But when they concede [that they found it together] or have witnesses to prove it, they divide it without taking an oath.

- [I.A] Said R. Huna, "There it is taught:
- [B] "A woman who was riding along on a beast, with two *men* leading it,
- [C] "[and she comes to court and claims,] 'These are my slaves, and the ass and its burden belong to me,'
- [D] "while this one says, 'This is my wife, and the other man is my slave, and the ass and its burden are mine,'
- [E] "and the other party claims, 'This is my wife, and the other man is my slave, and the ass and its burden are mine' –
- [F] "she requires a writ of divorce from each of the men, and she must also declare both of them free men.
- [G] "And both of them issue writs of emancipation to one another.
- [H] "And as to the ass and its burden, all three of them lay an equal claim [and divide it up]."

The Talmud's case is a variation on M.'s. That, sum and substance, is Yerushalmi to M. 1:1-2. Now to define the Yerushalmi in particular, we compare how the Yerushalmi and the Bavli intersect. First, let us compare the two Talmuds overall, then focus upon the one point at which they do come together. Y. to M. 1:1 commences with an introduction of a parallel case, which makes reference to our Mishnah rule. Y. proceeds to ask about the language that is used for the oath, but Y. 1:1 III turns out to pertain to the analysis of the passage in T. Shebu. 5:3, not here. Then Y. concludes with two Tosefta passages. Y. to 1:2 paraphrases M.'s case with a variation thereon. So much for the Yerushalmi. What we have is scarcely a sketch of a discussion.

If we had to spell out the Yerushalmi's framers' theory of making a talmud, it would be, show the interrelationships of Mishnah rules (the conception of an oath in tractate Shabuot and its use in tractate Baba Mesia) through an analysis of Tosefta's complement to the Mishnah – that much. Now within that program, we may not then say that the work we do have is primitive, since Y. 1:1 II-IV certainly prove to the contrary. In formal traits and intellectual morphology I could not distinguish this Talmud composition from any other. So what we have before us is not a "very early" or "undeveloped" talmud, not at all; we have a perfectly vivid and intellectually sophisticated talmud. Y. 1:1 V, VI, to be sure, seem perfunctory, and on the strength of Y. 1:2 I, we could never have predicted the genius of the Yerushalmi. Whether or not Yerushalmi Baba Mesia (and companions) is earlier than the rest of its Talmud, it is different from the rest.

Looking back to Chapter Three, we see that the Bavli's program is an elaborate and systematic one. The Bavli begins with a sustained analysis of the language of the Mishnah. As usual, that is the Bavli's favorite starting point. We proceed on the basis of that analysis to ask about the implications of our result. We move next to the principles that operate here, identifying the various premises that come into play. The third layer of analysis brings cases into juxtaposition and compares them through analogies. And at the end of our reading of M. 1:1 we move into entirely speculative territory, crossing the borders of the Mishnah paragraph entirely. It may be argued that the reading of M. 1:1 calls into action the most sophisticated minds of Talmud composition, so it is not only unfair, it is downright impertinent to compare the Yerushalmi at its worst with the Bavli at its best. But Bavli's reading of M. 1:2 brings us back to earth. Here, the Bavli investigates the principles in play through a clarification of the possibilities of reading the Mishnah rule itself. Its real point of interest is in the theory behind acquiring title to an object, that is, the basic conception of transferring ownership.

Clearly, the later Talmud, the Bavli, has no interest in the earlier one and finds nothing to copy or carry forward in the prior document, if its authors knew it at all. Yet, since the two Talmuds meet at the Mishnah (and the Tosefta), comparison between them for the purpose of differentiating the later from the earlier writing is certainly justified. In this mass of material, is there no point of intersection? Happily, there is one, and here we are able to see how the two Talmuds treat precisely the same statement:

[V.A]	It was taught: **Two who were laying hold of a document [bond]** –	5. A.	We have learned on Tannaite authority:
[B]	this one says, "It is mine, and I lost it!"	B.	"**Two were holding on to a bond** –
[C]	And that one says, "It was in my possession, and I already paid you for it!" –	C.	"the lender says, 'It's mine and fell from me and I found it.'
[D]	"Let the document be confirmed through	D.	"The borrower says, 'It's yours, but I paid it off' –
		E.	"let the bond be confirmed by its

the signatures of the witnesses which it bears," the words of Rabbi.

[E] And (Rabban Simeon b.) Gamaliel says, "Let them divide it [the money] between them" [T. B.M 1:15]. [Rabbi's position is that the former admits that he has written the bond and it is necessary to confirm the bond. If the creditor is able to do so, he has a valid claim and divides up the money covered by the bond. If not, the creditor has no share in the proceeds of the bond. Simeon Bavli Gamaliel's position is that it is not necessary even to confirm the bond; in any event the claimants divide the funds at issue.]

[F] R. Eleazar said, "All follows the circumstance of which of the claimants holds the part on which the witnesses have signed their names. [The party holding the part of the bond containing the confirmation by witnesses is the one who wins the case.]"

[G] Said R. Hisda, "If you accept this view, you accord with the position of R. Simeon [b. Gamaliel]. [But Rabbi will want the witnesses to confirm the bond in court.]"

F. signatories [verifying their signatures]," the words of Rabbi. Rabban Simeon Bavli Gamaliel says, "Let them divide it up."

G. If it came into the possession of a judge, he may never again produce it.

H. R. Yosé says, "Lo, it remains subject to the presumption pertaining to it [that it is valid, and the creditor may demand return of the document and collect on the strength of it]."

6. A. [Analyzing the passage just now cited,] a master has said, "'Let the bond be confirmed by its signatories [verifying their signatures]'" – *and may the lender then collect on the strength of the bond the whole of the debt confirmed therein?! Does not the master concur with our Mishnah paragraph:* **Two lay hold of a cloak?**

B. *Said Raba said R. Nahman, "In a case in which the document is confirmed [in court, with the witnesses verifying their signatures and the judges the endorsement], all parties concur that the two litigants are to divide the contested sum. Where they differ is in a case in which the document is not confirmed in court.*

C. *"Rabbi takes the view that if the debtor concedes that he has written* a bond, nonetheless it is necessary to confirm the signatories, and, if it is confirmed in court, then the contested sum is divided, and if it is not confirmed in court, there is no division at all. What is his reasoning? It is a mere sherd [if the document is not confirmed in court, and has no value whatever]. For, under these conditions, by what testimony is the bond validated anyhow? It is by the testimony of the borrower – who also maintains that he has paid!

D. "And Rabban Simeon Bavli Gamaliel takes the view that in the case of one who concedes in the case of a bond that he has written it, it is not necessary to confirm the document, and even though it is not confirmed, the litigants divide the contested sum." [Daiches: Even if the bill is not endorsed, the borrower cannot plead that he has paid the debt when the lender produces the document. The validity of the document does not depend on the plea of the borrower to that extent. Hence they divide the amount.]

The Tosefta passage is identical in both Talmuds. The Yerushalmi (F) explains the positions taken in the Tosefta passage and their implications (G). The Bavli draws the passage into relationship to our Mishnah rule and proposes that it conforms to the premise of that rule (6.A). Then we proceed to isolate the situation concerning which Rabbi and Simeon

Bavli Gamaliel his father disagree, 6.B-C. As is clear from 6.C, this speculative reading draws us far afield. Now at issue is the status of the bond.

So how do the Talmuds compare? The first Talmud analyzes evidence, the second investigates premises; the first remains wholly within the limits of its case, the second vastly transcends them; and the first wants to know the rule, the second asks about the principle and its implications for other cases. The one Talmud provides an exegesis and amplification of the Mishnah, the other, a theoretical study of the law in all its magnificent abstraction – transforming the Mishnah into testimony to a deeper reality altogether: to the law behind the laws. We shall continue this comparison when we return to describe the Bavli in its own framework. It suffices to say quite simply: The Yerushalmi is a work of competence; the Bavli is a work of genius. But that judgment on the quality of mind of the two documents hardly answers our question: How shall we characterize the Bavli's theory of how the great tradition is to be written down, and of what does the great tradition consist?

IV. The Rule and Its Reason in the Bavli

To this point we have concentrated on the facts generated solely by the documents under examination. Here I introduce the first, and only, fact we require from history. It is beyond any doubt: The Bavli exercised hegemony in Judaism from its closure to the present day. That fact places a new light on the problem with which we deal.

From the presentation of the Bavli, that document has served as the summa of Judaism. Through the Bavli, all prior Judaic writings deemed canonical, except for Scripture, reached posterity; and Scripture was mediated through the prism of the Bavli as well. Viewed theologically, the Judaic systems that succeeded from then to now have referred back to the Bavli as authoritative; formulated their statements in relationship to the Bavli, often in the guise of commentaries or secondary expositions of statements made in it; taken over the Bavli as the backbone for the law and culture that these continuator and successor systems proposed to set forth.

More than any other single characteristic, the hegemony of the Bavli over the intellect of that Judaism for the community of the believers distinguishes the true from the heretical in Judaism. To establish a truth, appeal to the highest court formed by those who have mastered the Bavli, its commentaries, codes, and accompanying response, alone would serve. And, finally, studying the Bavli so as to reconstruct the ancient conversations and arguments preserved there in notes and not in fully spelled-out form constituted an act equivalent in Judaic religious life to prayer, on the one side, and acts of supererogatory grace, on the other: study, prayer, acts of loving kindness together defined the Judaic way of life. And study meant, and now means, starting with the Bavli.

Why the Bavli and not the Yerushalmi? What distinguished the Bavli from that and all other writings? As I shall now explain, the Bavli's unique contribution was to insist that truths form one truth, so that, understood at the most profound levels of abstraction, the Torah's rules of thought and life really could be stated in a few, simple, comprehensive, and utterly cogent ways: abstract truth sustaining concrete truths. The power of the Bavli's analytical method lay in the demonstration of the unity and coherence of truth, on the one side, and the priority of critical, sustained, contentious argument in the discovery of truth, on the other. Since (in this context) these form theological judgments about religious truth and intellect, we may say, the Bavli reframed the very character of tradition. The Bavli is a theological statement of a religious system. Then how do the Talmuds compare, and why do I find in the results of comparison the Bavli's uniqueness in the context of how ancient writers wrote down their ancient, encompassing traditions? The Bavli is in quality and character different from the Yerushalmi, so different that the two Talmuds are incomparable.

The Yerushalmi talks in details, the Bavli, in large truths. The Yerushalmi tells us what the Mishnah says, the Bavli, what it means. By its dialectical arguments, the Bavli exposes how the Mishnah's laws form law, the way in which its rules attest to the ontological unity of truth. The distinction between the documents lies in the quality of mind that characterizes each. The Bavli not only thinks more deeply about deep things; its authors think about different things from those that occupy the writers of the Yerushalmi. The first Talmud analyzes evidence, the second investigates premises; the first remains wholly within the limits of its case, the second vastly transcends them; and the first wants to know the rule, the second asks about the principle and its implications for other cases. The one Talmud provides an exegesis and amplification of the Mishnah, the other, a theoretical study of the law in all its magnificent abstraction – transforming the Mishnah into testimony to a deeper reality altogether: to the law behind the laws.

To make these points stick, we turn to examine in some detail how the two Talmuds read Mishnah-tractate Gittin 1:1.[2] The Bavli continues the analysis for many pages; I give only its initial components, the

---

[2]Further examples and full discussion will be found in my seven-volume monograph, *The Bavli's Unique Voice. A Systematic Comparison of the Talmud of Babylonia and the Talmud of the Land of Israel* (Atlanta, 1993: Scholars Press for South Florida Studies in the History of Judaism).

Ways of Writing Down Great Traditions in Israel and Iran 179

character of the rest being clear from these. For the Yerushalmi I present the entire unit. What we compare is the structure of analysis, and that will become clear when the sequence of initiatives is fully exposed. Let us first look at the passage and the way that the Yerushalmi reads it.

Yerushalmi to Mishnah-tractate Gittin 1:1

[A] [43a] He who delivers a writ of divorce from overseas must state, "In my presence it was written, and in my presence it was signed."

[I.A] Now here is a problem. In the case of one who brings a deed of gift from overseas, does he have to state, "Before me it was written and before me it was signed"? [Why is the rule stricter for writs of divorce?]

[B] R. Joshua b. Levi said, "The case [of writs of divorce] is different, for [overseas] they are not expert in the details of preparing writs of divorce [properly]."

[C] Said R. Yohanan, "It is a lenient ruling which [sages] have provided for her, that she should not sit an abandoned wife [unable to remarry]."

[D] And is this a lenient ruling? It is only a stringent one, for if the messenger did not testify, "In my presence it was written, and in my presence it was signed," you are not indeed going to permit the woman to remarry [at all], [so what sort of a lenient ruling do we have here]?

[E] Said R. Yosé, "The strict requirement which you have imposed on the matter at the outset, requiring the messenger to testify, 'Before me it was written and before me it was signed,' turns out to be a lenient ruling which you have set for the case at the end. For if the husband later on should come and call into question the validity of the document, his cavil will be null."

[F] [As to the denial of credibility to the husband's challenge to the validity of the writ of divorce,] R. Mana contemplated ruling, "That applies to a complaint dealing with matters external to the body of the document itself."

[G] But as to a complaint as to the body of the document itself [do we believe him]? [Surely we take seriously his claim that the document is a forgery.]

[H] And as to a complaint [against the writ] which has no substance [one may not take the husband's cavil seriously].

[I] And even in the case of a cavil which has substance [should he not be believed]? [Surely he should be believed.]

[J] Said R. Yosé b. R. Bun, "[No, the original statement stands in all these cases.] [That is to say,] since you have said that the reason you have applied in the case a more stringent requirement at the outset, that the messenger must declare, 'Before me it was [written, and before me it was] signed,' is that you have imposed a lenient ruling at the end, for if the husband later on should come and call into question the validity of the document, his cavil will be null, and we must conclude that there is no difference at all whether the complaint against the validity of the document pertains to matters external to the body of the document or to matters internal to the body of the document, nor is there any difference whether the complaint deals with matters of no substance or matters of substance. [Once the necessary formula is recited by the messenger, the document has been validated against all future doubts.]"

[K] And yet should one not take into account that invalid witnesses may have signed the document?

[L] Said R. Abun, "The husband is not suspect of disrupting [the wife's future marriage] in a matter which is in the hands of Heaven, [but is suspect of doing so only in a matter which lies before a court]. [Hence we do not take account of the husband's issuing such a complaint as is entered at G.]

[M] "In a court proceeding he is suspect of disrupting the wife's [future marriage]. For since he knows full well that if he should come and register a complaint against the validity of the document, his complaint will be deemed null, even he sees to it [when he prepares the writ] that it is signed by valid witnesses."

Unit I clarifies the force of the required declaration. Once the messenger so states, the husband cannot later on invalidate the document. Since, in the meantime, it is assumed that the wife will remarry, the importance of limiting the original husband's power is self-evident. That, sum and substance, is what interests the Yerushalmi.

Now let us see how the Bavli reads the same paragraph. I give only part of the discussion, the first four units of a score of paragraphs – enough so that the point is abundantly clear.

Bavli to Mishnah-tractate Gittin 1:1

A. He who delivers a writ of divorce from overseas must state, "In my presence it was written, and in my presence it was signed."

B. Rabban Gamaliel says, "Also: He who delivers [a writ of divorce] from Reqem or from Heger [must make a similar declaration]."

C. R. Eliezer says, "Even from Kefar Ludim to Lud."

D. And sages say, "He must state, 'In my presence it was written, and in my presence it was signed,' only in the case of him who delivers a writ of divorce from overseas,

E. "and him who takes [one abroad]."

F. And he who delivers [a writ of divorce] from one overseas province to another must state, "In my presence it was written, and in my presence it was signed."

G. Rabban Simeon b. Gamaliel says, "Even [if he brings one] from one jurisdiction to another [in the same town]."

The interest of the Bavli is in the premise of the opening rule, and we shall see how the Bavli presents the two competing theories on the operative consideration behind the requirement of M. Git. 1:1A.

I.1   A.   What is the operative consideration here?

B. Said Rabbah, **[2B]** "Because [Israelites overseas] are inexpert in the requirement that the writ be prepared for the particular person for whom it is intended."

C. Raba said, "Because valid witnesses are not readily found to confirm the signatures [and the declaration of the agent serves to authenticate the signatures of the witnesses]."

D. *So what is at issue between these two explanations?*

E. *At issue between them is a case in which two persons brought the writ of divorce [in which case Raba's consideration is null], or a case in which a writ of divorce was brought from one province to another in the Land of Israel [in which case the consideration of Rabbah is null], or from one place to another in the same overseas province.*

We proceed to challenge each position in sequence, giving the other party the opportunity for a full and thorough reply. So the remainder is made up of thrust and parry, proposal and counterproposal, evidence and argument, contrary evidence and refutation.

I.2 A. *And from the perspective of Rabbah, who has said, "Because [Israelites overseas] are inexpert in the requirement that the writ be prepared for the particular person for whom it is intended,"* there should still be a requirement that the writ of divorce is brought by two persons, such as is the requirement in respect to all acts of testimony that are spelled out in the Torah [in line with Deut. 19:15]!

B. An individual witness is believed where the question has to do with a prohibition [for example, as to personal status, but not monetary matters].

C. *Well, I might well concede that we do hold,* an individual witness is believed where the question has to do with a prohibition, *for example, in the case of a piece of fat, which may be forbidden fat or may be permitted fat, in which instance the status of a prohibition has not yet been assumed. But here, with regard to the case at hand, where the presence of a prohibition is assumed,* namely, that the woman is married, it amounts to *a matter involving prohibited sexual relations, and a matter involving sexual relations is settled by no fewer than two witnesses.*

D. Most overseas Israelites are expert in the rule that the document has to be written for the expressed purpose of divorcing this particular woman.

E. *And even R. Meir, who takes account of not only the condition of the majority but even that of the minority [in this case, people not expert in that rule], concedes the ordinary scribe of a court knows the law full well, and it was rabbis who imposed the requirement. But here* **[3A]** *so as to prevent the woman from entering the status of a deserted wife [unable to remarry], they made the rule lenient.*

F. *Is this really a lenient ruling? It is in fact a strict ruling, since, if you require that the writ of divorce be brought by two messengers, there is no possibility of the husband's coming and challenging its validity and having it invalidated, but if only one person brings the document, he can still do so!*

G. Since the master has said, "As to how many persons must be present when the messenger hands over the writ of divorce to the wife, there is a dispute between R. Yohanan and R. Hanina. One party maintains it must be at least two, the other three." *Now, since that is the fact, the messenger will clarify the husband's intentions to begin with, and the husband under such circumstances is not going to come and try to invalidate the writ and so get himself into trouble later on.*

I.3 A. *Now from the perspective of Raba, who said that the operative consideration is,* "Because valid witnesses are not readily found to confirm the signatures [and the declaration of the agent serves to authenticate the signatures of the witnesses]," *there should still be a requirement that the writ of divorce is brought by two persons, such as is the requirement in respect to all acts of confirming the validity of documents in general!*

B. An individual witness is believed where the question has to do with a prohibition [for example, as to personal status, but not monetary matters].

C. Well, I might well concede that *we do hold,* an individual witness is believed where the question has to do with a prohibition, *for example, in the case of a piece of fat, which may be forbidden fat or may be permitted fat, in which instance the status of a prohibition has not yet been assumed. But here, with regard to the case at hand, where the presence of a prohibition is assumed, namely, that the woman is married, it amounts to a matter involving prohibited sexual relations, and a matter involving sexual relations is settled by no fewer than two witnesses.*

D. Well, in strict law, there should be no requirement that witnesses confirm the signature on other documents either, in line with what R. Simeon b. Laqish said, *for* said R. Simeon b. Laqish, "Witnesses who have signed a document are treated as equivalent to those who have been cross-examined in court." *It was rabbis who imposed the requirement. But here so as to prevent the woman from entering the status of a deserted wife [unable to remarry], they made the rule lenient.*

E. Is this really a lenient ruling? It is in fact a strict ruling, since, if you require that the writ of divorce be brought by two messengers, there is no possibility of the husband's coming and challenging its validity and having it invalidated, but if only one person brings the document, he can still do so!

F. Since the master has said, "As to how many persons must be present when the messenger hands over the writ of divorce to the wife, there is a dispute between R. Yohanan and R. Hanina. One party maintains it must be at least two, the other three." *Now, since that is the fact, the messenger will clarify the husband's intentions to begin with, and the husband under such circumstances is not going to come and try to invalidate the writ and so get himself into trouble later on.*

I.4 A. So how come Raba didn't give the operative consideration that Rabbah did?

B. He will say to you, "Does the Tannaite rule state, **In my presence it was written** for the purpose of divorcing this woman in particular, **and in my presence it was signed** for the purpose of divorcing this woman in particular?"

C. And Rabbah?

D.	Strictly speaking, it should have been formulated for Tannaite purposes in that way. But if you get verbose, the bearer may omit something that is required.
E.	Yeah, well, even as it is, the bearer may omit something that is required!
F.	One out of three phrases he may leave out, but one out of two phrases he's not going to leave out.
G.	So how come Rabbah didn't give the operative consideration that Raba did?
H.	He will say to you, "If so, the Tannaite formulate should be, **In my presence it was signed** – and nothing more! What need do I have for the language, **In my presence it was written**? That is to indicate that we require that the writ be prepared for the sole purpose of divorcing this particular woman.
I.	And Raba?
J.	Strictly speaking, it should have been formulated for Tannaite purposes in that way. But if it were done that way, people might come to confuse the matter of the confirmation of documents in general and hold that only a single witness is required for that purpose.
K.	And Rabbah?
L.	But is the parallel all that close? There the required language is, "We know that this is Mr. So-and-so's signature," while here it is, "In my presence...." In that case, a woman is not believed to testify, in this case, a woman is believed to testify. In that case, an interested party cannot testify, here an interested party can testify.
M.	And Raba?
N.	He will say to you, "Here, too, if the agent says, 'I know...,' he is believed, and since that is the fact, there really is the consideration [if he says only, 'In my presence it was signed' (Simon)], *people might come to confuse the matter of the confirmation of documents in general and hold that only a single witness is required for that purpose.*"

At their reading of M. Gittin 1:1, where the Talmuds intersect but diverge in the reading of the Mishnah paragraph, we are able to identify what is at issue. Here is an occasion on which we can see the differences between the Yerushalmi's and the Bavli's representation of a conflict of principles contained within a Mishnah ruling. The Yerushalmi maintains that at issue is the inexpertness of overseas courts vs. a lenient ruling to avoid the situation of the abandoned wife; the Bavli, inexpertness of overseas courts vs. paucity of witnesses.

The Bavli stands on its own not only because its framers think differently; nor merely because their modes of thought and analysis in no way correspond to those of the Yerushalmi. The governing reason is that, for the framers of the Bavli, what is at stake in thought is different from the upshot of thought as conceived by the authors of the Yerushalmi's compositions and compilers of its composites. Specifically, for the sages who produced the Bavli, the ultimate compilers and redactors of the document, what is at issue is not laws but law: how things hold together at the level of high abstraction. After we have compared the Talmuds at this crucial point, I shall point to the evidence that sustains that theory of the document. I set side by side the whole of the Yerushalmi's discussion and just part of the Bavli's. The comparison makes the case, and a quick reference back to the passage we have just examined will justify the generalizations I offer at the end.

[I.A] Now here is a problem. In the case of one who brings a deed of gift from overseas, does he have to state, "Before me it was written and before me it was signed"? [Why is the rule stricter for writs of divorce?]

[B] R. Joshua b. Levi said, "The case [of writs of divorce] is different, for [overseas] they are not expert in the details of preparing writs of divorce [properly]."

[C] Said R. Yohanan, "It is a lenient ruling which [sages] have provided for her, that she should not sit an abandoned wife [unable to remarry]."

[D] And is this a lenient ruling? It is only a stringent one, for if the messenger did not testify, "In my presence it was written, and in my presence it was signed," you are not indeed going to permit the woman to remarry [at all], [so what sort of a lenient ruling do we have here]?

[E] Said R. Yosé, "The strict requirement which you have imposed on the matter at the outset, requiring the messenger to tes-

I.1 A. What is the operative consideration here?
B. Said Rabbah, [2B] "Because [Israelites overseas] are inexpert in the requirement that the writ be prepared for the particular person for whom it is intended."
C. Raba said, "Because valid witnesses are not readily found to confirm the signatures [and the declaration of the agent serves to authenticate the signatures of the witnesses]."
D. *So what is at issue between these two explanations?*
E. *At issue between them is a case in which two persons brought the writ of divorce [in which case Raba's consideration is null], or a case in which a writ of divorce was brought from one province to another in the Land of Israel [in which case the consideration of Rabbah is null], or from one place to another in the same overseas province.*

I.2 A. *And from the perspective of Rabbah, who has said, "Because [Israelites overseas] are inexpert in the requirement that the writ be prepared for the particu-*

Ways of Writing Down Great Traditions in Israel and Iran

[F] tify, 'Before me it was written and before me it was signed,' turns out to be a lenient ruling which you have set for the case at the end. For if the husband later on should come and call into question the validity of the document, his cavil will be null."

[F] [As to the denial of credibility to the husband's challenge to the validity of the writ of divorce,] R. Mana contemplated ruling, "That applies to a complaint dealing with matters external to the body of the document itself."

[G] But as to a complaint as to the body of the document itself [do we believe him]? [Surely we take seriously his claim that the document is a forgery.]

[H] And as to a complaint [against the writ] which has no substance [one may not take the husband's cavil seriously].

[I] And even in the case of a cavil which has substance [should he not be believed]? [Surely he should be believed.]

[J] Said R. Yosé b. R. Bun, "[No, the original statement stands in all these cases]. [That is to say,] since you have said that the reason you have applied in the case a more strin-

lar person for whom it is intended," *there should still be a requirement that the writ of divorce is brought by two persons, such as is the requirement in respect to all acts of testimony that are spelled out in the Torah [in line with Deut. 19:15]!*

B. An individual witness is believed where the question has to do with a prohibition [for example, as to personal status, but not monetary matters].

C. *Well, I might well concede that we do hold,* an individual witness is believed where the question has to do with a prohibition, *for example, in the case of a piece of fat, which may be forbidden fat or may be permitted fat, in which instance the status of a prohibition has not yet been assumed. But here, with regard to the case at hand, where the presence of a prohibition is assumed, namely, that the woman is married, it amounts to a matter involving prohibited* gent requirement at the outset, that the messenger must declare, 'Before me it was [written, and before me it was] signed,' is that you have imposed a lenient ruling at the end, for if the husband later on should come and call into question the validity of the document, his cavil will be null, and we must conclude that there is no difference at all whether the complaint against the validity of the document pertains to matters external to the body of the document or to matters internal to the body of the document, nor is there any difference whether the complaint deals with matters of no substance or matters of substance. [Once the necessary formula is recited by the messenger, the document has been validated against all future doubts.]"

[K] And yet should one not take into account that invalid witnesses may have signed the docu-ment?

[L] Said R. Abun, "The husband is not suspect of disrupting [the wife's future marriage] in a matter which is in the hands of Heaven, [but is suspect of doing so only in a matter which

sexual relations, and a matter involving sexual relations is settled by no fewer than two witnesses.

D. Most overseas Israelites are expert in the rule that the document has to be written for the expressed purpose of divorcing this particular woman.

E. *And even R. Meir, who takes account of not only the condition of the majority but even that of the minority [in this case, people not expert in that rule], concedes the ordinary scribe of a court knows the law full well, and it was rabbis who imposed the requirement. But here [3A] so as to prevent the woman from entering the status of a deserted wife [unable to remarry], they made the rule lenient.*

F. *Is this really a lenient ruling? It is in fact a strict ruling, since, if you require that the writ of divorce be brought by two messengers, there is no possibility of the husband's coming and challenging its validity and having it invalidated, but if only one person brings the document, he can still do so!*

G. Since the master has said, "As to how many persons must be present when the messenger hands over the writ of divorce to the wife, there is a dispute between R. Yohanan and R. Hanina. One lies before a court]. [Hence we do not take account of the husband's issuing such a complaint as is entered at G.]

[M] "In a court proceeding he is suspect of disrupting the wife's [future marriage]. For since he knows full well that if he should come and register a complaint against the validity of the document, his complaint will be deemed null, even he sees to it [when he prepares the writ] that it is signed by valid witnesses."

party maintains it must be at least two, the other three." *Now, since that is the fact, the messenger will clarify the husband's intentions to begin with, and the husband under such circumstances is not going to come and try to invalidate the writ and so get himself into trouble later on.*

The Bavli proceeds in the same fair and balanced manner to expose the dispute of Yohanan and Joshua b. Levi. But enough has been given to provide a full grasp of the Bavli's intellectual morphology. Here the Yerushalmi, as much as the Bavli, presents a sustained argument, not just a snippet of self-evidently informative information, as at its reading of M. B.M. 1:1. So we now examine a fully exposed argument in the Yerushalmi as against its counterpart in the Bavli.

The Yerushalmi presents two theses, A-C, then challenges the second of the two, D-E. This produces a secondary inspection of the facts of the matter, F-I, and a resolution of the issues raised, J; then another secondary issue, K-M. Is there an *Auseinandersetzung* between the two conflicting parties, Joshua b. Levi and Yohanan? Not at all. There is, in fact, no exchange at all. Instead of a dialogue, formed into an ongoing set of challenges, we have the voice of the Talmud intervening, "And is this a lenient ruling at all?" There is no pretense that Joshua asks a question to Yohanan, or Yohanan to Joshua. The controlling voice is that of the Talmud itself, which sets up pieces of information and manipulates them. B. I.5, by contrast, presents us with one of the Bavli's many superb representations of issues, and we see that the goal of contention is not argument for its own sake, nor is the medium the message, as some have imagined. B. at I.1 states the contrary explanations and identifies the issues between them. Then one position is examined, challenged, defended – fully exposed. The second position is given equal attention, also challenged, also defended, in all, fully exposed. The two positions having been fairly stated and amply argued, we proceed to the nub of the matter: if X is so right, then why has Y not adopted his position? And if Y, then why not X? This second level of exchange allows each position to be redefended, reexplained, reexposed – all on fresh grounds. Now at this point, we have identified two or more principles that have been combined to yield a position before us, so the question arises, what authority, among those who stand behind the law, holds these positions, which, while not contradictory, also are not commonly combined in a single theory of the law? I.5 then exposes the several possibilities – three major authorities, each with his several positions to be spelled out and tested against the allegations at hand.

We may now generalize on the case at hand. What characterizes the Bavli and not the Yerushalmi is the search for the unitary foundations of diverse laws through an inquiry into the premises of those discrete rules, the comparison and contrast of those premises, the statement of the emergent principles, and the comparison and contrast of those principles with the ones that derive from other cases and their premises – a process, an inquiry, without end into the law behind the laws. What the Bavli wants, beyond its presentation of the positions at hand, is to draw attention to the premises of those positions, the reasoning behind them, the evidence that supports them, the argument that transforms evidence into demonstration, and even the authority, among those who settle questions by expressing opinions, who can hold the combination of principles or premises that underpin a given position.

Now, when we observe – as we might – that one Talmud is longer than the other, or one Talmud gives a fuller account than the other, we realize that such an observation is trivial. The real difference between the Talmuds emerges from this – and I state with emphasis, since here we come to the Bavli's quite original conception of what it is that comprises the great tradition: *the Bavli's completely different theory of what it wishes to investigate.* And that difference derives from why the framers of the Bavli's compositions and composites did the work to begin with. The outlines of the intellectual character of the work flow from the purpose of the project, not the reverse; and thence, the modes of thought, the specifics of analytical initiative – all these are secondary to intellectual morphology. So first comes the motivation for thought, then the morphology of thought, then the media of thought, in that order. And that leads us to the view that the Bavli has a different theory of what it is that comprises the great tradition. Clearly, the great tradition is made up of rules; on that, all parties, Judaic and Zoroastrian, concur. But what more is required? Those who add myths of origin and authority wish to persuade believers in one way, the Bavli's writers, providing their elaborate notes for the constitution of processes of analytical reasoning, wish to persuade them in another.

The difference in the definition of tradition encompasses a profound disagreement about how people are persuaded. Those who present the rules with their myth appeal to authority. The Bavli's framers who present the rules with their analytical apparatus appeal to intellect for its power of persuasion through fair and balanced argument, uncompromising contention, the power of compelling reason and fully exposed rationality. We need not reach outward toward the Zoroastrian formulations of tradition, the rivayats before us, to make that point; it would be unfair and indeed grotesque to offer such a comparison. Rather, let us continue to focus upon the Yerushalmi, where, after all, comparison is invited: two readings of a single prior document.

The difference between the Yerushalmi and the Bavli is the difference between jurisprudence and philosophy; the one is a work of exegesis in search of jurisprudential system, the other, of analysis in quest of philosophical truth. To state matters simply, the Yerushalmi presents the laws, the rule for this, the rule for that – pure and simple; "law" bears its conventional meaning of jurisprudence. The Bavli presents the law, now in the philosophical sense of the abstract issues of theory, the principles at play far beneath the surface of detailed discussion, the law behind the laws. And that, we see, is not really "law," in any ordinary sense of jurisprudence; it is law in a deeply philosophical sense: the rules that govern the way things are, that define what is proportionate and orderly and properly composed.

The reason that the Bavli does commonly what the Yerushalmi does seldom and then rather clumsily – the balancing of arguments, the careful formation of a counterpoint of reasons, the excessively fair representation of contradictory positions (why doesn't X take the position of Y? why doesn't Y take the position of X? Indeed!) – is not that the Bavli's framers are uninterested in conclusions and outcome. It is that for them, the deep structure of reason is the goal, and the only way to penetrate into how things are at their foundations is to investigate how conflicting positions rest on principles to be exposed and juxtaposed, balanced, and, if possible, negotiated, if necessary, left in the balance.

Rising above the limits of the case, let's take a metaphor from music. The Yerushalmi is an eighteenth-century fugue, the Bavli, a twentieth-century symphonic metamorphosis: not merely more complicated, but rather, a different conception altogether of what music is – and can do. And while, in the end, neither kind of music is the only valid kind, taste and judgment come into play; while we value and enjoy the simplicities of the baroque, the profundities, the inventiveness, the abstraction of our own day's music speak to us and reshape our hearing. So, too, while anyone can appreciate the direct and open clarity of the Yerushalmi (in those vast spaces of the text that are clear and accessible), no one can avoid the compelling, insistent, scrupulously fair but unrelenting command of the Bavli: see to the center of things, the core of mind, the workings of intellect in its own right.

What I find interesting therefore is that even when the facts are the same, the issues identical, and the arguments matched, the Bavli's authorship manages to lay matters out in a very distinctive way. And that way yields as a sustained, somewhat intricate argument (requiring us to keep in the balance both names and positions of authorities and also the objective issues and facts) what the Yerushalmi's method of representation gives us as a rather simple sequence of arguments. If we say that the Bavli is "dialectical," presenting a moving argument, from point to point, and the Yerushalmi is static, through such a reductive understatement we should vastly misrepresent the difference. The Yerushalmi's argument unfolds; the Bavli's argument assumes a formally static position at I.2. Rather, the Bavli's presentation is one – as we have seen before – of thrust and parry, challenge and response, assertion and counterassertion; theoretical possibility and its exposure to practical facts ("if I had to rely...I might have supposed..."); and, of course, the authorities of the Bavli (not only the framers) in the person of Abbayye are even prepared to rewrite the received Tannaite formulation. That initiative can come, I should think, only from someone totally in command of the abstractions and able to say, the details have to be this way; so the rule of mind requires; and so it shall be.

The Yerushalmi's message is that the Mishnah yields clear and present rules; its medium is the patient exegesis of Mishnah passages, the provision and analysis of facts required in the understanding of the Mishnah. That medium conveys its message about not the Mishnah alone, but – through its silences, which I think are intellectual failures of millennial dimensions – about the laws. Whether or not the same may be said of the two rivayats can be shown only by a systematic comparison of all of the writings of tradition of the ninth-century priests, and that project lies beyond the limits of this inquiry. But about the Bavli's message analyzed through the character of its medium we may be certain.

The Bavli conveys its message in a coherent and persistent manner through its ever-recurring medium of analysis and thought. We miss the point of the message if we misconstrue the medium: it is not the dialectical argument, and a mere reportage of questions and answers, thrust and parry, proposal and counterproposal – that does not accurately convey the medium of the Bavli, not at all. Where we ask for authority behind an unstated rule and find out whether the same authority is consistent as to principle in other cases altogether, where we show that authorities are consistent with positions taken elsewhere – here above all we stand in the very heart of the Bavli's message, but only if we know what is at stake in the medium of inquiry. That is the character of tradition: this rule, that law, the other theological verity, all sustained by an encompassing, extrinsic myth – or the sustained demonstration, through the internal paths of argument and contention, of how many things cohere, and all things say one thing. The intellectual prolixity of the Mishnah, the Yerushalmi, not to mention the book of Deuteronomy, the two Rivayats, and the Pursishniha, contrast with the intellectual economy of the Bavli, which needs no myth in its demonstration of the compelling authority of the truth.

V. The Bavli's Definition of Tradition

We have moved from the question of what to think to the issue of how to think, for everyone – the authors of the Iranian as much as the other Judaic writings that come down to us – but the framers of the Bavli defined tradition as the rules of right action, attitude, and conviction; they redefined tradition to encompass and lay emphasis upon modes of correct thought. Everyone else whose work we have read thought "the great tradition" consisted of information, with or without a compelling myth of authenticity and truth. The Bavli's framers define "tradition" in different terms altogether from all others. They think the tradition finds its definition not only in laws but in the law behind the laws, and they contribute to the definition of the great tradition the conception that correct logic and right reasoning define norms: attitude and modes of thought as much as action and modes of conduct. Without being told the rules, we can find the rules.

That definition emerges in the comparison with the Yerushalmi in particular. The difference is not so much in the details of law, which are mostly the same, or in the character of presentation, which in form is identical, but, rather, intellectual: the Bavli's composites' framers consistently treat as a question to be investigated the exegetical hypotheses that the Yerushalmi's compositions' authors happily accept as conclusive. All of the secondary devices of testing an allegation – a close reading of the formulation of the Mishnah, an appeal to the false conclusion such a close reading, absent a given formulation, might have yielded, to take the examples before us – serve that primary goal. The second recurrent difference is that the Bavli's framers find themselves constantly drawn toward questions of generalization and abstraction (once more: the law behind the laws), moving from case to principle to new case to new principle, then asking whether the substrate of principles forms a single, tight fabric. The Yerushalmi's authors rarely, if ever, pursue that chimera. Our comparison with the Pahlavi books should not at this point be forgotten. Like the Yerushalmi, they, too, tell us facts; like the Yerushalmi, they rarely expose the reasoning behind the facts, on the one side, or the logic that will transform facts into rules, laws into law. The Bavli stands by itself, and, I should claim, what makes it distinctive also accounts for its hegemony in Judaism and the power with which it has endowed Judaism.

But what gives the Bavli its compelling, ineluctable power to persuade, the source of the Bavli's intellectual force, is that thrust for abstraction, through generalization (and in that order, [1] generalization, toward [2] abstraction). To spell out in very simple terms what I conceive to be at issue: The way that the law behind the laws emerges is, first, generalization of a case into a principle, then, the recasting of the principle into an abstraction encompassing a variety of otherwise freestanding principles. This observation calls to mind how the Mishnah's cases time and again point toward a single abstraction, the hierarchical order of all being.[3] Here, in the Bavli, I find the counterpart and completion of the Mishnah's deepest layer of thought, which is, the intellectual medium to match the philosophical message.

That message is a theological one in philosophical form. Understanding the nature of being, the character of creation, is how the Mishnah uncovers the evidences for one God in the here and now of oxen that gore, farmers contending over a piece of property, a woman whose betrothal or writ of divorce from a prior marriage is subject to question, small things that scarcely matter, except if your ox has been gored, your land swiped, your children's status called into question because of a dubious writ of divorce. That is where people live, so that is where God must live, too. The Bavli forms the medium of the message, the instrument of tradition. The definition of tradition in the Bavli extends to the rules of rigorous, rational reasoning and applied logic which govern in the Torah. For the framers of the Bavli, the tradition hands on the rules of not only conduct but intellect, such that, without the rules in hand at all, through right thought we could ourselves construct them. So tradition is redefined by the Talmud to show age succeeding age not only what, but how God wants humanity to think, in full rationality, in rigorous inspection of contending principles to reveal the law of the gored ox, the stolen land, the miserable marriage: the broken heart of frail, injured humanity, where God lives.

---

[3] I refer to my *Judaism as Philosophy. The Method and Message of the Mishnah* (Columbia, 1991: University of South Carolina Press).

Index

Aaron, 146
Abbayye, 46, 80-81, 95, 121, 190
Abin, 78
Abin bar Hiyya, 78
Abin bar Kahana, 78
Ablat, 110
Abodah Zarah, 108
Abot, 10, 82-83, 137-138, 147-148, 169
Abraham, 113
Abun, 180, 186
Achaemenid, 4
Adda bar Ahba, 101, 110
adultery, 156
Adurbad, 147
agglutination, 13
Aha of Difti, 46, 80
Aibu, 112
Akkadian, 149
Alexander, 26-28
All-Merciful, 45, 95, 101
altar, 119
Ammi bar Hama, 45, 100-101
analogy, 77, 94, 100, 103, 120-121, 131
animal sacrifice, 30

Anklesaria, Behramgore Bahmuras, 10-11, 53, 90, 107
anoint, 155
anonymity, 21, 24, 49, 75-76, 105, 120, 130
apostasy, 1, 18-19, 24, 53, 110, 112, 133
Aqiba, 108, 119-120, 160
Aqiba b. Joseph, 160
Arab, 18
Aramaean, 112
Aramaic, 21, 34, 36, 105
argument a fortiori, 40-42
Asa, 53
Ashi, 109, 122
Assi, 78, 80-81
atonement, 66, 68, 98, 118
Aturfarnbag, 9, 11, 14, 21, 29, 51, 53, 70-71, 75-77, 82-84, 88, 90, 92-94, 97-98, 101-103, 105-110, 112-113, 117, 119, 122-123, 127, 133-134, 160, 165-166, 170
authorship, 21, 23, 26, 85, 93-94, 105, 127, 165, 168, 170, 190
Avesta, 5, 12, 21, 27-28, 55, 66, 118, 129, 131, 136, 154

Baba Mesia, 36, 150, 157, 171, 173-174

Baba Qamma, 13

Babylonia, 1-2, 4-5, 7-8, 12-13, 17, 19, 26, 29-30, 33-34, 36, 47, 49, 80, 123, 151, 170, 178

Babylonian, 12, 30, 129

Babylonian Talmud, 13, 36

Bailey, H.W., 21, 25-28

Bavli, 6-15, 17-18, 20-25, 28-29, 33-35, 38, 47-49, 53-54, 70, 76-79, 84-86, 87-90, 92-93, 97, 103, 106-107, 112, 114, 116, 123, 127-131, 133-135, 137-141, 143, 146, 151, 153-154, 159-161, 166-168, 170-178, 180, 183-184, 187-192

Ben Nannus, 39-40, 43-44

Ben Zoma, 148

betrothal, 79-81, 91-93, 192

blemish, 139

blood, 139-140

Byzantine, 18-19, 30

canon, 24-25, 29, 34, 135, 145, 177

catalogue, 148-149

childless, 91

children of Israel, 168-169

Christianity, 2, 5, 16, 18-19, 25, 28-30, 67, 106-107

cleanness, 144-145

cogency, 17, 29, 43, 47-48, 77-79, 82, 84-85, 178

commandment, 46, 61, 151, 168

comparison, 2-3, 5-11, 13-14, 16, 17, 19-22, 28-29, 42-43, 49, 53, 70, 76, 79, 83-86, 87-89, 92-93, 105, 107, 122, 127, 130, 143, 145, 149, 156, 159-160, 168, 170, 174, 177-178, 184, 188-192

comparison, documentary, 7, 10, 22, 76, 88-89, 107

comparison, episodic, 10, 88

comparison, systemic, 6-7, 10, 88

compilation, 12, 14, 22, 29, 33-34, 47, 82, 97, 110, 112, 122, 154, 170

composite, 34-35, 48-49, 79, 81-82

composites, free-standing, 48

consecration, 120-122

continuity, 19, 28

contrast, 2-3, 5, 7-9, 13, 16, 19-25, 28, 34, 43, 75, 77-78, 85, 92, 103, 110-111, 116, 128, 130, 132, 137-138, 140-141, 145, 160, 166, 168, 170, 187-188, 191

conversion, 134

corpse, 143-145

corpse uncleanness, 53, 143-144

creation, 192

cult, 84, 111

Dadestan i Denig, 9-12, 18, 21, 125, 127-128, 130, 132, 159, 167

Daiches, 37, 42, 44, 46, 176

de Menasce, 10, 21-23, 131

death, 11, 15, 19, 22, 26, 58-59, 62, 64, 80, 90, 100-101, 114-115, 128-129, 135, 141, 161

debt, 45, 64, 113-116, 171, 175-176

Index

Denkart, 10, 21, 25
Deut., 37, 78, 91, 108, 151, 169, 181, 185
Deuteronomy, 34, 168-169, 191
dialectic, 33, 49, 70, 77, 167, 178, 190
dialogue, 134, 187
Dimi, 111
disciple, 14, 17, 82-83, 112, 136-138, 145-149, 151, 160, 169
divorce, 22, 61, 70-74, 78-80, 92, 120-122, 153, 173, 179-182, 184-186, 192
doctrine, 2, 12, 15, 23, 27, 47, 131
dowry, 95-96
drink-offering, 108
Dual Torah, 34, 47, 135
Egypt, 27, 168-169
Egyptian, 144, 149, 168
Eleazar, 116, 137-138, 146, 175
Eleazar ben Arakh, 137
Eliezer, 137-138, 152, 180
Eliezer ben Hyrcanus, 137
Elijah, 42-43
English, 11, 22, 107
Epicurean, 166
Erubin, 146
eschatology, 14, 133
estate, 65, 94-97, 99-100, 113-116, 122
ethics, 25, 54
European, 9, 12
Ex., 114, 168

exegesis, 34-35, 48-49, 87, 97, 105, 108, 120, 123, 177-178, 189-191
exile, 30
Exodus, 168-169
expiation, 68, 98
Ezra, 112
festival, 84
fire, 1, 3-4, 11, 14, 128-129, 140-141, 161, 169
flux uncleanness, 144
forbidden, 90, 92, 100, 107-109, 111, 181-182, 185
fornication, 92
fraud, 45-47, 156-158
Freedman, H., 71, 121, 158
Gathas, 5, 21
gentile, 107-112
Gittin, 139, 178-180, 183
gloss, 35
God, 2, 4-6, 26, 29, 43, 47, 79, 83, 101, 111, 127-131, 133-134, 138, 146, 149, 159-161, 167-169, 192
good deed, 17, 65-66, 68, 98, 117-119, 134-136, 140, 148-151, 167
Greek, 149
guardianship, 53-61, 69, 72-74, 90, 93, 132
guilt, 83
Haggai, 155
Hama, 116
Hananiah, 137
Hanina, 182, 186

harmonization, 25, 33, 35, 43-44, 120
Heaven, 79, 128-129, 159, 166, 180, 186
Hebrew, 34, 36, 144
Helbo, 112
hermeneutics, 97, 123
hierarchy, 85, 192
high priest, 21, 130
Hillel, 137, 169
Hisda, 45, 99, 115, 175
history, 1, 3, 12, 19, 21-22, 26, 29, 85, 177
history of Judaism, 13, 178
Hiyya, 46, 109-110, 153, 172
Hiyya bar Judah, 155
Hiyya the Elder, 171-172
Holy Land, 30
Holy One, 128, 149, 160-161
Holy Place, 20, 30
Horeb, 168
House of Hillel, 91-92, 153
House of Shammai, 91-93, 153
Huna, 44-45, 155, 173
Huna b. R. Joshua, 115, 121
Huna b. Raba, 26
husband, 53-56, 58-61, 63, 69-74, 78-80, 84, 90-97, 114, 121-122, 129, 152-155, 179-182, 185-187
Hyman, A., 26
hypothesis, 110, 145, 191
Idi, 46
Idi bar Abin, 45, 96
idiom, 4, 17
idolatry, 106-108, 110-111

Ilaa, 109, 121
inheritance, 25, 48, 53, 94-96, 98, 100-102, 115, 166
intentionality, 98-100, 102, 119, 131
interpretation, 6, 8, 33-34, 145
Iran, 1, 5, 17-19, 21-22, 29-30, 49, 106, 131, 145, 165
Iranian, 1, 4, 9, 12, 17-19, 24, 29-30, 61, 67, 143, 154, 161, 168, 170, 191
Isa., 166
Isaac, 113
Ishmael, 18
Islam, 1-2, 4-5, 8, 16, 17-19, 21, 24-25, 28-30, 49, 131, 133-134
Israel, 4, 8, 12-13, 18-20, 24, 29-30, 33-34, 47, 80, 85, 106, 113, 122-123, 129, 138, 145-146, 165, 168-170, 178, 181, 184
Israelites, 26, 30, 81, 91, 107, 110-112, 166, 168, 181, 184, 186
Jacob, 113, 148
Jer., 95
Jeremiah, 121
Jeremiah bar Abba, 81
Jerusalem, 30, 33
Jew, 1, 3-4, 19, 26, 28-30, 145
Job, 160
Joseph, 92, 109, 112
Joshua, 82-83, 137-138, 169, 187
Joshua b. Levi, 179, 184, 187
Joshua b. Perahyah, 83
Joshua ben Hananiah, 137
Judah, 15, 79, 83, 91, 144, 146, 151, 160

Index

Judah b. Tabbai, 83

Judah the Patriarch, 94, 111-112, 131, 169

Judaism, 1-6, 12-13, 15-16, 17-21, 23-26, 28-31, 34, 47, 82, 86, 87, 89, 107, 112, 116, 120, 123, 143, 145-147, 149, 152, 154, 159, 161, 165, 177-178, 188, 191-192

judgment, 15, 47, 62, 64, 66, 80, 82-83, 107, 116, 118-119, 149-150, 169, 175, 177, 189

Kadi, 38

Kahana, 111

Ketubot, 95, 114, 122, 152

kings of kings, 18, 20, 149

Land of Israel, 8, 12-13, 18-19, 24, 30, 33-34, 122-123, 138, 170, 178, 181, 184

law, 2, 6-13, 15, 17, 22-23, 25, 27-30, 33, 35-36, 39, 41, 44, 47-48, 66, 69, 78, 82, 84-85, 89, 92-93, 96-97, 102-103, 109-111, 113, 116, 118, 120, 131, 134, 143-147, 149-150, 155, 158-160, 166, 168-169, 177-178, 181-183, 186, 188-192

laws of uncleanness, 143, 145

Leah, 113

leavening, 122

Lev., 15, 101-102, 144, 168

Levi, 139

levirate marriage, 80, 91

Leviticus, 5, 34, 145, 168-169

liability, 122

libation, 3, 108-110

literature, 12, 22, 85-86, 149

loan, 45-46, 63-65, 113-116, 138

logic, 8-9, 14, 33, 35, 48, 75-76, 83-85, 88, 141, 157, 191-192

Lord, 14, 27, 114, 129, 136, 160-161, 168-169

M. B.M., 42, 172, 187

M. Git., 71, 73-74, 79, 180, 183

M. Kel., 151

M. Ket., 114, 120

M. Nedarim, 119

M. Negaim, 144

M. Shebu., 39, 42

M. Sukkah, 4

M. Tam., 151

M. Yeb., 96

Magi, 26

Mana, 156, 179, 185

Manushchihr, 21, 29, 130

Mar Uqba, 79

marriage, 14, 22, 53-61, 69, 71, 78, 80-81, 89-97, 114, 132, 152, 155-156, 180-182, 185, 187, 192

marriage contract, 92, 95-96, 152

Matigan-i Hazar Datastan, 11

meat, 108, 139

media, 3, 12, 77, 165, 188

Meir, 120, 151, 181, 186

Menahot, 160

menstruation, 14, 34, 58, 90, 93, 132

Messiah, 30

metaphor, 189

metaproposition, 13

method, 178, 190, 192

Middle East, 1, 17, 30

midras uncleanness, 144
Midrash compilation, 29
Mishnah, 11, 13, 15, 18, 23, 29-30, 33-42, 44, 47-49, 69, 75, 79, 81-82, 84-85, 90-95, 97, 99-103, 106-110, 114, 117, 119-120, 122-123, 131, 133, 135, 137-138, 140, 143-146, 150-158, 165-166, 169-180, 183, 190-192
monotheism, 133
Moses, 2, 17, 26, 28-29, 82-83, 129, 138, 146, 159-160, 168-169
myth, 29, 146, 165-170, 188-189, 191
Nahman, 46, 71, 73, 80, 96, 115, 158, 175
Nahman bar Isaac, 78, 112
Nedarim, 119, 121
Negaim, 15
negative commandment, 46
Neziqin, 36
Niddah, 34
Nittai the Arbelite, 83
nonpriest, 81
Num., 145
Numbers, 5, 145, 169
oath, 15, 22, 36, 38-47, 66, 113-116, 118, 153, 171-173
Ohrmazd, 3, 13-14, 127-129, 132, 134-138, 141, 146-147, 149-150, 159, 161, 166-169
Old Testament, 159
Omnipresent, 138
omniscience, 128-129, 141, 159, 161, 167
Oral Torah, 146, 159
Oshaia, 100

paganism, 108
Pahlavi, 1, 5, 7, 9-12, 17-18, 20-21, 23-26, 28-29, 51, 53, 71, 97, 107, 123, 125, 127-128, 130-133, 138, 159, 167, 170, 192
Pahlavi books, 1, 5, 7, 9-10, 17-18, 20-21, 23-25, 28-29, 138, 170, 192
Palestinian, 33
Pappa, 38, 92, 96, 102, 115, 121
Parthian, 4, 19
Pentateuch, 4-5, 166, 168-169
pericope, 35, 167
perjury, 172
Persian, 10, 22, 25
philology, 12, 21, 130
philosophy, 8, 12, 25, 97, 117, 131, 189, 192
politics, 1, 4, 19-20, 165
prayer, 3, 178
priest, 1-2, 5, 12, 15, 18-19, 21, 23-24, 28-30, 81, 84, 86, 87-89, 112, 116, 119, 122, 130-131, 137, 139, 146, 154, 159, 161, 165, 168, 190
priestly code, 5
prohibition, 34, 107-111, 120-122, 152, 181-182, 185
prooftext, 35, 166
property, 22, 40-46, 53-54, 60, 63-66, 84, 91-92, 94, 96, 99-100, 102, 113-114, 117-119, 136, 150-151, 192
prophet, 2, 26, 82, 127, 134, 159, 167, 169
proposition, 8, 20, 33, 35, 69, 75-76, 78, 93-94, 128, 138, 141

Index

Prov., 148
Ps., 108, 138, 148
purity, 5, 12, 53, 84, 131, 145
Pursishniha, 4, 9, 14-15, 146-147, 152, 154, 166, 191
Qarna, 79
Qiddushin, 13, 70
Qonam vows, 120
Rab, 79, 81, 115-116, 151, 158, 160
Raba, 70-73, 75, 77-78, 80-81, 92, 95-96, 100-101, 116, 122, 151, 181-184
Rabbah, 45, 92-93, 109, 181-184
Rabbah bar Abbuha, 108
Rabbah bar R. Huna, 41, 115, 140
Rabbanai, 37
Rabbi, 17, 29, 100, 111-112, 137-138, 172, 175-176
rabbinic, 12, 34, 127
rabbis, 19, 38, 40-44, 79, 91-92, 95-97, 101-102, 109-112, 146, 151, 172, 181-182, 186
Rabina, 26, 46, 80
Rachel, 113
Rami bar Hama, 115
religion, 1-3, 5-7, 9, 11-16, 17-21, 24-25, 28-29, 47, 53, 55, 61, 67-68, 88, 98, 116, 130-134, 136-137, 140, 148, 166, 177-178
remarriage, 53, 91, 96-97, 179-182, 184, 186
resurrection, 14, 129, 133, 149, 166
revelation, 2, 20, 29, 47, 127, 130, 146, 149, 159, 167, 169

rhetoric, 3, 8, 48-49, 69, 88, 122, 140-141
right of refusal, 79-80, 89, 91-93
rivayat, 7-14, 16, 18, 21, 23, 33, 35, 49, 51, 53, 68-69, 75-79, 84-86, 87-90, 92, 94, 97, 105-106, 117, 122-123, 125, 127-128, 130-133, 138, 140-141, 143, 146, 149-152, 154, 156, 158-160, 165-168, 170, 189-191
Rome, 18-19, 26-27, 30, 149
Sabbath, 84, 168
sacrifice, 22, 30, 108
sage, 1-3, 5-6, 8, 10, 12, 14-15, 17-21, 23, 25-26, 28-30, 38, 40-42, 44, 68, 75, 82, 85-86, 87-89, 93, 95, 102, 107-113, 116, 120, 122-123, 127, 130, 133, 136, 138, 147-151, 154-155, 159, 161, 165, 175, 179-180, 183-184
salvation, 135
Sam., 148
Sama b. Raba, 26
Samuel, 79-80, 91, 110, 115-116, 120, 151, 158
Samuel bar Judah, 112
Samuel bar R. Isaac, 155
sanctification, 112, 119-122
sanctuary, 30
Sanhedrin, 166
Sarah, 113
Sasanian, 1, 4, 10-11, 17, 19, 21-22
Sayings of the Fathers, 137
scribe, 181, 186

Scripture, 12-13, 18, 23, 35, 37, 48-49, 60, 75, 101, 108-109, 114, 151, 177
Sehora, 151
sexual relations, 14, 34, 91-92, 132, 181-182, 186
Shabbat, 13
Shabuot, 171, 173
Shammai, 137, 169
Shebuot, 172
Sherira Gaon, 26, 85
Sheshet, 46
Shimi bar Ashi, 38
Shisha b. R. Idi, 121
Sifra, 18, 29, 34
Sifré to Deuteronomy, 34
Sifré to Numbers, 34
Sifrés, 18, 29, 34
Silverstone, 114-115
Simeon, 100, 137-138, 175-176
Simeon b. Gamaliel, 108, 114-115, 152, 169, 175, 180
Simeon b. Laqish, 78, 80, 109, 182
Simeon b. Shetah, 83
Simeon b. Yohai, 95
Simeon ben Nethanel, 137
Simon, 183
sin, 3, 14-15, 53, 58-59, 61-63, 67-68, 90, 93, 98, 106, 129, 132-136, 140, 147-148, 157, 167
Sinai, 29, 82-83, 129, 137, 146, 160-161, 168-169
sinner, 58-59, 66, 118, 136
slave, 22, 70, 72, 122, 133, 152-153, 155-156, 173

Slotki, 97, 122
sociology, 145
Steinsaltz, Adin, 38
successor system, 177
Sukkah, 4
Sumerian, 149
Sumkhos, 40-41, 102
syllogism, 76, 141
synagogue, 26
T. B.M., 101, 151, 175
T. B.Q., 101
T. Shebu., 171-173
Talmud, 1, 5, 8, 13, 18, 20, 24, 26, 33-37, 43, 47, 49, 51, 75-77, 85, 90, 93-94, 97-99, 102-103, 105, 108, 110, 112-114, 117, 119, 122-123, 125, 127, 133, 135, 145, 150-151, 154-156, 158, 170-174, 176-178, 183-184, 188, 192
Talmud of Babylonia, 1-2, 5, 7-8, 13, 17, 33-34, 36, 47, 170, 178
Talmud of the Land of Israel, 8, 13, 18, 24, 33-34, 138, 178
Tanna, 37-38
Tannaite, 45-46, 71, 73, 99-102, 110, 146, 151, 153, 174, 182-183, 190
Tarfon, 157
taxa, 49
taxonomy, 9, 13, 122
Temple, 30, 84, 119-120
Testaments, 22
text criticism, 35
theology, 5-12, 14, 17, 21, 28-29, 33, 49, 82-83, 87, 89, 106,

Index 201

128, 131-135, 143, 159, 165-166, 168, 177-178, 191-192

topic, 1, 3, 5-6, 8-9, 11, 16, 23, 33, 48-49, 54, 78, 84-85, 88-89, 94, 106-107, 110, 112, 122, 132, 140-141

Torah, 5, 13, 23, 26, 29-30, 34, 41, 44-45, 47, 82-83, 95-97, 112, 114, 129, 135, 137, 146, 151, 159-161, 166, 168-169, 178, 181, 185, 192

Tosefta, 18, 29, 34-36, 49, 75, 110, 145, 151, 156, 170, 173-174, 176

Tractate Avot, 82-83, 147-148, 169

Tractate Qiddushin, 13

tradition, 1-4, 7-9, 11-13, 17, 19-20, 22-23, 25-30, 33, 82, 85-86, 88-89, 107, 110-113, 120, 123, 127-132, 137-138, 145-146, 148-149, 154-155, 159-161, 165-170, 177-178, 188-192

transgression, 46, 137

translation, 4, 9-11, 14, 18, 22-23, 26, 71, 128, 130, 141, 167

Ulla, 151

uncleanness, 15-16, 53, 108, 110-111, 143-145

unconsecration, 120

unit of thought, 53, 76

voice, 12-13, 21, 47-49, 75, 131, 159, 178, 187

vow, 15-16, 65, 116-117, 119-122, 152-153

wealth, 22, 53, 67-68, 98, 132, 135, 156-157

West, 9-11, 139

wickedness, 3, 15, 28, 53, 61, 63, 65, 113, 118, 129, 134, 136, 138, 141

widow, 63, 113, 155

wife, 15, 53-55, 57-63, 69, 72, 78, 81, 89-90, 93-94, 96-97, 113, 120-122, 129, 152-155, 173, 179-184, 186-187

Williams, A.V., 11-14, 18, 128, 130-134, 140-141, 145, 167

witness, 15, 36, 43, 45, 62, 83, 114-115, 136, 150, 159, 171-173, 175, 180-187

woman, 14, 19, 22, 27, 34, 54-60, 67, 69-70, 73-74, 84, 90-91, 95-96, 114, 120-122, 132, 139, 152-155, 173, 179, 181-186, 192

wrath, 27

writ of divorce, 70-74, 78-80, 92, 173, 179-182, 184-186, 192

Written Torah, 5, 23, 30, 151, 159

Yannai b. R. Ishmael, 109

Yebamot, 91

Yemar, 96

Yerushalmi, 8-9, 12, 24, 29, 33-35, 155-156, 166, 170-171, 173-174, 176-180, 183-184, 187-192

Yohanan, 41, 44, 46-47, 78-80, 95, 97, 111-112, 120, 171-172, 179, 182, 184, 186-187

Yohanan b. Beroqah, 114-115

Yohanan b. Nuri, 120

Yohanan ben Zakkai, 137

Yohanan Hassandlar, 120

Yosé, 26, 41-44, 137-138, 151, 175, 179, 184

Yosé b. R. Bun, 179, 185
Yosé bar Hanina, 79
Yosé the Priest, 137
Zab, 144
Zabim, 144
Zatspram, 21
Zebahim, 13
Zira, 78, 80

Zoroaster, 2, 4, 21, 26-28, 127-129, 131, 134-138, 146, 149-150, 159-161, 166-169

Zoroastrianism, 1-16, 17-21, 23-25, 28-31, 68, 86, 87, 89, 102-103, 106-108, 110, 112-113, 116, 119, 131, 133, 144-146, 149, 151-152, 154, 156, 159, 161, 165-166, 188-189

South Florida Studies in the History of Judaism

240001	Lectures on Judaism in the Academy and in the Humanities	Neusner
240002	Lectures on Judaism in the History of Religion	Neusner
240003	Self-Fulfilling Prophecy: Exile and Return in the History of Judaism	Neusner
240004	The Canonical History of Ideas: The Place of the So-called Tannaite Midrashim, Mekhilta Attributed to R. Ishmael, Sifra, Sifré to Numbers, and Sifré to Deuteronomy	Neusner
240005	Ancient Judaism: Debates and Disputes, Second Series	Neusner
240006	The Hasmoneans and Their Supporters: From Mattathias to the Death of John Hyrcanus I	Sievers
240007	Approaches to Ancient Judaism: New Series, Volume One	Neusner
240008	Judaism in the Matrix of Christianity	Neusner
240009	Tradition as Selectivity: Scripture, Mishnah, Tosefta, and Midrash in the Talmud of Babylonia	Neusner
240010	The Tosefta: Translated from the Hebrew: Sixth Division Tohorot	Neusner
240011	In the Margins of the Midrash: Sifre Ha'azinu Texts, Commentaries and Reflections	Basser
240012	Language as Taxonomy: The Rules for Using Hebrew and Aramaic in the Babylonia Talmud	Neusner
240013	The Rules of Composition of the Talmud of Babylonia: The Cogency of the Bavli's Composite	Neusner
240014	Understanding the Rabbinic Mind: Essays on the Hermeneutic of Max Kadushin	Ochs
240015	Essays in Jewish Historiography	Rapoport-Albert
240016	The Golden Calf and the Origins of the Jewish Controversy	Bori/Ward
240017	Approaches to Ancient Judaism: New Series, Volume Two	Neusner
240018	The Bavli That Might Have Been: The Tosefta's Theory of Mishnah Commentary Compared With the Bavli's	Neusner
240019	The Formation of Judaism: In Retrospect and Prospect	Neusner
240020	Judaism in Society: The Evidence of the Yerushalmi, Toward the Natural History of a Religion	Neusner
240021	The Enchantments of Judaism: Rites of Transformation from Birth Through Death	Neusner
240022	The Rules of Composition of the Talmud of Babylonia	Neusner
240023	The City of God in Judaism and Other Comparative and Methodological Studies	Neusner
240024	The Bavli's One Voice: Types and Forms of Analytical Discourse and their Fixed Order of Appearance	Neusner
240025	The Dura-Europos Synagogue: A Re-evaluation (1932-1992)	Gutmann
240026	Precedent and Judicial Discretion: The Case of Joseph ibn Lev	Morell
240027	Max Weinreich *Geschichte der jiddischen Sprachforschung*	Frakes
240028	Israel: Its Life and Culture, Volume I	Pedersen
240029	Israel: Its Life and Culture, Volume II	Pedersen
240030	The Bavli's One Statement: The Metapropositional Program of Babylonian Talmud Tractate Zebahim Chapters One and Five	Neusner

240031	The Oral Torah: The Sacred Books of Judaism: An Introduction: Second Printing	Neusner
240032	The Twentieth Century Construction of "Judaism:" Essays on the Religion of Torah in the History of Religion	Neusner
240033	How the Talmud Shaped Rabbinic Discourse	Neusner
240034	The Discourse of the Bavli: Language, Literature, and Symbolism: Five Recent Findings	Neusner
240035	The Law Behind the Laws: The Bavli's Essential Discourse	Neusner
240036	Sources and Traditions: Types of Compositions in the Talmud of Babylonia	Neusner
240037	How to Study the Bavli: The Languages, Literatures, and Lessons of the Talmud of Babylonia	Neusner
240038	The Bavli's Primary Discourse: Mishnah Commentary: Its Rhetorical Paradigms and their Theological Implications	Neusner
240039	Midrash Aleph Beth	Sawyer
240040	Jewish Thought in the 20th Century: An Introduction in the Talmud of Babylonia Tractate Moed Qatan	Schweid Neusner
240041	Diaspora Jews and Judaism: Essays in Honor of, and in Dialogue with, A. Thomas Kraabel	Overman/MacLennan
240042	The Bavli: An Introduction	Neusner
240043	The Bavli's Massive Miscellanies: The Problem of Agglutinative Discourse in the Talmud of Babylonia	Neusner
240044	The Foundations of the Theology of Judaism: An Anthology Part II: Torah	Neusner
240045	Form-Analytical Comparison in Rabbinic Judaism: Structure and Form in *The Fathers* and *The Fathers According to Rabbi Nathan*	Neusner
240046	Essays on Hebrew	Weinberg
240047	The Tosefta: An Introduction	Neusner
240048	The Foundations of the Theology of Judaism: An Anthology Part III: Israel	Neusner
240049	The Study of Ancient Judaism, Volume I: Mishnah, Midrash, Siddur	Neusner
240050	The Study of Ancient Judaism, Volume II: The Palestinian and Babylonian Talmuds	Neusner
240051	Take Judaism, for Example: Studies toward the Comparison of Religions	Neusner
240052	From Eden to Golgotha: Essays in Biblical Theology	Moberly
240053	The Principal Parts of the Bavli's Discourse: A Preliminary Taxonomy: Mishnah Commentary, Sources, Traditions and Agglutinative Miscellanies	Neusner
240054	Barabbas and Esther and Other Studies in the Judaic Illumination of Earliest Christianity	Aus
240055	Targum Studies, Volume I: Textual and Contextual Studies in the Pentateuchal Targums	Flesher
240056	Approaches to Ancient Judaism: New Series, Volume Three, Historical and Literary Studies	Neusner
240057	The Motherhood of God and Other Studies	Gruber
240058	The Analytic Movement: Hayyim Soloveitchik and his Circle	Solomon

240059	Recovering the Role of Women: Power and Authority in Rabbinic Jewish Society	Haas
240060	The Relation between Herodotus' *History* and Primary History	Mandell/Freedman
240061	The First Seven Days: A Philosophical Commentary on the Creation of Genesis	Samuelson
240062	The Bavli's Intellectual Character: The Generative Problematic: In Bavli Baba Qamma Chapter One And Bavli Shabbat Chapter One	Neusner
240063	The Incarnation of God: The Character of Divinity in Formative Judaism: Second Printing	Neusner
240064	Moses Kimhi: Commentary on the Book of Job	Basser/Walfish
240065	Judaism and Civil Religion	Breslauer
240066	Death and Birth of Judaism: Second Printing	Neusner
240067	Decoding the Talmud's Exegetical Program	Neusner
240068	Sources of the Transformation of Judaism	Neusner
240069	The Torah in the Talmud: A Taxonomy of the Uses of Scripture in the Talmud, Volume I	Neusner
240070	The Torah in the Talmud: A Taxonomy of the Uses of Scripture in the Talmud, Volume II	Neusner
240071	The Bavli's Unique Voice: A Systematic Comparison of the Talmud of Babylonia and the Talmud of the Land of Israel, Volume One	Neusner
240072	The Bavli's Unique Voice: A Systematic Comparison of the Talmud of Babylonia and the Talmud of the Land of Israel, Volume Two	Neusner
240073	The Bavli's Unique Voice: A Systematic Comparison of the Talmud of Babylonia and the Talmud of the Land of Israel, Volume Three	Neusner
240074	Bits of Honey: Essays for Samson H. Levey	Chyet/Ellenson
240075	The Mystical Study of Ruth: *Midrash HaNe'elam* of the Zohar to the Book of Ruth	Englander
240076	The Bavli's Unique Voice: A Systematic Comparison of the Talmud of Babylonia and the Talmud of the Land of Israel, Volume Four	Neusner
240077	The Bavli's Unique Voice: A Systematic Comparison of the Talmud of Babylonia and the Talmud of the Land of Israel, Volume Five	Neusner
240078	The Bavli's Unique Voice: A Systematic Comparison of the Talmud of Babylonia and the Talmud of the Land of Israel, Volume Six	Neusner
240079	The Bavli's Unique Voice: A Systematic Comparison of the Talmud of Babylonia and the Talmud of the Land of Israel, Volume Seven	Neusner
240080	Are There Really Tannaitic Parallels to the Gospels?	Neusner
240081	Approaches to Ancient Judaism: New Series, Volume Four, Religious and Theological Studies	Neusner
240082	Approaches to Ancient Judaism: New Series, Volume Five, Historical, Literary, and Religious Studies	Basser/Fishbane

240083	Ancient Judaism: Debates and Disputes, Third Series	Neusner
240084	Judaic Law from Jesus to the Mishnah	Neusner
240085	Writing with Scripture: Second Printing	Neusner/Green
240086	Foundations of Judaism: Second Printing	Neusner
240087	Judaism and Zoroastrianism at the Dusk of Late Antiquity	Neusner
240088	Judaism States Its Theology	Neusner

DATE DUE

MAY 16 1997			
			Printed in USA